DISTRUSTING EDUCATIONAL TECHNOLOGY

Distrusting Educational Technology critically explores the optimistic consensus that has arisen around the use of digital technology in education. Drawing on a variety of theoretical and empirical perspectives, this book shows how apparently neutral forms of educational technology have actually served to align educational provision and practices with neo-liberal values, thereby eroding the nature of education as a public good and moving it instead towards the individualistic tendencies of twenty-first-century capitalism.

Following a wide-ranging interrogation of the ideological dimensions of educational technology, this book examines in detail specific types of digital technology in use in education today, including virtual education, 'open' courses, digital games and social media. It then concludes with specific recommendations for fairer forms of educational technology. An ideal read for anyone interested in the fast-changing nature of contemporary education, *Distrusting Educational Technology* comprises an ambitious and much-needed critique.

Neil Selwyn is Professor of Education at Monash University, Australia.

DISTRUSTING EDUCATIONAL TECHNOLOGY

Critical Questions for Changing Times

Neil Selwyn
Monash University, Australia

Routledge
Taylor & Francis Group

NEW YORK AND LONDON

First published 2014
by Routledge
711 Third Avenue, New York, NY 10017

and by Routledge
2 Park Square, Milton Park, Abingdon, Oxon OX14 4RN

Routledge is an imprint of the Taylor & Francis Group, an informa business

Library of Congress Cataloging-in-Publication Data

Selwyn, Neil.
Distrusting educational technology : critical questions for changing times /
Neil Selwyn.
       pages cm.
   Includes bibliographical references and index.
   1. Educational technology.   2. Information technology.   3. Internet in
education.   4. Digital media.   5. Social media.   I. Title.
LB1028.3.S38882   2013
371.33—dc23   2013017407

ISBN: 978-0-415-70799-2 (hbk)
ISBN: 978-0-415-70800-5 (pbk)
ISBN: 978-1-315-88635-0 (ebk)

Typeset in Bembo
by Apex CoVantage, LLC

Printed and bound by CPI Group (UK) Ltd, Croydon, CR0 4YY

CONTENTS

PREFACE

Unlike most other writing on the topic of education and technology, this is not a particularly hopeful or optimistic book. This is a book that paints an awkward and difficult picture of education in the digital age. Readers should not expect the enthusiasm and praise that usually are directed towards 'virtual education', 'school 2.0', 'e-learning' and the like. This book is not a rehash of the familiar transformatory claims that recur within discussions of technology use in education. This is not a book that purports to tell you what *might* happen with digital technologies, or evokes a sense of high-tech wonder and anticipation that many educational technologists appear to revel in. Instead, this is a book that is deliberately distrustful of the ongoing digitization of education provision and practice. Although expressed rarely within academic writing on education and technology, this distrust is well founded. Digital technologies have long promised much in the way of changing education along more democratic, more equitable and fairer lines, but have usually delivered far less. Indeed, it could be argued that digital technologies have served primarily to *increase* socially inequitable and exclusive trends within education. Over the past 30 years, technology-based education provision appears to have been reshaped along ever more individualistic and market-driven lines, working primarily to satisfy the demands of contemporary capitalism. This book therefore concerns itself with addressing the digital degradation of education in close detail, and then considering what – if anything – can be done to counter it.

In this sense, the next eight chapters are an expression of my continuing unease with academic, political and professional discussions of 'educational technology' – not least the gulf that persists between the rhetoric of how digital technologies *could* be used in education and the realities of how digital technologies are *actually* used in education. In almost all of my own educational experiences of digital technology, the promises of what 'should' be happening have far outstripped the realities of what eventually has taken place. This disjuncture certainly characterized my schoolboy experiences of microcomputers during the 1980s. This is still my experience of working as a university academic and tutor 30 years on. Perhaps the most disconcerting aspect of my perennial 'digital disappointment' is the absolute certainty of enthusiasts and experts when 'talking up' the educational use of the very same technologies. Of course, some of these people are little more than 'hucksters' keen to turn a profit from the educational technology marketplace. Yet educational technology is not solely the domain of sharp-suited, silver-tongued salespeople chasing a quick buck. Many enthusiastic proponents of the apparent benefits of educational technologies are amongst the most astute, well-intentioned, right-minded and clear-thinking people one could meet. There is certainly more to the 'hyping' of educational technology than either plain ignorance or simple profiteering.

So why do so many intelligent and well-meaning people appear to suspend their disbelief when it comes to digital technology and education? Is educational technology really a site of mass 'computer delusion' as Todd Oppenheimer once put it – a 'consensual hallucination' on the part of techno-romantic educationalists? Is educational technology a bold but ultimately doomed attempt by those who are brave enough to 'dare to dream' of a better educational future? In my mind, it is all too easy for the critical onlooker to excuse the field of educational technology in these forgiving terms. For sure, some people in educational technology are driven by a blinkered passion for all things technological. Some people do see themselves as genuinely attempting to re-engineer forms of 'better' education. Yet excusing the constant failed state of educational technology as due simply to near misses and misguided romanticism is to overlook the wider societal significance of digital education. From a more sceptical perspective it could be argued that educational technology has never been intended to make a substantial difference to the fairness of education. As such the past 30 years have not seen any particular 'failure' of educational technology *per se*. Instead, educational technology needs to be understood as a profoundly political affair – a site of constant conflict and struggle between different interests and groups. In this sense, the educational use of digital technology has no one 'true' meaning or inherent 'potential' that some people are more able to see than others. Instead, the educational use of digital technology needs to be seen as an ideologically driven concern.

These arguments are all unpacked and expanded upon in the eight chapters of this book. As such, the book draws together a number of themes that have 'bubbled under' much of my previous writing on education, technology and society, yet have never been addressed to my complete satisfaction. This book was prompted by a nagging feeling that my writing had never fully 'nailed' the ideological nature of educational technology – despite long recognising that issues of ideology and politics lie at the heart of making sense of the topic. I hope that the book offers a more rounded account of these concerns and their consequences. It would be heartening to think that these arguments might go some way towards challenging and changing popular perceptions of educational technology as a largely value-free, benign area of contemporary education. If not, then I hope that the book at least reinforces the message that educational technology might be many things, but it is certainly not above the cut and thrust of contemporary capitalism.

Before these ideas are pursued in earnest, it is perhaps helpful to justify the premise of 'Distrusting Educational Technology'. This somewhat provocative title was chosen to convey a number of key convictions that run throughout the book. First is the contention that educational technology is not value-free but value-laden, and therefore something that can be trusted *and* distrusted, agreed *and* disagreed with. Second is the belief that the nature and form of educational technology are not predetermined and inevitable but negotiable. In a similar spirit, the specific notion of 'distrusting' was inspired by the title of a collection of William Gibson's writing – *Distrust That Particular Flavor*. This, it was suggested to me recently, is a fitting description of my own stance towards education and technology. Although my personal prejudices about science fiction readers leave me wary of science fiction writing in any form, the more that I reflected on the notion of 'distrusting that *particular* flavour' then the more that Gibson's sentiment seemed appropriate for my own writing. Thus in this spirit of a discerning (rather than indiscriminate) distrust, I would like to reassure the reader that this is not a wholly anti-technology book *per se*, but rather an attempt to construct a nuanced and helpful set of arguments concerning the current nature and form of digital technology use in education. While making a passionate case for the merits of taking a deliberately pessimistic approach, this remains a book that is concerned ultimately with finding better ways of using digital technology in education. So regardless of whether you agree with its arguments, please take this book in the spirit in which it was written – as a set of arguments that are constructively (rather than destructively) against educational technology.

ACKNOWLEDGEMENTS

This book was researched and planned largely in the UK, and then written largely in Australia. As such I would like to thank academic colleagues from both these countries for their advice and comments on my work and writing. At Monash University I would like to thank Scott Bulfin for his recommendations of further reading and various critiques of early arguments and ideas. I would also like to thank Nicola Johnson and Michael Henderson for their enthusiasm in getting me over to Australia in the first place, and Ilana Synder for her suggestion of 'distrust' as the overall 'flavour' that runs throughout this book. I would also like to thank a number of colleagues at the Institute of Education–University of London who also helped shape and sharpen my thinking on these issues. These include Martin Oliver, Carey Jewitt, John Potter, Andrew Burn, Magda Kolokitha, Ambrose Neville, Carlo Perrotta, Brock Craft, Richard Noss and Diana Laurillard.

Aside from colleagues in Melbourne and London, there are a number of other people who have played important roles in developing my reading, thinking and writing. Over the past 20 years I have benefitted immensely from talking with others on the subject – not least Keri Facer, Sonia Livingstone, David Buckingham and Charles Crook. Finally on a more practical note, I am always grateful for the editorial work that goes into the publishing process. So I would like to thank the New York production and editorial team at Routledge – notably Alex Masulis and Madeleine Hamlin. I would also like to thank Juliet Sheath at Full Focus Photography, London, for her work on the front cover image.

Of course, all these acknowledgements are accompanied by the usual caveats and get-out clauses. In particular, I would like to remind readers that while this book draws on the work, ideas and arguments of many others, ultimately I remain responsible for writing it. All errors, inconsistencies or inaccuracies are mine.

Neil Selwyn
Melbourne – June 2013

1

WHY DISTRUST EDUCATIONAL TECHNOLOGY?

Introduction

In comparison to other major educational problems of our times, the need to ask critical questions of digital technology in education is not immediately apparent. It is perhaps unsurprising that little serious attention has been paid to digital technology within recent critiques of contemporary education. Most critically minded authors understandably concern themselves with interrogating and examining the more obvious educational controversies and conflicts of curricular reform, social reproduction, marketization, identity politics, inclusion, the universal right to schooling and so on. In contrast, many people presume digital technology to be one of the least problematic elements of contemporary education provision and practice. Indeed, digital technologies of all shapes and sizes are now woven deeply into the everyday fabric of education – from 'virtual learning environments' and interactive whiteboards to Google searches and Wikipedia entries. Tools and applications such as these represent some of the most familiar cultural resources and symbols within contemporary educational settings and, at first glance, do not appear to be of particular cause for concern. If anything, the use of digital technology has now become a rather unremarkable aspect of education provision and practice.

Yet the use of digital technology in education should now be seen as a significant issue for everyone with a stake in education. The day-to-day lives of learners and educators are saturated with digital technology use – both in terms of personal uses of digital devices and the more hidden uses of technological tools and systems by educational institutions. Digital technology continues to be an important educational priority for governments, politicians and policymakers – especially in terms of national efforts to engineer new and improved education systems with the capability to "out-educate and out-hustle the rest of the world" (Obama 2011). The use of digital technology in education is certainly of significance to commercial actors involved in the selling of technology to educational consumers – a global marketplace that is estimated conservatively to be worth in excess of $5 trillion *per annum*. Obscured by these interests perhaps, but no less significant, educational technology is also a growing concern for parents, journalists, employers and most other education 'stakeholders'.

In short, digital technology should be seen as an integral part of the educational landscape, and as something that is shaped by the (in)actions of a wide range of different actors and interests. Indeed, as all but the most ardent technological determinist would acknowledge, digital technology is not something that simply comes down to us from 'on high' – fully formed and ready to use. Instead, any instance of digital technology use in education is shaped by a range of social interests – from designers and developers, financiers and marketers to technology-using educators and the educational institutions they work within (see Bromley 1997; Oliver 2011). While all acting upon different motivations and intentions, these groups share a common interest in stimulating and supporting the increased acceptance and use of digital technology in education. It is therefore understandable that educational technology tends to be promoted and publicized by actors from all sides of the 'education community' as a natural, necessary and largely neutral element of contemporary education. An orthodoxy appears to have developed in most parts of the world that digital technologies are an integral and inevitable feature of 'modern' forms of education, and therefore require little or no discussion. Certainly as far as many academic commentators are concerned, the only questions that need to be asked today of educational technology are technical and procedural in nature. How might we better 'harness' the educational potential of technology? How might technology use be more 'effective'? What changes do new technologies demand of existing educational ideas and understandings?

Questions such as these are all well and good, yet offer a highly partial picture of education and technology when addressed in isolation. In contrast, this book seeks to explore a set of more awkward and difficult questions. So while most people tend to think of technology as a necessary and even neutral feature of education, this book starts from the premise that educational technology is certainly *not* uncontested terrain. Approached in these terms, educational technology is not a straightforward, value-free process involving an individual using a piece of technology in order to learn something. Instead, all of the actors outlined so far in this chapter should be seen as having good reason to ensure that their interests and values are supported and advanced through the use of digital technology in education. While undoubtedly of great potential benefit, it is clear that educational technology is a value-laden site of profound struggle that some people benefit more from than others – most notably in terms of power and profit.

Thus despite all the prevailing talk of enhanced equality and democracy, it must be remembered that the application of digital technology in educational settings is almost always an unequal affair. To put it in crude terms, educational technology could be observed to involve a hierarchy of actors and interests ranging from those who generally 'do' educational technology through to those who generally have educational technology 'done' to them. In other words, it is important to acknowledge the differences that persist throughout educational technology between those who produce and those who consume, those who are empowered and those who are exploited. These are all 'outcomes' that are rarely acknowledged and written about in the academic educational technology literature. Indeed, part of my own long-standing concern with educational technology – and certainly a motivation for writing this book – lies with the apparently uncontroversial, unproblematic and apolitical manner in which educational technology tends to be discussed by otherwise highly critical commentators. Why is it that so many critically minded academic writers and researchers have an apparent 'blind spot' for the politics of educational technology? More importantly, what can be done to politicize the field of educational technology and establish it as an area of serious academic debate and discussion? It is these issues that this book concerns itself with. This is what is meant by '*distrusting* educational technology'.

One of the key prompts to write this book, therefore, is the fact that those who tend to be most disadvantaged by educational technology are usually those who think least critically about it. These people are usually described in pejorative terms within technology discussions as 'end users', despite encompassing a large majority of the population (and certainly a large number of readers of this book). In this sense, the reluctance of a majority of people to critique their relationships with educational technology is certainly not confined to education. Langdon Winner (2004) described a phenomenon of 'technological somnambulism' that seems to pervade Western society – that is, the tendency for a majority of people to sleepwalk through their mediations with technology. As Matthewman (2011, p. 173) writes, contemporary society suffers from a 'banal' tendency to overlook the role of digital technology in everyday life:

> We do not notice the obvious. Ubiquity creates invisibility. McLuhan famously compared us to fish that fail to see our water. Under such circumstances, as Heidegger said, we are only likely to notice our technologies when they stop working as anticipated.

Even though people may now consider themselves to be far more technologically sophisticated than might have been the case in the times of Heidegger or McLuhan, there has been little recent indication that the tendency to look past 'the digital' is diminishing. Given the recent mass fetishization of all things Apple, coupled with the apparent compulsion for people to spend every waking hour of their lives tweeting, posting and 'liking', it would seem that very few of us are overly concerned with developing critical knowledge of how we interact with digital technology. Winner (2004) sees this disinterest in the politics of technology as stemming from a number of factors. First is the ever-increasing separation between the minority who design, develop, make and sell 'new' technology and the mass of us who end up merely purchasing and using it. Second is a long-standing tendency within Western thought to view digital technologies as tools that largely are separate from the human condition and can therefore be used and then discarded without any long-term personal implications. A third – and perhaps most significant – reason relates to the ways in which digital technologies are believed commonly to create 'new' spaces and places in which people can interact and operate separately from their nontechnologically mediated 'offline' existences. As such, much of what goes on 'through' digital technology use is often somehow perceived as being situated *away* from the minutiae and messiness of the 'real' world. Given this dissonance, it is perhaps understandable that the majority of people tend to be concerned with the personally pleasurable aspects of their technology use, rather than fretting over how these technologies might be entwined with the wider economic, political, social and cultural conditions of everyday life.

This sense of 'sleepwalking' is certainly reflected in the apolitical manner in which educational technology has been understood and discussed by academic commentators over the past 30 years or so. Even within the specialized academic fields of 'technology-enhanced learning' and 'educational technology' those writers and researchers who devote much of their time engaging with the topic tend to do so in constrained ways. From the outset, then, it is my intention that this will *not* be a book that will be similarly compromised and curtailed. Instead, this book will examine educational technology in a profoundly political light – approaching digital technology as part of the complex ways that social, economic and political tensions are 'mediated' in educational settings. As such, this is a book that aims to unpack the issues, arguments and assumptions that underpin four recent forms of digital technology use in education that otherwise tend to be considered as largely benign and wholly beneficial: virtual, open, games and social technologies. In particular the book seeks to problematize these technological forms in order to uncover their latent *ideological* content. A number of questions are therefore pursued with regard to examining the ideological nature of these dominant aspects of the current educational technology orthodoxy. Just why have these forms of technology use been selected and promoted in the ways that they are? Whose technologies are these? Who selected them? Why are they being organized and provided in the ways that they are? What interests are benefiting from this use? What linkages are there between these forms of educational technology and wider societal (re)arrangements and organization?

On one hand, then, this book seeks to problematize what is being presented to us as 'educational technology' and ask whether there might be alternate ways of making fairer use of digital technologies in education. As Sonia Livingstone reasons, there are perhaps only three lines of questioning worth pursuing when considering digital technology use in this manner – that is, "what's really going on, how can this be explained, and how could things be otherwise?" (Livingstone 2012, p. 19). These questions certainly underpin much of this book's analysis. Yet the overriding concern in doing so is not to attempt valiantly to 'improve' educational technology *per se*. Instead, this book is concerned first and foremost with unpacking and problematizing the inherently political nature of what is seen usually as a profoundly apolitical aspect of contemporary education provision and practice. In this way, it should be possible to develop more concrete and complete understandings of the linkages between political and economic power and the forms of technology-based education that are being experienced by 'end users' around the world.

What We (don't) Talk About When We Talk About 'Educational Technology'

Before all these grand ambitions can be realized, it is perhaps helpful to first consider some fundamental matters of definition. In particular, what are we referring to when we talk about 'educational technology'? Moreover, why should it be approached in problematic terms? In addressing these basic questions, it is worth reminding ourselves that the development of increasingly 'powerful' digital technologies has undoubtedly been one of the defining features of the past 30 years. Indeed, the scale and pace of recent digital innovation – in particular the growth of computing, the internet and mobile telephony – have prompted many commentators to position digital technology as a key driver of societal development around the world (Castells 2006). One of the striking characteristics of many recent accounts and analyses has been the transformative (and often optimistic) ways in which the changes associated with digital technology are imagined. Many popular and academic perceptions of digital technology appear, for example, to be animated by common discourses of progress and the allure of 'the new', coupled with a belief that our current digitally inflected era represents a "pervasive sense of leaving the past behind" (Murdock 2004, p. 20). In particular, many discussions are informed by a belief that digital technologies herald distinctively new *and* improved social arrangements in comparison to preceding 'predigital' times. This sense of improved change has been described as a 'digital remediation' of everyday life and social processes (see Bolter & Grusin 1999), where digital technologies are reconfiguring social processes and practices for the better. This is not to say that 'new' digital forms are believed to be usurping *all* social practices and processes that have gone before, but rather that digitally based activities are able to borrow from, refashion and often surpass their earlier predigital equivalents. For many commentators, therefore, the ready answer to alleviating contemporary social problems is now assumed to involve some form of digital technology. As Steve Woolgar (2002, p. 3) reflects, "The implication is that something new, different, and (usually) better is happening".

Given these general trends, it is not surprising that the past 30 years have seen increasing enthusiasms for computerized, online and increasingly mobile forms of teaching and learning. Given the apparent transformatory power of contemporary digital technologies, it is understandable that these technologies are now seen by most commentators as being an essential and largely unquestionable element of contemporary educational arrangements. Indeed, the controversies that raged throughout the 1980s and 1990s over whether learning about digital technology should be a core component of education (the so-called issue of 'computer literacy') have long since been resolved. Now there is widespread acceptance that digital technologies should play an integral role in all aspects of learning throughout the life course. Thus widespread support now exists for the integration of computers into school, college and university contexts, as well as the online delivery of opportunities for study and training. There is also much enthusiasm for the digitally supported 'informal' modes of learning that are stimulated by general interests, pursuits and hobbies outside of the formal curriculum. In short, digital technology is now seen as an utterly integral but wholly unremarkable component of educational conditions and arrangements around the world.

At this point, it is important to note that 'educational technology' is not a single, homogenous entity. Instead, 'educational technology' is deceptively neat shorthand for a diverse array of socio-technical devices, activities and practices. Above and beyond the multitude of technological devices and artefacts themselves, 'educational technology' refers to a wide-ranging field of activities and practices – that is, what is done with these technologies in the name of education. Perhaps less obviously, 'educational technology' also refers to a commercial field of technology development, production and marketing, as well as a thriving field of academic study and scholarship. While all of these areas of activity are concerned with the use of technology in educational settings, they are so in very different ways, often for very different reasons. As such, 'educational technology' needs to be understood as a knot of social, political, economic and cultural agendas that is riddled with complications, contradictions and conflicts. It therefore makes little sense to talk of 'educational technology' as a neat single entity, just as it makes little sense to talk of 'society' in singular, monolithic terms. One of the first tasks in this book's development of a distrust of educational technology is to establish a sufficiently nuanced understanding of what 'educational technology' is in all its forms.

Taking this multifaceted approach certainly runs counter to the ways in which educational technology tends to be discussed in popular, political and academic circles. Despite its obvious complexity, educational technology tends to be perceived in alarmingly one-dimensional terms. This is the case even with the continually renewed range of products and devices that constitute the material face of educational technology. In fact, most discussions of 'educational technology' focus only on the most popular and prominent 'classroom' forms of digital technology. Instead, it is important to recognise from the outset that educational uses of digital technology range from the personal use of internet-connected portable devices such as tablet computers and 'smartphones' to multimedia immersive simulation environments for the military and medical professions. It is also important to note that educational applications of digital technology are not confined only to schools and universities. These technological devices are used throughout educational systems to support a diversity of forms of educational provision, from kindergartens to work-based training and community settings. We therefore need to remain mindful of this diversity throughout our subsequent discussions.

It is also worth moving beyond the limited, one-dimensional manner in which educational technology outcomes tend to be understood and portrayed. Indeed, in most popular, political and academic discussions, digital technologies tend to be associated with similar sets of potentially far-reaching shifts either in terms of individual learning and/or the organization and governance of educational provision. For instance, most digital technologies over the past 30 years have been accompanied by promises of widened participation in education, increased motivation and engagement, better levels of 'attainment', enhanced convenience of use and more 'efficient' and 'effective' provision of educational opportunities. Indeed, the field of education and technology is beset by exaggerated expectations over the capacity of the latest 'new' technology to change education for the better, regardless of context or circumstance. Typical of this thinking, for example, was Rupert Murdoch's assertion that current forms of internet technology offer the potential to "ensure the poor child in Manila has the same chance as the rich child in Manhattan . . . the key to our future is to unlock this potential" (cited in Willsher 2011, n.p.).

High-profile public proclamations of this sort typify the general belief amongst many powerful interests that digital technologies have the potential to enable fundamental educational change and renewal. One prominent discourse here is the notion of digital technology sustaining a genuinely democratic rearrangement of educational opportunity – in John Daniel's (2009, p. 62) words, heralding "a tectonic shift that will bring the benefits of learning and knowledge to millions". The notion of educational technology as a democratizing phenomenon is evident in numerous celebrations of the ability of digital tools and applications to allow educators and educational institutions to operate in 'borderless' and 'edgeless' ways, and for individuals to enjoy unprecedented levels of meritocratic educational opportunity. From an epistemological perspective, digital technologies continue to be associated with the 'de-territorialisation' and 'de-referentialization' of knowledge, where data, information and knowledge travel freely around the world and are unencumbered by boundaries. For some critical educators, then, digital technologies are seen as opening up possibilities for the development of cosmopolitan and communitarian forms of education, "powerfully contribut[ing] to the worldwide democratization, civic engagement and action-orientated social responsibility" of educators and educational institutions (Benson & Harkavy

2002, p. 169). There are many people who – for a variety of reasons – believe passionately along these lines that digital technology is an inherently 'good thing' for education.

This is not to say that the use of digital technology in education has been free from any dissent at all. Indeed, the past 30 years have seen a small but steady succession of commentators developing counterarguments to these celebratory discourses – asserting in essence that digital technologies are a generally 'bad thing' for education. Here educational technology has tended to be associated with a set of universalized problems – from increased physiological and neurological impairments and risks to diminished learning and general disengagement from education. Authors such as Clifford Stoll gained notoriety during the 1980s with books such as *High Tech Heretic* and *Silicon Snake Oil*, pointing out the excesses of the procomputer lobby in education. More recently, Mark Bauerlein in *The Dumbest Generation* offered a similarly dismissive analysis of the funding being directed towards educational technology, questioning whether it was helping people learn any better than they would without. Indeed, perennial concerns have been raised over the intellectual 'dumbing-down' associated with students' and teachers' use of digital technologies to access information and knowledge (Donnelly 2012). Similarly, biologists and psychologists have pointed towards technology-related declines in children's cognitive skills and mental performance, as well as the unbalancing of hormonal levels (Sigman 2009; Greenfield 2009). Aside from these supposed detrimental effects on intellect, cognition and 'traditional' skills and literacies, fears have long been raised that digital technologies may be contributing to an increased disaffection and disrespect amongst students for schools and classroom-based learning (Parsons & Taylor 2011).

Another small set of authors has sustained a strain of technology critique within the social sciences, philosophy and humanities that presents straightforward and dystopian visions of contemporary technology-based education. As Cooper (2002, p. 129) reasons, these are critics who "can do little else than simply say 'no' to technology". Perhaps the most well-known critique 'against' educational technology in these terms was Todd Oppenheimer's treatise *The Flickering Mind*, with its unequivocal subtitle of "The False Promise of Technology in the Classroom and How Learning Can Be Saved". Here Oppenheimer focused on what he describes as the ineffectual use of technology in formal education settings characterized by commercially driven 'False Promises' and practically related 'Hidden Troubles'. Similarly, Tara Brabazon's *Digital Hemlock* and *The University of Google* both pointed to the (over)use of digital technology in education as 'white bread for the mind'. While far less prominent than the proponents of educational technology, commentators such as these nevertheless could be said to constitute a vocal 'counterorthodoxy of pessimism' amongst some public figures and academics where, as William Wresch (2004, p. 71) puts it, "nothing good can be said about information technology".

Approaching Educational Technology in Critical Rather Than Celebratory Terms

This tendency for the majority of people to unthinkingly assume educational technology to be inherently beneficial and for a few others to oppose it in generally unconvincing and alarmist terms has limited the quality of debate and scrutiny in the area over the past 30 years or so. Polarized debates over the absolute 'rights' and 'wrongs' of educational technology have certainly marginalized more nuanced concerns over the politics of digital technology use in education. Clearly, given the increasing prominence, diversity and complexity of 'educational technology', it is time to move beyond such extreme received wisdoms. Instead, it surely makes better sense to set about developing an *appropriately* critical approach to making sense of the use of digital technology in education. A ready starting point for doing so can be found in Chris Bigum and Jane Kenway's critique nearly 20 years ago of the tendency of educational technology to be discussed mainly in terms of 'boosterist' claims of efficiencies of provision, choice and diversity, enablers and drivers, speed and convenience. As Bigum and Kenway (1998, p. 378) contended, these were proponents of educational technology

> characterized by an unswerving faith in the technology's capacity to improve education and most other things in society, often coupled with a sense of inevitability concerning the growth and use of computer technology. They have few doubts about the educational merits of their vision for change.

Conversely, many of the usual arguments *against* educational technology can be described as 'doomster' discourses. As Bigum and Kenway observe, these are visions that

> see much damage to society and education arising from the uncritical acceptance of new media forms ... nostalgic for the period when these technologies did not exist or for the practices and institutions that are being replaced by new technologies.
>
> *(ibid., p. 386)*

While the polarized nature of societal views of education and digital technology in excessively optimistic or excessively pessimistic terms is wholly understandable, they run counter to many of the recent realities of educational technology use. Instead, much of the use of digital technology in education is far 'messier' than the rhetoric of absolute change (for better or for worse) might suggest. Indeed, one of the common outcomes of digital technology use in education often appears to be that of largely unaltered 'business as usual'. As all but the most blinkered educational technology commentators would concede, many of the fundamental elements of 'traditional' learning and teaching have been neither transformed nor ruined by the waves of digital technologies that have been in-troduced inside and outside of classrooms over the past few decades. Despite repeated predictions of inevitable changes and impending transformations, digital technologies are used inconsistently in educational settings, usually with little large-scale conclusive 'effect'. Put bluntly, then, any stridently optimistic descrip-tion of technology-induced educational change should be seen more as a matter of faith than as a matter of fact.

This matter of people's strident faith or belief in the power of digital techno-logy to effect change is an important one, and shall be revisited throughout this book. As should already be evident, the use of digital technology in education is a matter for many people of intense conviction and passion. While the imperative to make 'best' use of digital technologies in education may appear irrefutable, it is important to remain mindful of the symbolic role that technology often plays in discussions and debates over societal change and improvement. In this sense, many of the promises, claims and justifications outlined so far in this chapter are perhaps more accurately seen as inspirational and exhortative rather than actual accounts of education and digital technologies. The field of educational technology could therefore be said to be imbued with a distinct sense of 'truthiness' – that is, "the quality of preferring concepts or facts one wishes to be true, rather than concepts or facts known to be true" (Spring 2012, p. 30). In this sense, educational techno-logy is as much a focus for wish fulfilment as it is a focus for accurate forecasting and reasoned analysis.

This notion of the use of digital technology in education being a matter of faith as well as fact suggests that educational technology might be best understood as akin to many other faith systems – that is, a "system of radical optimism" that persists despite the lack of immediate experience or evidence (Inge 1912/2003, p. xiii). Of course, as with any faith system, within this system of technological optimism and hope, a variety of positions can be taken. For example, Duncan-Andrade (2009) distinguishes between what he terms 'hokey hope', which reflects a naïve view that somehow things will get better, despite the lack of evidence to warrant this view, and 'mythical hope', which is based around a "profoundly ahis-torical and depoliticized denial of suffering that is rooted in celebrating individual exceptions" (Duncan-Andrade 2009, p. 184). Finally, there is the state of 'hope de-ferred', which sees the current economic, political or society 'system' as blocking the otherwise inevitable transformation. Educational technology can certainly be said to contain all these variations of hope, despite the lack of compelling tangible signs of their realization. Indeed, educational technology could be seen as a field that requires its participants to collectively sustain a blind, unwavering belief that the 'project' will be seen through to an ultimately successful conclusion.

These latter descriptions raise the point that 'educational technology' needs to be understood both as *process* and as *discourse* – a distinction that reiterates the argument that relatively little of what is presented under the label of 'educational technology' is a straightforward matter of fact rather than a more complex matter of hope and belief. Above all, then, it is important to acknowledge that notions such as 'technology-enhanced learning', 'learning technology' and 'e-learning' are largely sets of value preferences – that is, social imaginaries and ideological formations that present common (and often persuasive) understandings of how things 'should be' and 'will be'. Thus, we would do well as this book progresses to resist the temptation to take every 'educational technology' concept and explanation at face value. As Nicholas Garnham concludes, accepting unquestioningly big explanatory notions of digital technology and society does not "serve as a useful starting point" for any thorough social science analysis. Rather, the uncritical use of concepts such as these "merely and dangerously distracts – as is often intended – from the real issues" (Garnham 2000, p. 126). It therefore makes good sense at this stage of our analysis to treat the notion of 'educational technology' as 'problematic' – that is, as useful means of highlighting clusters of issues for investigation and consideration rather than a foolproof blueprint for the future of the world (Lyon 1988). In this spirit, a critical approach towards educational technology would seem not only sensible but also essential.

Assuming a Critical Stance Towards Educational Technology

As has been implied already, such is its apparent ubiquity throughout contemporary society that it is rare for digital technology to be subjected to a full, sustained critique. Most of the criticism that has been levelled towards digital technology in recent times has tended to be either 'medicalized' or 'moralized' (Lovink 2011, p. 9) – that is, questioning the psychological aspects of technology engagement, or else framing it in terms of what is considered to be morally acceptable in society. As Lovink writes, popular concerns and unease about digital technology are often expressed in terms of cognitive and neurological development, generational and age differences or the causation of violence and addictive behaviours. These concerns tend to cumulate in a psychopathologizing and individualizing of the 'problem' of technology use. Thus many recent popular critiques of technology appear uncertain where to attribute blame – often settling erroneously on blaming the individual. As Lovink (2011, p. 25) concludes, "In the information age we blame ourselves without knowing why we are at fault". It is notable that this reversion to individual blame does little to address the inherently *social* nature of digital technologies, and the shared political, economic, cultural and historical nature of the digital artefacts, processes and practices that we are seeking to critique.

This paucity of critique has certainly limited the academic study of education and technology, where little criticism of any sort tends to come from academic writers and researchers. Even in the 2010s, authors advancing a critical or negative analysis are likely to be ignored politely, or else shouted down as 'Luddites', 'technophobes' or 'naysayers'. Indeed, the academic study of educational technology is perhaps best understood as an essentially 'positive project'. Most people working in this area are driven by an underlying belief that digital technologies are – in some way – capable of improving education. This mind-set is evident, for example, in the tendency throughout the 2000s to refer to 'technology-enhanced learning' or before this, during the 1980s and 1990s, to 'computer-assisted learning' – descriptions that leave little doubt over the inherent connection between digital technology and the improvement of learning and teaching. As such, the *de facto* role of the academic educational technologist is understood to be one of finding ways to make these technology-based improvements happen and – to coin a phrase often used in the field – to 'harness the power of technology'. Of course, this positive approach reflects the desire amongst most educational technologists to make education (and, it follows, 'the world') a better place. Nevertheless, it could be argued that this inherent positivity has long been an all-encompassing – if not hegemonic – feature of educational technology thinking and writing that limits the validity and credibility of the field as a site of serious academic endeavour. In this sense, the apparently calm and consensual tone of most educational technology debates and discussions belies an implicit 'with-us-or-against-us' attitude. In short, most people working in the field are so convinced of the benefits of digital technology in education that they are unwilling to think otherwise.

Educational technology has therefore become a curiously closed field of study – populated by people who consider themselves to be in the somehow more informed position of properly understanding the educational potential of digital technology. This can sometimes lead writers and researchers to adopt an intellectual stance that is evangelical – if not righteous – in its advocacy of this 'truth'. As its heart, then, educational technology displays many of the features of what Kling and Iocono (1988) termed a 'computerization movement' – that is, an interest-driven field of practice whose advocates focus on digital technologies as instruments capable of bringing about some sort of new social order. Of course, most academic disciplines and fields have dominant traditions and shared theoretical assumptions. Yet unlike most other fields of academic study, educational technology appears particularly resistant to viewpoints that contradict its core beliefs and values – not least the orthodoxy that technology is a potential force for positive change.

The present book can be considered 'critical' in that it offers a counterpoint to this orthodoxy. In this sense, taking a critical approach does not imply some rigid, dogmatic adherence to a particular political viewpoint or philosophical tradition. Instead, we are pursuing what Popkewitz (1987, p. 350) describes as 'critical intellectual work' – that is, attempting to move "outside the assumptions and practices of the existing order and struggling to make categories, assumptions and practices of everyday life problematic". This involves not finding comfort in commonsensical assumptions and taking things for granted. Being 'critical' instead implies taking a sceptical view of the claims surrounding educational technology in terms of fairness and efficiency, and rejecting the notion that this is an inevitable process that is beyond challenge or change. This also involves problematizing and engaging in systematic doubt – what John Holloway (2002, p. 6) describes simply as "a refusal to accept". This involves considering alternative explanations and perspectives, and maintaining a generally questioning approach to the established order. As Robert Cox (1981, p. 126) describes it, the critical academic therefore "stands apart from the prevailing order of the world and asks how that order came to be". As all these descriptions suggest, this is not a glamorous, self-affirming or 'sexy' approach to take – especially in comparison to the generally breathless accounts usually produced about digital media and technology. As Geert Lovink (2011, p. 63) acknowledges, any critical study of new technology will be gruelling and unglamorous – "we need to keep in mind that criticism is a necessary yet boring job; developing a compelling argument of related concepts can be profoundly unsexy".

The Need for a Technological Pessimism in Education

These previous observations are not intended to demean or affront the majority of academics who choose not to approach education and technology in this manner. In many ways the embrace of a positive and optimistic position is a completely understandable stance to adopt with respect to the application of technology in education – fitting neatly with the 'techno-romantic' manner in which most technologies are framed within modern thought. Indeed, there is a long-standing intellectual tradition in Western thinking of viewing technology as the pinnacle of scientific accomplishment (Coyne 1999), stemming from an Enlightenment-informed ideal of 'progress'. Thus, as Leo Marx (1994) has observed, the act of technology being 'assigned a heroic role' in pursuit of this 'progress' is certainly not a new one. Moreover, it could be argued that a tendency to be optimistic about the role of technology in modern life is itself an example of the positive essence that lies at the heart of nearly all Western thought. With only a few exceptions (such as Nietzsche and Schopenhauer), it could be argued that optimism is an essential underlying component of Western philosophy. As Dienstag (2006, p. 34) observes, most Western thought is based around "the notion that there *must* be an answer to our fundamental questions, even if we have not found it yet, and that this answer will deliver us from suffering".

Set against this orthodoxy of optimism, it is perhaps to be expected that the academic study of educational technology is driven by an almost unconscious urge to improve the human condition through technology. After all, this is simply how we are brought up to think about the role of technology in modern society. Yet while maybe justifiable from a philosophical point of view, the fact remains that this optimism and positivity have nevertheless served to limit the credibility and usefulness of educational technology within the wider social sciences. Even in terms of its 'parent' field of education studies, educational technology tends to be viewed as something of a lesser endeavour – a peripheral distraction from the more pressing 'real' issues of education and society. How, then, can educational technology discussion and debate be reinvigorated and reorientated towards becoming a more realistic, rigorous and ultimately relevant academic form? It is here that a case can be made for the field to adopt an avowedly critical and – above all – pessimistic perspective. In other words, to think *against* educational technology.

Given all that we know about the social complexities of technology use in education, it could be argued that a pessimistic stance is the most sensible, and possibly the most productive, perspective to take. As such, this book starts from the premise of simply accepting education, technology and society *as it is* – for better and (more often) for worse. It is important to note that this does not entail the adoption of dogmatic blanket negativity towards education and technology. Instead, this is to be a carefully focused and well-directed negativity and distrust. Holloway (2002, p. 5) writes,

> It is not because we are maladjusted that we criticise, it is not because we want to be difficult. It is just that the negative situation in which we exist leaves us no option: to live, to think, is to negate in whatever way we can the negativeness of our existence.

In its purest sense, then, pessimism still allows room for an acceptance that specific things are getting better. However, it also acknowledges the fact that life has long remained the same for most people in most circumstances, and that many social inequalities continue to persist regardless of changes elsewhere. Thus at one level, the pessimistic observer is simply one who adopts a mindset that is willing to recognise – and work within – the current and historical limitations of educational technology rather than its imagined limitless potential. As Dienstag (2006, p. 25) points out,

> Pessimists do not deny the existence of 'progress' in certain areas – they do not deny that technologies have improved or that the powers of science have increased. Instead, they ask whether these improvements are inseparably related to a greater set of costs that often go unperceived. Or they ask whether these changes have really resulted in a fundamental melioration of the human condition.

When seen in this light, it could be reasoned that pessimism is a rewarding and heartening position from which to approach education and technology. As Dienstag (2006, p. 40) contrasts, "The pessimist expects nothing – thus he or she is more truly open to every possibility as it presents itself . . . the optimist, on the other hand, must suffer through a life of disappointment, where a chaotic world constantly disturbs the upward path he feels entitled to tread". The pessimistic position certainly relieves the educational technologist from the burden of having to offer grand solutions to problems that can never be solved. As Dienstag (2006, p. 269) writes, the pessimistic mindset "rejects the idea that . . . human existence [is] a question or a problem waiting to be solved. Human existence just is – it has no predicate". In this sense, pessimism provides an ideal means of breaking free from the recurring cycle of 'hype, hope and disappointment' that has so often beset educational technology over the past 30 years (see Gouseti 2010).

In these terms alone, concentrating on the negative – instead of the positive – aspects of educational technology should lie at the heart of any attempt to establish a 'better' field of scholarship and practice. If there is anything to be learnt from the past 30 years of 'computer-assisted learning' and 'technology-enhanced learning' it surely is that there is little to be gained from maintaining a Pollyannaish stance towards technology use in education. Instead, contemporary discussions of educational technology need to foreground a host of usually overlooked critical issues and themes. Perhaps, as implied earlier in this chapter, the overriding change that this entails is shifting the field away from asking 'state-of-the-art' questions about technology, and towards asking questions that can be described as being concerned with the 'state-of-the-actual'. In other words, educational technology scholarship should look beyond questions of how technology *could* and *should* be used, and instead ask questions about how technology is actually being used in practice.

Thus at one level, the pessimistic perspective simply draws attention to the fact that the use of digital technology in education is never a completely predictable or certain affair. Given all the obvious limitations of the realities of educational technology use *in situ*, the 'glass-half-empty' view is perhaps a more rational approach to take than the 'glass-half-full'. The pessimistic educational technologist is at least willing to accept that digital technology is *not* bringing about the changes and transformations that many people would like to believe. Similarly, the pessimistic educational technologist recognises that to imagine otherwise for the future is to misunderstand wilfully the nature of social change. Yet to repeat a point made earlier, this is not to reconfigure educational technology into a defeatist endeavour. Instead, pessimism can provide an ideal basis from which educational technologists can achieve positive ends. While the field of educational technology clearly has much to gain from taking pessimism rather than optimism as the starting point for its activities, this should be done as an initial step towards then exploring how best to work alongside (and within) the imperfections of digital technology and education.

It is therefore important to note that what is being advanced here is the *purposeful* pursuit of pessimism. This is not what Michael Burawoy (2011) identifies as an 'uncompromising pessimism' that is engaged with for its own sake. The argument is certainly not being made for a revival of what Flanagan (1976, p. 1) termed 'the occupational masochism' of some aspects of social science that revel in a 'jaded sense of impotency'. Similarly, it is not being suggested that we succumb to what Leo Marx (1994) identifies as a 'postmodern pessimism' centred on the fatalistic acceptance of the 'domination' and 'menace' of life by large technological systems. All that is being advocated here is that educational technology is approached from a position that *expects* nothing – a position that is not to be confused with the nihilistic position of wanting nothing, or even the sceptical position of knowing nothing. Pessimistic educational technologists should neither celebrate nor welcome the constantly unsatisfactory situation of education and technology – rather they should "simply consider it their duty to call attention to it" (Dienstag 2006, p. x).

This suggests approaching educational technology from a position similar to Gramsci's notion of being "a pessimist because of intelligence, but an optimist because of will" (Gramsci 1929/1994, p. 299). In other words, this should be a pessimism that recognises the usefulness of starting from a position that acknowledges the parameters and boundaries of any technological endeavour, and holds realistic expectations of the political struggles and conflicts that surround any social change. This knowledge can *then* be used to go on to inform political action conducted in a more optimistic spirit. As Holloway (2002, p. 8) reasons, "If the hope is not grounded firmly in that same bitterness of history, it becomes just a one-dimensional and silly expression of optimism". Thus, while pessimistic educational technologists recognise that they may well be defeated in their ultimate ambitions, they should be in no way defeatist in their actions. It is therefore being proposed that the field of educational technology engages in pessimistic thought not from a sense of despondency, but as a sensibility from which political intervention and actions can be derived. Pessimism should not result in a passive resignation to one's fate, but as an active engagement with continuous alternatives. Pessimism can therefore provide a powerful basis for exploring ways that educational technologies can be used by individuals to better survive within an inherently imperfect world. As Dienstag (2006, p. ix) concludes,

> In the right hands, pessimism can be – and has been – an energizing and even liberating philosophy. While it does indeed ask us to limit and eliminate some of our hopes and expectations, it can also provide us with the means to better navigate the bounded universe it describes.

Steps Towards Distrusting Educational Technology

It should now be clear that educational technology is not as straightforward as we are often led to believe. In particular, this chapter has advanced the case that educational technology is *not* a neutral force for good that simply needs to be used in the 'right' or 'best' way to pay dividends. Instead, educational technology should be seen as a vehicle for a number of ideological agendas that subtly shape what educational technology is, and what educational technology does. Given all that has been discussed so far in this chapter, there would seem to be a pressing need to attempt, wherever possible, to challenge this current *status quo* of educational technology. In particular, there is a need to challenge the dominant ideological underpinnings of the educational application of digital technology, and therefore go some way to redressing the contradictions and conflicts that these forces suppress. While the vast majority of people working with educational technology appear willing to ignore or 'work around' these contradictions, there is an urgent need nevertheless for these issues to be thought (and fought) 'against'.

As such, our starting position of 'distrusting' educational technology involves simply being willing to see digital technology for what it is, while also attempting to imagine digital technology for all that it might be. First and foremost this involves questioning, challenging and carefully deconstructing the nature of the presumed digital transformations and changes with regard to contemporary forms of education that many commentators describe wholeheartedly and uncritically. Secondly, this needs to be done with a full awareness of the dominant ideological concerns of much educational technology reform to date. Thus we need to pursue a critical form of scrutiny which is perhaps less forward-looking, often less obvious and certainly less confirmatory than is usually found in academic writing on educational technology.

There are a number of characteristics and qualities that we should strive to take forward into the remainder of this book. The first characteristic is to deliberately slow down the pace of our discussions in the face of the fast-moving, rapidly changing and often ephemeral nature of the topic. Indeed, the new media landscapes of Facebook, Twitter and the iPad can often come across erroneously as somehow too fast-moving and mercurial to demand serious scrutiny. Jodi Dean (2010, p. 1), for one, has bemoaned the intellectual 'challenge' faced by any academic who attempts to think critically and politically "about media practices in a setting where they are fast, fun and ubiquitous". In order to counter these distractions, there is a clear need for a deliberate de-acceleration of our discussions of digital technology and education. Amidst the speed, churn, ephemerality and plurality of the contemporary digital landscape, there is a danger that "we lose the capacity to grasp anything like a system" (Dean 2010, p. 3). Yet if one looks beyond the seemingly ephemeral surface features of digital culture, then a number of entrenched issues of central importance to the contemporary educational condition are apparent. Given the endurance of these issues, a strong argument can therefore be made for adopting a more de-accelerated, detached and disinterested gaze towards education and technology than is usually the case in popular discourses of digital technology. Although many people may consider it to be a dying, outmoded format, the cumbersome, long form of a printed book certainly allows for a detached, more considered and de-accelerated perspective on technology.

Alongside this need to slow down, care also needs to be taken to not associate digital technology too readily with discourses of inevitable progress, transformation and the allure of 'the new'. Indeed, academic researchers should always take care that the apparent novelty of the technological near-future does not seduce them into overlooking the rather less novel realities of the present. As Peter Golding's (2000) description of 'type one' and 'type two' technologies reminds us, technologies rarely enable *new* forms of activity that were previously impracticable or inconceivable (type two). More often than not, technologies allow *existing* social action and process to occur *perhaps* in a speedier, more efficient or more convenient manner (type one). Thus it is important to resist the temptation to unthinkingly associate digital technologies with the inevitable change and progress associated with 'type two' technology. Instead researchers should remain mindful of the continuities, recurrences and repetitions associated with most 'new' technologies that are being used in education. In many instances, the cliché of 'old wine in new bottles' remains an appropriate description of the nature and forms of digital technology use in education. As such, one of the first steps when taking a distrustful approach to technology and new media is being able to move beyond the never-ending 'noise' of technical upgrades and product reversioning, and instead identify the often obscured but nevertheless substantive social issues that persist beneath (Wessels 2010). It is therefore crucial to lose any residual 'wonder' or 'awe' that one might have for the digital spectacular. As Geert Lovink reasons, in no sense should these technologies be perceived as fantastical. These are technologies that are now woven into the mundanity of everyday life and are therefore deserving of a dispassionate analysis:

> Let's get real. We should start with the observation that the internet is now a mainstream technology. While its ever-changing qualities continue to fascinate us, there is nothing spectacular about it. We've gone post-spectacle. This is the information society made real.
>
> *(Lovink 2011, p. 68)*

Following this lead, it is important to ground our analysis in the present-day uncertain realities of educational technology. Indeed, there is a need to be confident in the messy, uncertain nature of education and technology, and not feel obliged to present too certain or too neat a picture. While there is a tendency for discussions of education and technology to gravitate towards technicist notions of 'best practice,' 'effectiveness' and 'what works', it is far more accurate to see technological 'progress' as anything but predictable. To paraphrase Knud Løgstrup (1997), 'absolute certainty' about the benefits of educational technology equates to 'absolute irresponsibility'. Instead digital technologies are subjected continually to complex interactions and negotiations with the social, economic, political and cultural contexts into which they are situated. Thus this book should strive to develop an analysis of the messy, uncertain present-day realities of education and technology as they are currently manifest. As John Holloway (2002, p. 67) concludes, "The study of society . . . is the study of what *is*. The question of what ought to be may be interesting too [but] we must not confuse reality with dreams. As long as they are kept separate, there is no problem".

Conclusions

This opening chapter has covered a lot of ground – much of which has pointed to the need to engage with the politics of education and technology. Above all, the sense has emerged that digital technology is certainly not an uncontested or uncontroversial area of education. Instead, it can be concluded that the use of digital technology in education needs to be understood as an intense site of conflict. Indeed, as Andrew Feenberg (1991, p. 14) puts it, "Technology is not destiny but a scene of struggle". Education and technology can therefore be seen as a set of struggles that take place across a number of fronts – from the allocation of resources and the design of curricula to the maximizing of profit and attempts to overcome patterns of exclusion. As Wiebe Bijker (2010) reminds us, 'how to use technology?' is an inherently political question. Seen in this light, many of the key issues underpinning education and digital technology would appear to be the fundamentally political questions that are asked continually of education and society – that is, questions of what education is, and questions of what education should be. Developing a fuller sense of how and why digital technologies are being used in educational settings in the ways that they are therefore demands a broad recognition of issues of power, control, conflict and resistance. Put bluntly, any account of technology use in education needs to be framed in explicit terms of societal conflict over the distribution of power. As has also been argued throughout this chapter, such an approach demands a willingness to engage with the negative. As Apple, Ball and Gandin conclude,

> [We] must bear witness to negativity. That is, one of the primary functions is to illuminate the ways in which educational institutions, policies and practices are connected to the relations of exploitation and domination – and to struggles against such relations – in the larger society.
>
> *(2010, p. 5)*

Yet care has also been taken during this opening chapter to retain a sense of purpose. As has been stated before, the pessimistic approach does not imply that we need to adopt a nihilistic negativity with no hope or purpose. This approach also compels academic researchers to engage in work that aims to actually make a difference and that considers how education, technology and society might be made fairer. As implied throughout this chapter, the most valuable aspects of academic scrutiny of education and technology stem from a commitment to foster and support issues of empowerment, equality, social justice and participatory democracy. While no easy task, it should be possible to position the development of a critical analysis of education and technology within the underpinning aim of developing a critical disposition for "overt political struggle against oppressive social structures" (Harvey 1990, p. 20).

Taking these issues forward therefore demands a refocusing of our attention. In developing an interest in the politics of education and technology, the next chapter further examines the specifics of contemporary educational technology as a site of struggle and contest. In particular, the case is made for approaching educational technology as ideology – thereby linking our specific concerns with digital education with wider struggles for power and control amongst social groups and elites. Above all, this involves identifying the connections between educational technology and contemporary capitalist society, as well as the social relations associated with the 'new economy'. When seen in this light, then there is certainly much about education and technology that we might consider ourselves to be distrustful of.

2

UNDERSTANDING EDUCATIONAL TECHNOLOGY AS IDEOLOGY

Introduction

As highlighted in Chapter 1, the reluctance of many people to think critically about digital technologies in education contrasts sharply with the political nature of technology. While some appetite was shown for oppositional thought during the 1980s and 1990s (see, for example, the writings of Michael Apple, CA Bowers, Hank Bromley, Larry Cuban, Ivor Goodson and Neil Postman), the vast majority of academic discussion of educational technology has tended to lie somewhere between a disinterested acceptance and a deep-rooted belief in the inherent benefits of technology for education. The framing of digital technology as a generally 'good thing' has become an orthodoxy within education thinking – that is, part of a shared consensus where digital technologies have become "gradually accepted and virtually un-noticed", often without "those who are affected registering the fact" (Lefebvre 1981/2007, p. 78). It could be argued that educational technology is now something that appears to barely require thinking about at all. In many ways, the use of digital technology in educational settings has reached a state of being 'ideologically invisible' (Nye 2007), with the basic rationality of educational technology accepted largely without question.

This normalization of educational technology certainly requires critical attention. While the hopes, beliefs and promises that surround digital technology may have a strong intuitive resonance, the commonsensical 'stories' of digital technology that are repeated and 'retold' throughout educational discussions and debates need to be problematized. Indeed, despite its comforting overtones one should always be highly suspicious of commonsensical thinking. As David Harvey (2005, p. 39) cautions, the commonsensical can be "profoundly misleading" – masking, obfuscating or disguising real problems and leaving important realities closed to questioning. With these warnings in mind, this chapter seeks to move beyond the orthodoxy of educational technology as a 'good thing' and, instead, prepare the ground for a deliberately political analysis of education and technology. In particular, it is argued that the ways in which digital technology is talked about and understood within educational circles reflect the ideological function of educational technology. Thus from this point in the book onwards, we need to look beyond the "overbearing matter-of-factness" (Adorno 1981, p. 126) that characterizes most debates of education and technology and creates an illusion that these issues are free of political substance. Instead, this chapter develops a framework for identifying what these shaping ideological interests are, and exploring the consequences and outcomes of their dominance.

Understanding Ideology

First we need to develop a clear sense of what ideology is and how it operates. In a popular sense, the term 'ideology' is most often used to denote a general system of ideas, beliefs and values that guide action. For example, sports teams and multinational corporations are often said to have core guiding 'ideologies' that shape their success – such as the Dutch philosophy of 'total football' or Google's much-cited maxim of 'don't be evil'. Yet this bland everyday use of the word belies the significance of 'ideology' as a political concept, and its importance in understanding patterns of power and dominance in contemporary society. For this we need to look over the past 150 years of political thought, starting with the work of Karl Marx. For Marx, the concept of ideology was related to the masking of the contradictions produced by the capitalist system in ways that contributed to its reproduction. These contradictions included the exploitation and domination of the working classes, and the dehumanizing social relations and inequalities that result throughout society. Put simply, Marx described ideologies as functioning to invert the relationships between different elements of the capitalist system, thereby concealing the real patterns of power.

In this sense, Marx saw ideology as functioning to make these arrangements appear necessary, normal and congruous, and thereby helping to reproduce the dominance of one interest over the interests of others. Marx developed the understanding that ideologies are inherently political devices centred on the notions of 'inversion' and 'concealment'. One enduring example of the ideological concealment of contradiction can be seen in the ways in which markets tend to be presented and perceived as imbued with values of freedom and equality of opportunity, despite their underpinning inequalities and unfreedoms. Inversions such as these, Marx argued, lead to a 'distorted consciousness' throughout society that masks social and political contradictions. As such people's collective attention is focused on 'the sphere of appearances' (e.g., the illusion of the free and equal market) as opposed to the 'sphere of inner relations' (e.g., the unequal realities of production). Thus for Marx, ideology represented "illusion, false consciousness, unreality, upside-down reality" (Williams 1985, p. 156), which functioned to offer justification and consolation for oppression under capitalism.

While Marx's original reading of ideology can be criticized as being overly holistic and unified, there is obvious merit in his analysis. In particular this reading highlights a number of key features of ideology that pertain to our current discussions of educational technology – not least the idea that ideologies are endowed with crucial political functions, ordering the social world and directing it towards certain activities while legitimating some practices and de-legitimating others. In other words, Marx demonstrates how ideologies exercise power by creating a framework within which decisions can be taken and sense be made of these decisions. Crucially, Marx highlights the fact that the dissemination of ideology can be an act of deliberate manipulation, but also can be an unconscious or self-deceptive process. As such, ideologies contain levels of meaning that are hidden from their consumers and often from their producers. Marx's analysis is also useful in highlighting the pervasiveness of dominant ideologies in a society. These dominant ideologies often appear to 'belong' or be 'driven' by no one in particular. Instead, they are seen as part of the wider cultural and social milieu and moulded by long-standing social and historical circumstances. One of the key challenges of any study of ideology, therefore, is to attempt to identify and then decode these dominant ideologies – "identifying structures, contexts, and motives that are not readily visible" (Freeden 2003, p. 11).

Of course, these initial definitions prompted 150 years of subsequent debate and refinement. As Raymond Williams describes, many writers after Marx saw ideology less as a holistic mass illusion and in more bounded terms of specific forms of domination by "a given set of material interests or, more broadly, from a definite class or group" (Williams 1985, p. 156). Thus subsequent political philosophers and theorists have refined the notion of ideology away from the idea of a class-wide distortion and instead described it in more specific terms of the domination of one interest over others. For example, György Lukács wrote of ideology as the individualist consciousness of the bourgeois classes. Conversely, Karl Mannheim highlighted the pluralist potential of ideologies to play a central part in the attempts of different groups to exercise power – thus raising the possibility of competing ideological systems emerging from different modes of existence.

One of the key twentieth-century descriptions of ideology was that of Antonio Gramsci. In his writing Gramsci also moved away from the idea that ideology acted as a distorted form of mass consciousness, but instead described it as a system of ideas with a "capacity to inspire concrete attitudes and give certain orientations for action" (Larrain 2007, p. 86). Gramsci wrote of ideologies functioning to allow one class to exercise 'hegemony' over others – that is, winning consent to position a system of ideas or 'worldview' as the common sense of the majority. In this sense the notion of ideology as hegemony does not describe the imposition of false ideas from the dominant onto the dominated. Rather hegemony refers to a continually negotiated and often compromised 'common sense' that takes place between dominant and less dominant groups. As Raymond Williams (1980, p. 37) observed, these processes are often so all-encompassing that they often escape close attention:

> [hegemony] supposes the existence of something which is truly total ... but which is lived at such a depth, which saturates society to such an extent, and which even constitutes the substance and the limit of common sense for most people under its sway, that it corresponds to the reality of [their] social experience.

Crucially in Gramsci's analysis, ideological hegemony can be exercised not just through state force but also through various cultural means – thus drawing attention towards the "manufacturing of consent among the population at large, so that the masses would regard their own assent as spontaneous" (Freeden 2003, p. 20). This understanding of the cultural and social manufacturing of consent and compliance was extended in the work of Louis Althusser, who highlighted the existence of ideology in a material form across a wide range of social practices – most obviously the actions and behaviours of social institutions such as the family, religious and educational organizations. These latter writers highlight the necessary production of compromise between dominant ideological interests and subordinate groups, alongside the importance of the underlying forces that produce an illusion of voluntarism, free choice and consent. Later writers have therefore tended to view ideology as a pervasive means of manipulation and persuasion, rather than a means of direct repression. Jürgen Habermas, for example, wrote of the construction of 'reason' and 'uncoerced consensus' through what is said as well as what is done. This reading usefully highlights the importance of language and what Habermas referred to as 'systematically distorted communication' in the construction and maintenance of ideological thought. Rather than attempting to identify all-encompassing ideologies, Habermas recognised the importance of 'fragmented' rather than 'false' consciousness in advanced industrial societies. In this sense, Habermas described what he saw as the replacement of all-encompassing ideologies with more fragmented and partial frameworks of knowledge emanating from 'expert cultures'. This fragmented consciousness produced a divisive condition of 'obscurity' rather than total concealment or distortion.

As these latter examples imply, contemporary writers and thinkers have tended to approach ideology in less holistic terms than Marx's initial analysis. Rather than describing the universal repressive imposition of the beliefs and will of one dominant interest over all others, the notion of ideology is now understood in more nuanced terms as the manipulation of understandings in an attempt to legitimate the interests of particular groups and interests. Approached in this manner, the notion of ideology is concerned with ongoing struggles for meaning and understanding throughout a society. Indeed, as John Thompson (1990, p. 56) has argued, it is meaning rather than any other form of interaction that best "serves to establish and sustain relations of domination". As such, ideology is perhaps best understood as seeking to 'de-contest' or naturalise the meanings of political terms by converting the variety of possible meanings and interpretations into a reduced, simplified certainty that becomes the common consensus (Freeden 2003). For writers such as Laclau and Mouffe (1985), ideology is pursued increasingly through discursive practices that shape both the subject and the nature of reality itself – that is, what is said about something eventually *becomes* that thing. In this sense ideologies can be understood as attempting to naturalise subject positions by seeking to (re)establish closure wherever there are 'open' areas of discussion or disagreement.

Thus in taking these arguments forward in our analysis of educational technology, we need to recognise the complexity of ideology in contemporary society – not least the deep-rooted permeation of the values of dominant ideological interests into the fabric of everyday social processes and practices. Indeed, despite the sophisticated and ever-changing times that we now consider ourselves to be living in, many areas of contemporary society continue to be beset by dominant paradigms and mindsets, commonsensical thinking, worldviews, understandings of the '*status quo*', 'neutral' assumptions and facts. Thus as Zygmunt Bauman (2001, pp. 10–11) describes,

> Ideology is not so much an articulated creed, a set of verbal statements to be learned and believed; it is, rather, incorporated in the way people live – 'soaked in' by the way people act and relate. Once the hegemony has been achieved, hints and clues pointing in the wrong direction (wrong from the point of view of the actors' interests) are densely scattered all over the world within which the actors put their lives together; there is no more possibility of avoiding them or of unmasking their fraudulence so long as it is just their own life experiences that the actors much rely on in setting their 'life projects' and planning their actions. No brainwashing is required – the immersion in daily life shaped by the pre-set and pre-scripted rules will be quite enough to keep the actors on the set course.

The Dominant Ideologies of Contemporary Society and Technology

When seen in these terms, strong arguments can be made for digital technology acting as one of the key 'mechanisms' for giving dominant ideologies a 'real existence' in contemporary society (Boltanski & Chiapello 1999/2005). There is certainly widespread acceptance across the broader social science literatures of the ideological nature of technology. Indeed, over 30 years of writing and research from within the sociologies of technology, knowledge and science have detailed how all technologies are laden to some extent with values and embedded social relations. As Andrew Feenberg (1999, p. 83) contends, technology therefore should be seen as "a site of social struggle" through which hegemonic positions are developed, legitimated, reproduced and challenged. Indeed, the idea of *digital* technology as ideology was a recurrent theme throughout the work of Henri Lefebvre during the 1970s and 1980s, arguing that the emerging computerized and telecommunications technologies of the time served mainly to imbue, reinforce and 'nourish' ideology. Similarly, at the beginning of the 1990s Neil Postman coined the phrase 'technopoly' to denote the pervasive conflation of information technology and ideology throughout the latter half of the twentieth century. Paul Virilio also pointed to the ways in which digital technologies are bound within a distinctly militarist ideology. More recently, writers such as Nicholas Garnham (2000) critiqued the dominant views of 'digital age' and 'information society' as profoundly ideological in their role in engineering consent and acceptance of major economic, cultural and social reorderings of society.

If we are to develop a similar analysis for contemporary forms of educational technology, it is important to first identify the dominant ideologies that inform and underpin the prevailing 'major economic, cultural and social reorderings of society', and therefore could be said to drive contemporary enthusiasms for digital technology. Thus before we go on to consider the specific details of educational technology as ideology, it is necessary to consider the deep-rooted ideologies that permeate contemporary society and contemporary forms of digital technology. While not *always* apparent or *wholly* consistent, it could be argued that digital technology has long been intertwined with a closely related set of dominant contemporary ideologies – that is, libertarianism, neo-liberalism and what can be termed the 'new' capitalism. The nature of these ideologies will now be outlined in further detail.

I. Libertarian Ideology

One increasingly dominant ideology over the past 50 years has been the libertarian belief in the primacy of the individual. Indeed, libertarian discourses have long pervaded the meanings and understandings attached to digital technology – a trend described by writers such as Langdon Winner (1997) as 'cyber-libertarianism'. Here, the power of technology and the power of the individual – what Kelemen and Smith (2001, p. 371) describe as "two ideas which lie at the heart of modern civilization" – are seen as creating new forms of action and organization that do not require the appropriation of traditional spaces or structures. Of course, libertarian ideology long precedes the advent of digital technology – originating in debates surrounding slavery and feudal rights, and therefore spanning back to the concerns of the founders of the US bill of rights. Indeed, a basic trust in the moral and political primacy of the individual and a corresponding sense of self-ownership can be traced back to John Locke's (1690/2010, para. 27) assertion that "Every man has a Property in his own Person". As this demonstrates, an enduring tenet of libertarian thinking is the primacy of the individual. Libertarianism sees the control for one's actions coming from within the individuals themselves, with everyone having the right to strive for whatever goals and outcomes they see fit. In this sense, society is seen as being best organized along meritocratic lines of self-ownership and individual control of resources.

This notion of individuals pursuing their own rational self-interest has proved to be especially seductive within North American culture, which it could be argued "has always celebrated radical individualism, as epitomized by the image of the frontiersman" (Palley 2005, p. 21). Thus the libertarianism of the early twenty-first century could be seen as a particularly American strain of individualism – with its emphasis on personal responsibility, self-management and self-sufficiency, coupled with reduced levels of government control and control from the state (Sennett 2012). Yet we should not overlook the humanist tone of libertarian ideology. In its purest form, libertarianism presents a generally trusting and positive view of human nature, in which people learn from their mistakes and rationally try their best. As Moseley (2007, p. 88) describes it, "The general vision . . . is that of a man [sic] set free from men, developing his talents and exchanging freely with others voluntarily". Ayn Rand, a key influence on recent libertarian thinking, argued for an ethical and moral dimension, where people should be protected against those who impose violence or a threat, while striving for an independence from others. This, then, is not an exclusively individualist doctrine – a social life is seen as necessary for individual advancement, and the benefits of cooperating, collaboration and exchanging are seen as key to survival and success. Libertarianism therefore acknowledges "the relations that exist amongst people but maintains that the acting individual always acts of his own volition – even when running with the crowd" (Moseley 2007, p. 87).

It is perhaps not surprising that libertarian ideology has been aligned closely with the development of digital technology. It can be argued that digital technology offers a ready canvas for various strains of libertarian thinking to be imagined and (in part) operationalized – in particular the privileging of the sovereign user and the principles of self-responsibilization and self-determination. For example, computer use has long been based upon a valorisation of the empowered individual user, living "a world where anyone can learn to become a creator of information or code that can help to transform their lives and societies" (Palfrey & Gasser 2011, p. 195). Conversely, celebrants of the new digital economy – the so-called 'digerati' of *Wired* magazine, Silicon Valley and the NASDAQ – hold similar deep-rooted views of the potential for individually driven progress through technology. As Geert Lovink describes, this is an area of business that is devoid of traditional political beliefs but based around a loose 'freewheeling ethic' where the internet offers a largely "unregulated sphere" for individual entrepreneurship (Lovink 2011, p. 1). The majority of academic writing and research on digital technology and media takes a similar line on the empowered individual. As Miller (2011, p. 230) argues, "Much of the field buys into individualistic fantasies of reader, audience, consumer or player autonomy – [the] intellectual's wet dream of music, movies, television and everything else converging under the sign of the empowered fans".

It is therefore clear that ideologies of individualism and libertarianism are embedded deeply within many aspects of the application of digital technology in society. This, it would seem, is consistent regardless of political conviction or social standing. As Harper (2009, p. 148) observes, "According to the majority of internet pundits, whether e-business billionaires or left-wing academics: internet equals freedom". Thus the notion of 'techno-libertarian utopia' has proved to be a 'strong meme' throughout the history of digital technology and media, not least the idea of digital technology "as a tool for personal freedom" (Lovink 2011, p. 39). However, it is important not to be seduced into a technological determinist reading of digital technologies somehow *causing* these shifts to occur. The key point here is that libertarianism and individualism are cultural and ideological shifts that have long informed the organization of many societies and "whose logic is finally simply playing itself out in our technological and social institutions" (Song 2010, p. 270).

II. Neo-liberal Ideology

The second set of meanings and understandings attached to contemporary digital technology is that of neo-liberalism. As an ideological form, neo-liberalism extends libertarian notions of individual liberty, self-responsibility and personal entrepreneurism with an explicit belief in consumer choice and market freedom, coupled with the dominance of private interests over the workings of the state (Ball 2012). For many commentators, neo-liberalism has been a dominant ideology across societies for the past 30 years. As David Harvey (2005, p. 3) argues, "Neoliberalism has, in short, become hegemonic as a mode of discourse. It has pervasive effects on ways of thought to the point where it has become incorporated into the commonsense way many of us interpret, live in and understand the world". While some people now claim wishfully that the dominance of neo-liberalism was undermined fatally by the global economic crises of the late 2000s and early 2010s, neo-liberal ideology has proved remarkably adaptable and resilient. As Peters (2011, p. 5) observes, "It is undeniably still the ruling ideology even though it has transmuted in form a number of times".

It is important to distinguish between the often flawed application of neo-liberal ideology in practice and its more abstract form as what Charles Taylor (2004) describes as a 'social imaginary' – that is, as a set of ideas and ideals telling us what is normal and what is possible. In this sense Nick Couldry (2010) makes the distinction between the economic 'workings' of 'neo-liberal proper' and the theoretical forms of political and social organization suggested by 'neo-liberal doctrine'. In this more theoretical sense of doctrine, neo-liberalism can be understood as an unfinished project seeking to remould the world in its image. As such, "the neoliberal model does not purport so much to describe the world as it is, but the world as it should be" (Clarke 2005, p. 58). Neo-liberalism should not be seen simply as a business template concerned with increasing the prominence of the market and diminishing the power of the nation state and other market 'impediments'. Instead, as a social imaginary, neo-liberalism "involves a broader range of underlying principles, ultimately political values that are deeply embedded" (Couldry 2010, p. 22).

Echoing the libertarian ideology, one key set of values in neo-liberal thought is the primacy of unimpeded individual action. Neo-liberalism therefore promotes individual responsibilization and the self as enterprise, with the onus placed on the values of self-interest, individual entrepreneurialism and competition (Hilgers 2010). As Harvey (2005, p. 65) details, "Each individual is held responsible and accountable for his or her own actions and well-being". Against this individualism, it is the 'spontaneous order' of the market that is seen as the best means of preserving individual freedoms while also establishing a societal order. Indeed, markets are seen as optimal and self-regulating social structures that function best without restraint. This leads to an occupancy of a language of 'choice' and relations of competition as the most efficient way of allocating resources, as well as the most efficient way of achieving human freedom (Munck 2005). One of the key tenets of this privileging of the market is the removal of 'artificial distortions' from the path of free and equal exchange (Colás 2005). Neo-liberalism is therefore imbued with a strong opposition to state-led 'social engineering', not least the welfare state. As such, neo-liberalism seeks to cede responsibility of the state to individual self-concerns, with the role of the state reduced, at most, to creating and preserving an institutional framework appropriate to strong private property rights, free markets and free trade – ideally at the global level (Harvey 2005).

In many ways, neo-liberalism has lent philosophical support to the twentieth-century free market economics of Hayek, Popper and Berlin and the corresponding view of the individual *homo economicus* as "an egoistic, rational, utility maximizer" (Hind 2010, p. 83). Seen in this light, "every area of human life [becomes] subject to reorganization on economic principles, with economic thought becoming coterminous with rationality itself" (Couldry 2010, p. 28). Yet it is important not to portray neo-liberal thought solely in terms of individual economic rationality. Neo-liberalism can be seen as offering an alternative societal model to centralism and thereby offering an escape from government domination for those who previously were unable to exercise choice. Neo-liberalism does not necessarily oppose the social and the communal. Indeed, neo-liberalism offers a model of a shared communal market – albeit one that individuals are not obliged to participate in. As Couldry (2010, p. 135) describes, the key moral underpinning of neo-liberal ideology is "the *individual's* sense of control over his or her own life . . . On this view, cooperation, though often desirable, is purely a matter of individual will".

III. The Ideology of 'New Economy'

Clearly neo-liberal ideology is linked intrinsically with the organization of capitalism and capitalist relations. Indeed, for some commentators, neo-liberalism is primarily a system of justification and legitimization for "re-establish[ing] the conditions for capital accumulation and to restore the power of economic elites" (Harvey 2005, p. 19). As Andrew Glyn (2007) puts it, neo-liberalism is 'capitalism unleashed'. The fact that the term 'capitalism' has been obscured largely by the term 'neo-liberalism' over the past 30 years is, for some commentators, indicative of the hegemony of capitalist relations and "capitalism's ideological triumph" (Žižek 2008, p. 337). Thus we must also look beyond 'neo-liberal' ideology and consider the meanings and understandings attached to digital technology relating to the nature and needs of contemporary capitalism.

As has been noted widely, the nature of capitalism has shifted considerably over the past 40 years or so. Throughout the 1970s and 1980s a number of structural changes in economic relations were being described by commentators in terms of 'post-industrial' society, 'post-Fordist' modes of production, the 'knowledge economy' and the information society. All these labels reflected shifts towards what Harvey (1990) terms 'flexible accumulation' – that is, the emergence of flexible labour markets and labour processes, as well as increasingly flexible patterns of production and consumption. These structural changes in capitalism were based around a decline in traditional industry and industrial economies, with the significance of industrial labour usurped by "a more heavily financialized and image-based system of global exchange" (Brennan 2011, p. 1).

Key to the changes associated with the rise of the 'new economy' is the notion that these new forms of production, consumption and profit are largely immaterial in nature. As Ekman (2012) notes, the organization of the new economy is based largely around the privatization of 'immaterial' assets that were previously outside the realms of capital accumulation – such as knowledge, genetic material and reproduction processes. This has been a key thesis developed by the 'autonomist' Marxist school of thought, which points to the extension of labour, production and exploitation beyond the established boundaries of industrial capitalism. In terms of the principal modes of production under these new conditions, the autonomist writers have highlighted the growing significance of 'immaterial labour' – that is, "labour that creates immaterial products, such as knowledge, information, communication, a relationship, or an emotional response" (Hardt & Negri 2004, p. 108). In this sense, profit is gained from the production of knowledge and ideas rather than industry, therefore requiring new models of capital accumulation. Christian Fuchs (2008, p. 103), for example, contrasts traditional forms of manual labour that work primarily to change the physical condition of objects with what he termed 'informational labour', which works to change "the emotional and communicative aspects of human relations".

As Fuchs and others suggest, digital technologies are an integral element of these recent shifts towards globally networked capitalism, just as the steam engine and other industrial-age technologies were central to earlier 'mutations' of capitalism (Savat 2009). The computer can therefore be described with some justification as the 'universal instrument' of recent times – "today the computer corresponds to what the electrical motor was a century ago, and the steam engine before then" (Maraizzi 1994/2011, p. 68). Commentators have identified a number of 'new' varieties of capitalism that are predicated upon computerized processes and practices – such as digital capitalism, virtual capitalism, high-tech capitalism, informatic capitalism and informational capitalism. One significant description is 'cognitive capitalism' (Vercellone 2007), highlighting the importance of 'cognitive labour' that is intellectual, communicative, symbolic and emotional in its substance, and therefore concerned with working with forms of language and communication that can be digitalized. The notion of cognitive capitalism also foregrounds the importance of networked and highly social modes of cooperative production within contemporary capitalism. These themes are extended into the notion of 'communicative capitalism', which highlights the growing commodification of everyday life – not least online communication and interaction (Dean 2012). As Maraizzi (1994/2011) contends, the emphasis here is on forms of information, language and communication that are ultraprecise, ultralogical (i.e., that have shared rules and grammar that can be used anywhere) and ultraformal (i.e., 'abstract, artificial, completely symbolic'). These are forms of information, language and communication that thereby lend themselves to easy symbolization, codification and instrumentalized calculation (Maraizzi 1994/2011). Also along these lines is the growth of 'algorithmic capitalism', reliant on the use of technology-based systems in easily sequentialized and logicized areas of society such as financial markets and the law.

All these digitally based forms of capitalism are seen as having created an altered set of economic demands. For example, in terms of forms of work, the new economy is seen as demanding the extension and intensification of post-Fordist forms of labour. Thus the work skills of the new economy are based around skills and dispositions relating to multitasking, autonomy, creativity, 'innovation' and networked and cooperative forms of working, as well as malleability of working practices (Boltanski & Chiapello 1999/2005). This has been reflected in the recent popularisation of concepts of 'lean production', team concepts, 'just-in-time' production, mobile capital and the diversification of commodities for niche markets. The importance of these qualities reflects the fact that the work of the new economy is less bounded and delineated – leading to a totalized and permanent state of work. For example, Negri (1984) noted the move from the industrial 'mass worker' producing consumer goods in a factory to the 'social worker' whose work has expanded beyond the workplace and into most aspects of society. In this sense, the new economy is seen as encompassing most areas of everyday life as potential sources of profit generation. This blurring of boundaries is also seen as existing between the domains of production and consumption. In the new economy, it is argued, one of the key individual subjectivities is the ability to consume as well as the ability to produce. Contemporary capitalism, therefore, is seen as built around a dominant 'consumerist life pattern' across all areas of life, where "consumer markets expand, thrive and profit by commodifying the pursuit of fun, comfort and happiness" (Bauman 2012a, p. 116).

Understanding Educational Technology as Ideology

There are clear links between the development of digital technology and all of the dominant ideologies just described – especially in terms of the understandings and meanings that are popularly attached to digital devices and digital practices. It could be reasoned that digital technologies have a two-way relationship with ideologies of individualism, neo-liberalism and the new economy – clearly being shaped by these dominant values and interests, but also acting to perpetuate the dominance of those values and interests in wider society. Indeed, digital technologies can be seen as a key material form of these ideologies over the past few decades – embodying the values, dispositions and mindsets of libertarianism, neo-liberalism and new forms of capitalism while extending them into the social practices and relations of everyday life. There is a growing literature that details the full extent of these connections between everyday digital technology use and the hegemony of contemporary individualized, neo-liberal, capitalist society. Dyer-Witheford and de Peuter's (2009) analysis of video gaming, for example, demonstrated how each stage of the production and consumption of video games (from the design studio to the bedroom) can be linked to the cultural, political and economic interests of global capital. Conversely, Melissa Gregg's (2010) study of white-collar 'office' technologies of laptop computers and email showed how these digital devices and applications extend flexible capitalist working practices into every aspect of everyday life, fuelling a growing alienation and disaffection with work and family life. Similar studies have highlighted the ideological nature of web-searching, mobile telephony and social networking (Eichstaedt 2011; Mager 2012; Sevignani 2012). These correspondences may not always be consistent and are rarely obvious, but must be taken seriously when trying to make sense of the significance of digital technology in contemporary society.

In this sense, we now need to begin to consider how these dominant ideologies may correspond with the specific domain of *educational* technology. Thus, while it may not appear immediately obvious, we now need to explore the idea that the digital technologies used increasingly throughout education are also best understood as ideological in character and form – that is, shaped by dominant sets of values and interests, and then acting (however subtly) to perpetuate the dominance of those values and interests. This – in itself – is not an especially novel set of contentions to make. Ivor Goodson and John Marshall Mangan, for example, made a persuasive series of arguments nearly 20 years ago that computers in schools were key sites for the expression, maintenance and extension of dominant ideologies of economic competitiveness and the development of 'high skills'. These authors argued that it was essential to approach the technologizing of education as what they termed an "ideologically freighted innovation" (Goodson & Mangan 1996, p. 65). Similarly, as Michael Apple argued 10 years before,

> The debate about the role of the new technology in [education] is not and must not be just about the technical correctness of what computers can

and cannot do. These may be the least important kinds of questions, in fact. Instead, at the very core of the debate are the ideological and ethical issues concerning what [education] should be about and whose interests they should serve.

(Apple 1986, p. 153)

Despite their voracity, these arguments have remained largely absent from the academic study of education and technology. Most people, it would seem, are happy to assume that educational technologies are 'neutral' tools that are essentially free from values and intent (or, at most, shaped by generally optimistic understandings and meanings associated with educational change and improvement). In this sense, it is difficult at first glance to see educational technology as entwined with any aspect of the dominant ideologies just described. Yet, as was noted earlier, one of the core characteristics of hegemony is the ability of dominant ideologies to permeate commonsensical understandings and meaning. Following this logic, then, the fact that educational technology appears to be driven by a set of values focused on the improvement of education does not preclude it also serving to support and legitimate wider dominant ideological interests. Indeed, if we take time to unpack the general orthodoxy of educational technology as a 'positive' attempt to improve education, then a variety of different social groups and with different interests, values and agendas are apparent. As will now be argued, while concerned ostensibly with changing specific aspects of education, all of these different interests could be said to also endorse (or at least provide little opposition to) notions of libertarianism, neo-liberalism and new forms of capitalism. Thus educational technologies can still be said to be 'ideologically freighted', although this may not always be a primary intention of those involved in promoting their use.

These are complex contentions, and clearly require further justification. Thus before these arguments are explored in further detail, the remainder of this chapter will unpack briefly the general consensus of educational technology as a 'positive project'. What values and interests lie beneath the promotion of educational technology over the past 30 years, and to what extent could they be said to constitute an ideology of educational technology? In considering these points, a number of distinct values and agendas can be identified that could be said to constitute the positive project of educational technology, and therefore merit closer consideration.

I. Learner-centred Learning

Perhaps most obviously, digital technologies are seen by many educationalists as fitting neatly with a number of values and interests relating to the nature and organization of learning. In this sense, many people's interest in educational technology is underpinned by a dominant set of values stemming from progressive education ideals and/or social constructivist and sociocultural models of learning – all of which privilege learner-centred and learner-driven forms of education. These approaches share a view that learning is a profoundly social and cultural process and therefore emphasise the influence of the social environments that surround an individual's learning and cognitive development. Seen along the lines of sociocultural theories of learning – particularly the (post)Vygotskian tradition – digital technologies act as powerful social resources within an individual's learning context (see Luckin 2010). In particular, this approach frames digital technology as a key means of providing learners with enhanced access to sources of knowledge and expertise that exist outside of their immediate environment. There is now considerable interest, for example, in the field of 'computer-supported collaborative learning', where individuals collaborate and learn at a distance via digital tools. Similarly, there is much enthusiasm for the ability of digital technology to support social-cultural forms of 'situated learning' and the associated notion of 'communities of practice'. These terms describe learning as best taking place in the form of 'real-world' activities and interactions between people and their social environments.

For some educators, these pedagogic and epistemological values extend into a belief that digital technology can support 'progressive', nonauthoritarian forms of educational engagement. These include child-centred learning and open forms of teaching which emphasise meaning making and interpretation, as well as encouraging learner autonomy and dispersal of power. In this sense, enthusiasm for digital technology use in education chimes with the Deweyian philosophy that underpins much contemporary Western educational thought. Here education is seen as concerned primarily with the development of persons, and helping individuals acquire the knowledge and understanding that enable them to live fully human lives as well as belonging to a wider community through appropriate actions and commitments (Pring 2010). Digital technologies are therefore seen as playing a key role in redefining most of the core aspects of education along these lines, not least the redefinition of the teacher's role, the reconceptualization of learner action and the relationship between learning and knowledge.

While these beliefs and assertions tend to be presented as empirical 'fact' it is important to view them as driven by both objective *and* subjective debate – much like other ideologically driven 'scientific' debates such as climate change or green economics. Indeed, many of the 'learning science' descriptions of digital technology are driven by wider beliefs of what constitutes 'good' or 'desirable' learning. As such, many of these justifications position digital technology as a form of pedagogic corrective – that is, a means to get particular learning values and philosophies into formal educational settings that are otherwise seen as lacking. Some educational technologists refer to this as the 'Trojan Mouse' approach – that is, using digital technology as a means to 'leverage' wider philosophies of teaching and learning into educational settings. As Eric Klopfer (2008, p. 12) acknowledges, "It isn't all about the technology . . . Many of these skills [have] been promoted by education reformers for decades, and could be fostered without technology. Technology, however, is the vehicle for getting these intellectual capabilities into schools discretely".

II. The Efficiencies of Education

A further set of interests and values that are prominent within the general promotion of educational technology is concerned with issues of enhanced organizational effectiveness and efficiency, rather than individual or collective empowerment. As such, the use of digital technology in education is also justified as fulfilling various criteria relating to the 'economics' of education (see Ball 2007). These include the idea of technology contributing to the efficient logistics of educational provision; the idea of technology contributing to the profitability and commoditization of education; and the idea of technology contributing to countries' economic competitiveness and efficiency of labour and knowledge production.

In terms of the first criterion, for example, clear linkages are made by some social groups between educational technology and a general desire to see the 'modernization' and 'incentivization' of public sector services through techniques of management derived from the for-profit sector. These values therefore position educational technology within issues of efficiency, effectiveness, modernization, rationalization and the reduction of spending costs (Deem 2004). In this sense, digital technology is seen as supporting the recasting of education along more business-orientated centralized 'data-driven' lines. Indeed, there has been a steady rise of discernible technology-supported managerial practices that are now prevalent throughout many sectors of education – from systems of self-evaluation and performance management, intensified managerial control of curricula, standardized labour processes and the introduction of accountability mechanisms. The enrolment of digital technologies into these debates therefore lends a distinctly technocratic air to how contemporary education is being imagined – with many discussions imbued with a sense of 'digital Taylorism' (Brown, Lauder & Ashton 2011), reflecting what Lasch (1987, p. 87) termed "technology and the ideology of total control".

There is also a clear sense amongst some social groups that digital technology can contribute to the profitability and commoditization of education. A notable belief here is the use of technology as a vehicle for the establishment of 'genuine' markets in education – characterized by "no state intervention of any kind, in funding, provision or regulation" (Tooley 2006, p. 26). In one sense, these arguments are driven by a procorporate interest in supporting the expanding marketplace for technology-based education. Yet these values also convey a desire to reorganize and rearrange all aspects of education along market-based lines. It is important to note that these arguments are not profit-driven *per se*; indeed there are a growing number of market fundamentalists who are "inspired by the non-commercial possibilities of social production and social networks" (Freedman 2012, p. 77). Nevertheless, the technology-supported removal of the state from the provision of public education has been anticipated by a range of articulations of the 'end of school' and realizing the "dream of education without the state" (Tooley 2006, p. 22).

Finally, the use of digital technology in education has long been promoted as contributing to countries' economic competitiveness and efficiency of labour and knowledge production. In particular, much government interest in educational technology is imbued with a belief that digital technology can act as a means of increasing a nation's economic competitiveness in the knowledge-driven economies of the post-industrialized world. As such, it can be argued that national educational technology agendas have been conceived and perpetuated by nation states as a concerted attempt to reconfigure the economic 'mindset' of future workers towards a technologically based global competition. The emphasis here is on upgrading the skills base of emerging generations of young people and creating the 'workforce flexibility' to counter the threat of a global labour market. As Lefebvre (1976/2009) notes, one of the primary pressures facing the nation state in the modern world is the relatively autonomous nature of technological and economic growth. In this sense, the totemic value of educational technology for states should not be overlooked, with governments using educational technology agendas as a high-profile means of being seen as actually 'doing something' about the digital age.

III. Communitarianism

In addition to these agendas, a strong strain of counterestablishment thinking also underpins many other people's endorsement of digital technology as a means of reorganizing educational provision and practice. Regardless of whether consciously held, these values reflect the influence of 1960s' counterculturalism on development of digital technology. Indeed, the significance of late 1960s' Californian 'hippie' philosophy in informing the beginnings of the home-brew computer movement, early programmer communities and, more recently, the notions of open-source software and social software has been well documented (Markoff 2005). As such, progressive and subversive countercultural values and philosophies have long underpinned the development of computer technology from the 1960s onwards. As Steven Jones (2006, p. 189) contends, over the past 50 years this has seen the steady growth within countercultural movements of a "pro-technology faction [who] believed that it was possible to create a new kind of counter-technology, an appropriately scaled and designed technology that, come the revolution and the collapse of the military-industrial complex, would rise to the occasion".

The influence of this "wild hippie culture" (Lovink 2011, p. 39) is evident in what can be described as the 'communitarian' understanding of computer technology as a ready means of reimagining and reorganizing all aspects of society and culture (including education) by "promot[ing] togetherness through the fostering of mutual empathy and understanding" (Curran 2012, p. 38). These views therefore reflect the 'New Communalist' strand of the 1960s' San Francisco countercultural movement, which imbued computing with values of "collaboration, flexibility and utopian social change" (Dean 2010, p. 19). Such thinking led to popular reconceptualizations of computing in terms of the progressive values and artistic sensibilities of the time. Persuasive arguments have therefore been made over time for the development of computer-based communes and 'global villages', and the framing of computer-based action as a "loose-knit, collaborative effort with an open social structure" (Mason 2006, p. 145).

During the 1960s and 1970s, this computer-based communitarianism was largely a political attempt to reposition the computer as a 'social machine' rather than a 'war machine'. In this sense, these values reflected the "psychedelic social ideas" (Mason 2006, p. 143) of the hippie movement alongside traditions within academic science of openness and reciprocity (Curran 2012). Yet communitarian ideals have persisted throughout the subsequent development of computer and internet technology. Indeed, the use of digital technology to support the re-creation of what Jodi Dean (2010, p. 8) describes as "society without antagonism" now has a relatively long heritage in technology terms – linking back to the development of the Whole Earth 'Lectronic Link (or WELL), alongside MUDS, MOOs and other forms of 'virtual community' in the 1980s and 1990s, to the virtual worlds and 'blogosphere' of the 2000s and 2010s. The recent trend for Silicon Valley billionaire entrepreneurs to invest their money in the construction of real-life offshore island communities and space transportation is therefore a logical extension of these values.

IV. Anti-institutionalism

The communitarian philosophy frames digital technology as "a form of relatively slow and benign sabotage – that is, as a means of using human-scale technology to resist and gradually undermine the dominant technocracy" (Jones 2006, p. 195). In contrast, another strand of countercultural-inspired thinking about digital technology and education is more direct in its framing of technology as a means to resist and oppose establishment interests. This is what Richard Wise (2000) identifies as the 'disruptive' anti-institutional wing of the computing counterculture – that is, those "believ[ing] that cheap computing power in the hands of citizens could be a powerful resource for democracy and a weapon against overbearing government and big business" (Wise 2000, p. 26). These ideas celebrate the empowerment of computer-using individuals at the expense of dominant institutions – be they military, bureaucratic, corporate or government. The key here is the perceived ability of digital technologies to support 'self-organization' within networks that is decentralized, distributed and bottom-up, therefore opposing the planned and controlled nature of institutional organization. Seen along these lines, then the facilitation of a "do-it-yourself, self-reliant approach" (Atkinson 2010, p. 79) is an inherent outcome of computer use – reflecting "a widespread desire for connection and cooperation in a context free of the private and public hierarchies that so often dominate our lives" (Streeter 1999, p. 60).

These ideas of anti-institutional forms of self-organization have been expressed in a number of ways with regard to digital technology and education. For example, educators working in the traditions of 'critical pedagogy' and 'democratic education' have seized upon digital technology as a potential "means for revolutionary ends" of allowing individuals to transcend the limitations of conventional schooling and educational expectations (Suoranta & Vadén 2010, p. 177). Such thinking therefore positions digital technology as realizing the critical pedagogic philosophy of Paulo Friere and the arguments for the 'deschooling' of society by the likes of Goodman, Holt, Lister, Kozel, Reimer and, most prominently, Ivan Illich. During the 1960s and early 1970s these writers condemned institutionalized learning as inhibiting individual growth due to its function as a product of capitalist society and emphasis on 'progress' through mass production and consumption. These views are therefore seen as prophetically anticipating contemporary rhetorics of digital technologies and education. As Charles Leadbeater (2008, p. 44) reasoned, "In 1971 [deschooling] must have sounded mad. In the era of *eBay* and *MySpace* it sounds like self-evident wisdom".

In these terms, support for individuals' self-determination of their learning via digital technologies feeds into wider enthusiasms shared amongst many in education for the inherent benefits of episodes of informal learning that take place outside the control of formal education organizations and settings (see Sefton-Green 2004). Digital technology has therefore been aligned readily with arguments for the deinstitutionalizing of education (Downes 2010), and the encouragement of 'unlearning' – that is, "learning how to learn independently" (Chokr 2009, p. 6). In these terms, digital technology is seen as a potential means of resisting the 'banking model' of accumulating 'knowledge content', and instead supporting open discussion, open debate, radical questioning, continuous experimentation and the sharing of knowledge.

V. Techno-fundamentalism

A final core (but often less obvious) value underpinning many people's interest in educational technology is what Vaidhyanathan (2011) describes as a 'techno-fundamentalism'. While acknowledged rarely, this can be described as a straightforward enchantment with technology and desire to benefit from continued technological progress. As Steven Jones (2006, p. 2) describes, this line of thinking reflects a popular "willingness to buy into two widely shared assumptions: i) that technology's place in our daily lives is central; and ii) that it will inevitably increase in the future". As such the techno-fundamentalist mindset reflects an implicit belief that technology offers a means to substantially improve current forms of everyday life and social relations – including education. Jodi Dean identifies this as a 'core faith' throughout many sectors of contemporary society, often reflected in a belief that "technology will save the world . . . the credo that the proper tools make anything possible: the computer thus appears to make anything possible; the computer thus appears as the universal tool making *everything* possible" (Dean 2010, p. 20).

One prominent feature of the techno-fundamentalist mindset is a belief in what has been termed 'computationalism' (see Golumbia 2009; Lanier 2010). Computationalism frames the world in terms of adjustable and refinable statistical algorithms, thereby offering what Savat (2009, p. 4) describes as "the simplicity of increased control offered by Boolean logic and the binary digit". As such, any aspect of society – including education – can be seen in terms of a computational problem that can be addressed through computational thinking and logic. From this perspective, digital technology offers a ready means to "route around conflict, as if working code were the solution to any problem rather than a particular set of problems" (Dean 2010, p. 23).

These beliefs and values are rarely expressed or acknowledged, yet underpin many justifications for the use of digital technology in education. A techno-fundamentalist perspective certainly underpins the framing of discussions of education and technology in terms of future-orientated belief, speculating on how technology 'can and will' rather than how technology 'has and does' (Njenga & Fourie 2010, p. 201). These assumptions are apparent within expectations of even the newest of technology users, reflecting the unconscious nature of many people's inherent faith in technological progress and the 'technical fix'. Indeed, this deep-rooted faith in technology could be said to have assumed a quasi-religious status within contemporary society. Some authors have pointed toward the 'awe' with which digital technology is regarded in Western society (Jones 2006), alongside the 'almost religious intensity' that pervades popular discourses around technology (Thomas 2011; see also Lewin 2011). For some commentators, then, this 'infatuation' with digital technology has "gain[ed] the aura of a new religion" (Campanelli 2010, p. 37) in our otherwise increasingly secular times. As Jaron Lanier (2010, p. 178) concludes, "Those who enter into the theatre of computationalism are given all the mental solace that is usually associated with traditional religions".

Thinking Against the Orthodoxy of Education and Technology

The use of digital technology in education is clearly intertwined with a diversity of values, interests and agendas – from a straightforward faith in the transformatory 'power' of technology to matters of global economic competitiveness and organizational efficiency. As such, educational technology is perhaps best understood as a 'culturally contested zone' where a variety of social groups "create, negotiate, and give differing and sometimes conflicting forms, meanings and uses to technologies" (Oudshoorn & Pinch 2003, p. 24). What is particularly interesting about the umbrella term of 'educational technology' is its apparent ability to accommodate all these agendas (from the countercultural to the commercial) with little sense of incompatibility or conflict. This is an area where different social groups (from corporate interests to critical educators) with different values and interests appear to more or less coexist alongside each other, united by their cumulative support for the orthodoxy of educational technology. Given this complexity of values and interests, it is certainly worth questioning how educational technology appears to exist as an uncontroversial and relatively harmonious area of education.

One obvious conclusion – which shall be explored throughout this book – is that this lack of controversy and conflict reflects the underlying ideologically driven nature of educational technology. Indeed, the fact that apparent consensus can arise from such seemingly contradictory interests fits well with the messy and compromised nature of sustained ideological dominance. As Freeden (2003) reminds us, dominant ideologies need to constantly attract and retain a wide range of interests and 'significant groups', and rely on the ongoing negotiation of some sort of compromise. While logical inconsistencies will inevitably creep into this process, "ideologies are adept at reconciling such tensions mainly because the polysemic manner in which [these ideas are] formulated allows for enough interpretative leeway to find an area of logical consistency among them" (Freeden 2003, p. 56). Thus while new age spiritualism, sociocultural psychology, countercultural deinstitutionalization and technocratic notions of new managerialism may appear unlikely bedfellows, such sentiments have proved to find common ground under the general banner of achieving some sort of 'transformation' and 'change' through educational technology. This relates back to the observation in Chapter 1 about educational technology being an essentially 'positive project' – that is, involving groups who share a common interest in using technology to change or 'transform' education along better lines (whatever they might understand 'better' to mean). In these terms, one can begin to see the ways in which educational technology might be said to have become an area dominated by what Friesen (2008, p. 2) terms "ideologically-charged common sense". In other words, it is an area where diverse groups are all working to pursue their various visions of a 'better' education, while also legitimating and supporting a wider range of largely obscured dominant ideological interests.

The key issue that now needs to be considered is how the ideological character of educational technology is actually taking form 'on the ground' and with what outcomes. At this early stage of our analysis it is therefore important to maintain an open mind about what lies ahead. Of course, implicit in this book's stated mission of 'distrusting educational technology' is a suggestion that these dominant shapings are an unwelcome and ultimately restrictive imposition on education. However, in highlighting the ideological nature of educational technology, it should not be assumed that there are no benefits at all associated with current forms of educational technology. Indeed, it *could* be that many of the individualized, neo-liberal, new capitalist promises of education and technology are justified and valid. It could well be that these technologies support meaningful and fulfilling forms of educational engagement within the conditions of contemporary society. It could well be that digital technology is successfully allowing the "privilege and convenience" of education to be provided "without the unsightly mess" of state inefficiencies and restrictions (Dean 2002, p. 3).

Regardless of whether one is prepared to start this analysis with a completely open mind, it is certainly sensible to remain circumspect about the realities of education and technology. As such, it seems appropriate to conclude this chapter with a set of questions that can be carried through the next six chapters. In challenging the ideology of education and technology these are some of the main issues and questions that are worthy of attention:

- What are the ideological dimensions of educational technology? What meanings and understandings of education are being conveyed through digital technologies? How do these technologies disseminate ideas about political and economic structures? What is the language that is being associated with education and digital technology?
- What forms of educational engagement are being promoted through digital technology use, and what forms are being obscured and silenced? In whose interests does the common consensus about educational technology work? How persuasive does this manipulation of understandings and meanings appear to be?
- What freedoms and unfreedoms are associated with digital technology use in education? How are these being experienced by different individuals and social groups? To what extent are educational technologies situated in dominant structures of production and power? To what extent do educational technologies disrupt dominant structures of production and power?
- How is technology-based education altering the relationship between the individual and the commons, as well as the public and private? Are new technologies fostering a sense of obligation and communal sense of education? Are all individuals self-responsibilized and empowered by educational technology?
- What are the emotional, 'human' outcomes of increased technology use in education? In what ways are digital technologies enhancing or diminishing a sense of pleasure, engagement and enchantment with education?
- What are the continuities and discontinuities between 'new' forms of digital education and the forms of education that preceded? In what ways are existing practices and processes altered? In what ways are existing structures and relations superseded altogether?

Conclusions

These questions are a reminder that rather than simply noting the potential links between educational technology and dominant ideologies, we also need to explore the '*how*' of these ideologies (Ball 2012). How are these dominant ideologies being promoted – if at all – through educational technologies? How are libertarian, neo-liberal and new capitalist values and dispositions being enacted through the increased use of technology in education? These questions certainly suggest the need to spend time examining the 'real life' of various forms of digital technology use in education. They also warn against approaching these issues in a wholly detached manner. Instead, any critical analysis of education and technology needs to be able to offer a set of alternative counterhegemonic suggestions of ways in which more 'palatable' future forms of education and technology might be secured. As such, our pessimistic investigation of education and digital technology is not one that is totally devoid of hope.

So how, then, to best take these intentions forward? Rather than concentrating on specific devices and applications that are being currently valorised and celebrated in academic discussions of educational technology (e.g., speculative discussions of the educational merits of tablet computers, Twitter or 'MOOCs'), the next four chapters pursue the questions just outlined through detailed analyses of four main *genres* of contemporary educational technology – that is, 'virtual', 'open', 'social' and 'games' technologies. These genres reflect a set of dominant cultural logics in recent educational technology thinking, and all have had a lasting influence on the nature and flavour of contemporary educational technology. The next four chapters will therefore now go on to explore the ideological nature and form of the 'virtual', 'open', 'games' and 'social' technologies that are increasingly being used in education. Most importantly, each chapter will consider the fundamental question that has lurked beneath all of our discussions so far – that is, to what extent should we be distrustful of the ideological underpinning of these technologies?

3

DISTRUSTING 'VIRTUAL' TECHNOLOGIES IN EDUCATION

Introduction

While the arguments presented in Chapter 2 make neat theoretical sense, developing realistic understandings of the connections between educational technology and dominant ideologies requires further work. We now need to apply the critical concerns and concepts outlined in Chapters 1 and 2 to some tangible examples. The next four chapters of this book therefore stand against, and explore in detail, four prominent genres of digital technology in education – that is, the use of 'virtual', 'open', 'games' and 'social' technologies. Of course, in differentiating between these 'types' of digital technology it should be recognised that what we are taking to be their distinct characteristics are actually in evidence across many different forms of digital education. For example, such is the ongoing convergence of digital devices and digital practices that most contemporary forms of technology could be said to have 'social' characteristics. Notions of 'open' architecture and 'open' access are common features of many contemporary forms of digital technology. Games and gaming activities are also now incorporated into many different types of technology. Perhaps most obviously, any digital technology is by definition 'virtual'. However, as will be reasoned in each chapter, these broad categories can be used as helpful shorthand in identifying specific sets of tools, applications and services that lie at the heart of digital technology use in contemporary education. Thus while they might appear to be somewhat arbitrary distinctions to make, these four genres provide a useful 'way in' to exploring and better understanding the ideological nature of educational technology.

We can start this process by examining what can be identified as 'virtual' technologies. Of course, virtuality has become a widely accepted and rarely commented upon feature of contemporary digital technology – in contrast to the novelty of the term during the 1980s and 1990s. Indeed, during these latter decades of the twentieth century, authors such as Pierre Levy and William Gibson made great play of promoting the notion of the 'virtual' as a contemporary buzzword alongside the general excitement for 'cyberspace', the 'information superhighway' and the prefixing of 'e' to most areas of economy and society. Nearly 30 years later, while the social science literature now rarely makes mention of concepts such as virtual communities, virtual reality or virtual teams, the concept of 'virtual' technologies nevertheless remains a key part of contemporary digital technology use. In particular, this chapter will concentrate on the genre of digital technologies that seek to represent, and often replicate, forms of educational provision and practice. These range from virtual classes and courses, virtual schools and universities to other forms of 'virtual learning environments' and 'virtual worlds'. While subsequent chapters will go on to explore genres of technology that are perhaps considered by technologists to be more innovative and 'disruptive' by contemporary standards, the virtual technologies described in this chapter certainly represent some of the most widely implemented and frequently encountered forms of digital technology in education. As such they are an appropriate set of digital technologies with which to begin our discussion.

What Are Virtual Technologies?

Most forms of digital technology rely on the concept of representing and replicating more complex physical forms and associated 'real-life' practices in a 'virtual' form. For example, the ubiquitous 'office' computer applications of word processors, spreadsheets and databases can all be seen as virtual forms of older analogue technologies such as typewriters, accounts ledgers and filing cabinets. Indeed, computerized technologies tend to be presented to the user in the form of a 'virtual machine' – that is, a simple-to-use, imaginary device that the operating system presents as a facade. In the case of a personal computer's virtual 'desktop' or the user interface of a smartphone, this engineered virtuality is generally so successful that most users do not stop to think that the 'machine' they are viewing and interacting with is a very simplified virtual version of the actual hardware. In this sense, all digital devices rely on the presentation of different forms of simulated virtual environment, albeit with varying degrees of realism. In contrast, digital technologies can also be used to support highly complex, lifelike representations of 'real-life' phenomena. The 1980s and 1990s, for example, saw much enthusiasm for the use of computer hardware and software to create the effect of fully immersive three-dimensional environments that users could move through and interact with. Crucially, these environments created the effect of objects having a three-dimensional spatial presence, independent of both the user and the computer technology. Thus whereas virtual applications usually require the user to suspend his or her disbelief and imagine a virtual environment, 'virtual reality' technology was seen as distinct in actually creating such environments through human senses such as sight, sound and touch. Whereas the speculated virtual reality technology of the 1990s was never realized fully, the use of digital technologies to sustain immersive environments continues in the form of 'augmented reality' (i.e., the imposition of computer information in real-life environments) and highly realistic simulation environments that rely on forms of tangible 'haptic' feedback.

In many ways, then, virtual technologies can be seen as distinct from the material and concrete elements of the physical world. As Rob Shields (2003, p. 2) puts it, these are technologies that convey "the nature of activities and objects which exist but are not tangible". In other words, virtual technologies constitute 'real' forms of action and consequence, albeit in an abstracted form. As the 'reality' element of virtual reality implies, something is actually happening when one uses these technologies. Thus, as Shields (2003, p. 25) writes, "the virtual is real but not actual". In this sense, virtual technologies are often seen as supporting wholly different and distinct environments within which social interactions can take place. One of the obvious differences of virtual technologies lies in their support of disembodied action, "allow[ing] the overcoming of the constraints of embodiment, enabling the subject to engage with the world outside of a specific embodied location in time and space" (Cooper 2002, p. 7). This discontinuity between the body and location, as well as between the self and others, is therefore seen by some commentators to support the reconstitution of social relations. For example, Cooper (2002) points to the 'qualitative shift' of offering individuals the chance to engage with and consume cultural objects outside of the socio-historical locus of their production. Similarly, the ability to interact with others regardless of physical distance or proximity is seen as having significant implications for the presentation of self and the (re)constitution of identity. As Shields (2003, p. 13) puts it, virtual technologies can allow "users to imagine leaving behind identities in one realm to become something/someone else or to play an entirely different role".

These issues notwithstanding, it would be a mistake to assume that virtual technologies are *completely* distinct and differentiated from the concrete actualities of the physical world. Indeed, in a prosaic sense it is important not to overlook the underpinning material elements of any 'virtual' technology. For example, the material realities of any form of virtual computing remain rooted in the global network of hundreds of thousands of miles of cabling, alongside the huge warehouses of servers in North Carolina, Ireland and other centres of data storage and processing around the world. Viewed in these terms, it was estimated that maintaining the 'life' of each citizen of the popular 'virtual world' Second Life involved an average annual electricity consumption equivalent to that of a real-life adult living in Brazil. While enthusiasts of Second Life may dismiss this as a pedantic and trivial point, it highlights the continuities as well as discontinuities between the 'virtual' and the 'concrete' that lie at the heart of any virtual technology. The same can also be said for the immediate context of use of these technologies (e.g., the bedroom, the classroom or the office), or issues of offline language proficiency or socio-economic conditions. Thus, virtual environments might be better classed as ambiguous 'liminal' spaces. In one sense, these are spaces and environments that are participated in on a temporary basis, and are distinguished from some notion of commonplace 'everyday life'. Yet these are spaces and environments that are also "integrated within existing offline practices and social relationships, rather than creating a 'reality' that is completely separate and removed from offline life" (Song 2010, p. 266). Thus as Rob Shields (2003, p. 79) concludes, virtual technologies should be seen as a complex combination of the fantastic and the concrete:

> The digitally virtual is thus embedded in the on-going life of the concrete, standing in close relationship as a fantastic escape attempt, a simulation of possible events, or a rendering which is used as the basis of decisions on and actions in the material world . . . the digitally virtual is an important extension of notions of reality and the context of action.

This correspondence between the concrete and the virtual is reflected in the well-established spatial metaphors that are often used to define and structure virtual environments. As Payal Arora (2012) notes, many of these metaphors position virtual environments as 'utilitarian-driven spaces' that are of functional and practical use to society (the 1990s' notion of the 'information superhighway' being a good example of this). Virtual environments are also often described in terms of being 'context-driven spaces' – oriented towards specific situated and embedded practices. The computer 'desktop', for example, conveys a clear sense of the type of work that the computer can be used for, implying expected forms of organization and management. These spaces are often 'value-driven' in nature – that is, based on emotive elements through personal association and sentiment (such as the notion of the 'virtual museum'). In contrast, other spaces are described in terms that convey less emphasis on functionality and appear to be more open and 'play-driven' in nature, such as the seemingly endless socially orientated 'islands' of the Second Life virtual world. As Arora (2012) concludes, tethering virtual spaces to real places in this manner serves to shape perceptions and influence user actions – ultimately acting to replicate pre-existing social structures and forms of organization in virtual form.

Virtual environments should therefore be seen as aligned closely with real-life, concrete spaces and places – sometimes complementing and extending the features of physical spaces, and sometimes offering substitutes and alternatives. In all cases, however, it could be argued that virtual environments have a number of common underpinning features. Till Straube (2012), for example, reasons that virtual places can be understood in at least three different ways. Firstly, these are technology-mediated environments that have a primarily imagined materiality and location – be it in terms of 'entering' chat rooms or maintaining documents with hierarchies of organized folders. This sense of rootedness in a particular materiality and location is enforced by the tendency of many forms of virtual technology to convey a sense of technology-mediated 'telepresence'. This involves manipulating the user's senses to provide a feeling of being present in a setting other than his or her actual location, and also being able to feel the presence of others who are similarly dislocated. Secondly, Straube (2012, n.p.) points to the mutual constitution of virtual spaces with physical places – as he puts it, "these imaginary qualities are always in reference to real places". Finally, virtual places can be seen as being built around the primacy of social processes and relations between the various users (or participants) of the virtual environment. As Straube (2012, n.p.) concludes, virtual places can therefore be thought of as "reification of social relations".

The Rise of Educational Interest in Virtual Technologies

As these descriptions and definitions suggest, virtual technologies are associated with a range of possible reconfigurations and realignments of real-life practices and processes across a number of different domains. As Brian Massumi (2002, p. 30) observes, the virtual is therefore a 'realm of potential' which combines the future and the past, offers new spaces for existing action and therefore constitutes "a lived paradox where what are normally opposites coexist, coalesce, and connect; where what cannot be experienced cannot but be felt – albeit reduced and contained". Given this sense of augmentation and improvement, it is understandable that virtual technologies have long attracted the attention and enthusiasm of educationalists keen to use these technologies as a means of improving and transforming education. For example, according to Tiffin and Rajasingham (1995, p. 7), virtual education should be seen as having many possibilities to 'advance the way we learn':

> [Virtual technology] offers us the possibility of a class meeting in the Amazon Forest or on top of Mount Everest; it could allow us to expand our viewpoint to see the solar system operating like a game of marbles in front of us, or shrink it so that we can walk through an atomic structure as though it was a sculpture in a park; we could enter a fictional virtual reality in the persona of a character in a play, or a non-fictional virtual reality to accompany a surgeon in an exploration at the micro-level of the human body.

These sentiments of allowing the learning of 'anything' regardless of place, space, time or physical constraints runs throughout discussions of the educational potential of virtual technologies. Indeed, beyond such abstracted descriptions, educational application of virtual environments, simulation and worlds is well established, centring around three different types of technology – simulations; virtual classrooms and virtual schools; and virtual worlds and virtual learning environments.

I. Simulations

Computer simulations can be divided into two broad types: simulations based on operational models and those containing conceptual models of real-life phenomena (De Jong & Van Joolingen 1998). As the term suggests, 'operational' simulations include sequences of tangible cognitive and noncognitive procedures that relate directly to the system being simulated. 'Conceptual' simulations – such as those that offer models of complex processes in economics and physics – are often more complex and hold more abstracted principles, concepts and facts related to systems being simulated. The use of computer-based operational simulations has a rich heritage in education and training. Sophisticated and immersive simulations have been developed for a variety of work-related areas of 'operational' training – such as flight simulators and vehicle simulators. The use of computer-based conceptual simulations also has a long history in schools and universities, especially in subject areas such as science. Here digital technology is used to present dynamic models of real-life systems and processes that would be too expensive, dangerous, time-consuming or microscopic to experience in real life. The ability of computers to repeat these simulations on multiple occasions is seen as allowing for discovery-based learning and the refinement of conceptual understandings (Rutten, Van Joolingen & Van der Veen 2012).

Recently, these domains of operational and conceptual simulation have converged in the form of highly sophisticated immersive simulations. In terms of medical training, for example, a range of clinical simulations has been developed, from computer-controlled mannequins (which are designed to replace the traditional use of cadavers) to fully immersive surgical simulation rooms that replicate operating theatres and similar clinical settings (see Weller, Nestel, Marshall, Brooks & Conn 2012). In the field of military training, increasingly sophisticated battle-field and naval war craft simulators have been developed to mimic some of the social and cultural elements of war-work as well as operational aspects of combat. These technologies are also used to a lesser extent in compulsory education. For example, the popularity of interactive whiteboards in schools has seen the development of education-related 'cave automatic virtual environments' where data projectors are directed on the walls of a classroom to simulate 'immersive virtual reality environments'. These trends continue through the emerging technologies of holography, retinal screens and other digital eyewear supporting the access of education through virtual studios.

II. Virtual Classrooms and Virtual Schools

Whereas simulation technologies all focus on specific, bounded situations, digital technologies are also used to replicate and represent general educational contexts and settings. One popular application is the 'virtual classroom' – usually a spatial representation of a classroom or lecture theatre that can be 'inhabited' by learners and teachers. Often these virtual spaces will support synchronous forms of 'live' instruction and feedback, with learners able to listen to lectures and view videos and visual presentations, while also interacting with other learners via text and voice. Other asynchronous forms of virtual classroom exist in the form of digital spaces where resources can be accessed and shared – such as audio recordings and text transcripts of lectures, supplementary readings and discussion forums.

Aside from virtual classrooms, digital technology is now used commonly to support the provision of formal education outside of the physical and spatial confines of school and university buildings, while retaining major educational structures and processes such as curriculum, assessment and certification. Although some proponents of virtual education such as Tiffin and Rajasingham (1995, p. 10) suggest using the term 'virtual learning institute' to "avoid the idea ... [of] a virtual version of educational systems as we know them now", most of these technologies replicate the familiar spaces of the school, college and university. This has been especially the case with regard to school-based education, with growing numbers of internet-based virtual schools now established to offer online 'out-of-school' schooling. One of the first major instances of this was the now defunct Hudson-Concord 'Virtual High School' programme in the US. Operating between 1997 and 2002, this programme was sponsored by $7.4 million of federal funding and, at its peak, boasted students from 10 countries. From these beginnings the majority of US states now operate online learning programmes for children and young people involved in compulsory schooling. Similar operations continue in the forms of the long-running 'World Virtual School' and 'Florida Virtual School' – the latter of which has been funded in part by the Gates Foundation and offers instruction on a global basis. While the Florida Virtual School is free of charge for residents of Florida, there are also a growing number of elite, fee-paying virtual schools, seeking to cater to the children of globally mobile families.

One sustained application of virtual schools has been the establishment of online 'charter schools' in the US – effectively online versions of independent, state-supported schools providing an alternative to traditional public education. Online charter schools grew twentyfold during the 2000s, positioning them as a significant element of compulsory education provision. The majority of states in the US now support individual 'cyber schools' as well as having district-level online programmes where 20 to 80 per cent of a student's academic instruction can be delivered via the internet (Watson, Gemin & Ryan 2008; Ellis 2008). It is estimated that nearly a quarter of a million US students are enrolled in full-time virtual schools (Miron & Urschel 2012), with over 1 million taking online courses alongside their classroom lessons each year (Means, Toyama, Murphy, Bakia & Jones 2009).

These forms of virtual schooling provide online access to conventional schooling that directly replicates the curriculum and culture of traditional 'bricks and mortar' schools without being delivered in a physical institution. Other forms of virtual schooling include complementary or 'secondary-credit' provision that adds to – rather than replicates – face-to-face schooling. One high-profile example was the Australian 'Virtual School for the Gifted' programme that operated during the 2000s. This programme used remote online tuition to offer supplementary learning opportunities for 'gifted and talented' students who were considered to be largely unchallenged by their conventional schoolwork. Other prominent instances of complementary virtual schooling include the provision of online supplementary learning resources by a range of public and commercial organizations. One example of this form of virtual schooling is the British Broadcasting Corporation's popular 'ByteSize' revision materials. A similar commercially provided equivalent is the fast food chain McDonald's provision of subsidized online tutoring programmes to secondary school pupils in Australia (Curtis 2009). As with 'official' virtual school provision, these programmes offer online means of helping students engage with aspects of their schooling without attending a physical school.

III. Learning in Virtual Worlds

Whereas these virtual technologies seek to replicate specific educational settings or forms of teaching and learning, interest is also growing in providing educational opportunities through less bounded and more open forms of 'virtual worlds'. The notion of virtual worlds came to popularity during the 2000s with the rise of applications such as 'Second Life'. These are online simulated environments which present a consistent and persistent modelled 'world' within which users can interact with each other – most commonly in the third-person form of controlling a personalized character (known as an 'avatar'). These applications are usually rendered in three-dimensional form, combining graphics, text, sound and gesture, and attracting large numbers of users. At its peak, for example, Second Life boasted an average of over 60,000 concurrent users with over 20 million registered accounts. Unlike the 'massively multiplayer online role playing games' these virtual worlds are not underpinned by games mechanics such as rules, points scoring, rewards and goals. Instead, these digital applications are designed primarily to support open-ended social interactions between users.

The capacity of virtual worlds to offer alternate spaces for interaction prompted many educational institutions to experiment with the virtual provision of classes and courses through Second Life during the 2000s – especially in the areas of college-level and university-level language learning and business subjects. A number of educational institutions still run virtual classrooms and educational spaces through virtual world applications, and the development of learning provision in virtual worlds remains a growth area of educational technology scholarship (Nelson & Erlandson 2012). As Jin (2011) has argued, virtual worlds place an emphasis on learning through social interaction and collaboration, as well as through visual communication. Aside from the use of mainstream virtual worlds such as Second Life, a number of virtual environments have been developed specifically for distinct educational topics. For example, the European Union–produced 'Citzalia' virtual world was heralded as "democracy in action . . . a role-playing game and social networking forum wrapped in a virtual 3D world that captures the essence of the European parliament" (Phillips 2010, p. 18). Ambitiously, this application was designed to offer a "mash-up of the three European parliament buildings in

Brussels, Strasbourg and Luxembourg and filled with real MEPs and European Commission civil servants". In this virtual world, school children and other interested parties were supposed to "re-enact the process of creating EU legislation" and "stimulate discussion about Europe" (Phillips 2010, p. 18).

IV. Virtual Learning Environments

These immersive and somewhat exotic applications notwithstanding, perhaps the most significant of the virtual technologies used in education are the 'learning management systems', 'managed learning systems' and 'virtual learning environments'. These are applications that seek to replicate the main functions of educational institutions in digital form – the provision of learning content and other resources, communication between learners, teachers, administrators and (where applicable) parents, the submission and assessment of coursework, and the monitoring of learning progress. The most popular of these applications – in particular the commercially produced 'Blackboard' system and its open-source equivalent, 'Moodle' – are now used widely through universities, colleges and school systems as a prominent means of managing and administrating teaching and learning processes.

Of late, these virtual technologies (which are concerned specifically with the organization of curriculum and pedagogy) have been integrated increasingly with digital technologies designed to support the routine processes of data collection, record keeping, monitoring and assessment, creation and distribution of learning resources, and coordination of students, teachers, parents, school leaders and administrators. These technologies include 'management information systems' that collate record-keeping functions such as payrolls, budgeting and accounting, lesson timetabling, scheduling and planning, as well as the management of student attendance, registration and admissions. The past 10 years or so have seen the increased convergence of these institutional technologies into integrated systems – thereby allowing institutionally related data, resources and other services to be accessed and used across the different aspects of a school or university organization. This has seen the integration of management information systems, virtual learning environments and communications technologies into virtual systems that are accessible to educational managers, administrators, teachers, students and parents. As such, school, college and university use of integrated management and administration-related systems now represents a significant feature of the educational technology landscape in many European, North American and Australasian contexts.

Positive Claims and Promises for the Use of Virtual Technologies in Education

While diverse in nature and form, the use of these virtual technologies in contemporary education is associated with a number of commonly perceived benefits and advantages. For many commentators, these virtual technologies introduce increased freedoms to any individual's engagement with education. A prominent argument in this respect is the role of virtual education in increasing choice and imposing 'market accountability' in the form of competition that drives educational providers (both online and offline) to improve as they compete to recruit and retain students (Miron & Urschel 2012). As such, forms of virtual schooling are often justified as introducing the benefits of market efficiency and competition into compulsory school systems. Indeed, virtual schools have tended to be developed and run by a variety of providers – from school districts and universities to small private companies and large multinational corporations (see Picciano & Spring 2013). Growing numbers of commercial companies also act as vendors for the delivery of virtual courses and the licensed use of virtual course materials. This 'learning marketplace' is bolstered by the considerable amount of content developed by educators and schools themselves. All told, virtual schooling is seen as making school systems more diverse and more competitive. This reflects what Anderson (2009) identified as the 'long tail' of digital provision, where purely digital products that are of marginal, niche interest can be produced and consumed at no additional material loss.

Besides these system-wide improvements, proponents of virtual forms of education also celebrate the benefits of personalization and flexibility for individual learners. For example, it is often argued that virtual schools provide individualized forms of instruction that better meet the specific needs and learning styles of students. Virtual schooling is seen as allowing flexibility in terms of scheduling and place, as well as expanding high-quality learning in specific subjects. While some students (or their parents) will actively choose virtual schooling, the virtual provision of education is also seen as playing a compensatory role for students who are unable physically to attend 'bricks and mortar' schools. As such virtual schooling is justified as a ready alternative for students who have long-term illness, who have been excluded from school or for whom schools are considered unsuitable. With increasing fears over school safety in the wake of campus shootings and other school-related crime, the option of the virtual school has gained popularity in urbanized parts of North America. Even when students continue to attend face-to-face classes, virtual learning environments are seen as extending the provision of the formal educational institution into the home and allow for additional learning opportunities outside of the classroom.

Virtual technologies are also celebrated as providing individual students an enhanced freedom from the physical constraints of the 'real world'. This is often expressed in terms of overcoming of barriers of place, space, time and geography, with individuals able to access high-quality educational provision regardless of their local proximity. When using simulations, for instance, students are seen as being able to experience otherwise inaccessible locations and experiences. Similarly, as the producers of the Second Life virtual world boasted, "virtual worlds allow teaching to go beyond the classroom, extending learning beyond the limitations traditionally imposed by geography" (cited in Salen 2008, p. 244). Additionally, virtual technologies are described as offering individuals an increased social and psychological freedom from their real-life circumstances. Enthusiasts argue that virtual technologies therefore have profound implications for the ways that students and teachers can communicate and interact with each other, with people no longer constricted by distance, time or physical attributes like location or body. In this sense, it is argued that users will be able to construct diverse 'virtual identities' and digital forms of embodiment through which they can experience these 'virtual' worlds. The key advantage here is that the individual user has control over both the environment and the presentation of self.

These issues all feed into the wider contention that virtual technologies can support what Bill Gates once termed 'friction-free' interactions and experiences. While Gates was talking primarily about the reduced environmental impact of virtual rather than material forms of production and consumption, this notion of friction-free benefit is often applied in social terms – reflecting "an impression of digital space as a radically democratic zone of infinite connectivity" (Murphy 2012, p. 122). These claims are accompanied by a sense that virtual technologies support forms of education that are somehow more efficient than would otherwise be the case. Purported benefits of virtual learning environments, for example, include the increased 'engagement' of students with 'personalized' educational provision, the 'democratizing' of school processes through the flattening of traditionally hierarchical relationships, and increased levels of school 'performance' and teacher productivity through the 'open' sharing of administrative and management data (see Selwood & Visscher 2007).

Arguments Against the Use of Virtual Technologies in Education

As with all forms of educational technology, these virtual technologies have attracted occasional criticism and unease as their use has increased. For example, specific virtual technologies have been criticized in terms of their apparent ineffectiveness in supporting the levels of learning that one might expect from corresponding 'traditional' forms of education. In a recent review of the performance of virtual schools in the US, Miron and Urschel (2012) pointed to sustained evidence of apparently poor performance in comparison to traditional 'bricks and mortar' school institutions. Focusing on one set of commercially provided virtual schools, these authors calculated that just over one quarter of the virtual schools had met the expected official targets for 'Adequate Yearly Progress' – criteria that are usually met by over half of the 'traditional' nonvirtual public schools in the US. This trend was especially pronounced in terms of reading and mathematics attainment. Miron and Urschel (2012) suggested a number of potential reasons for these shortfalls, including the fact that the company operating these virtual schools devoted considerably fewer resources to instructional salaries and benefits for employees, as well as having more than three times the number of students-per-teacher in comparison to student-teacher ratios in public schools.

In this manner, questions are raised regularly over the rigour and integrity of virtual forms of educational provision. In particular, a number of commentators question the threat of virtual technologies to the role of the teacher, not least in the tendency of these technologies to involve the total displacement of the teacher altogether. For example, the notion of the de-peopled 'virtual campus' and the idea of schools and universities that are hosted entirely online have obvious consequences for the role of the teacher. While not foreseeing the complete replacement of the teacher, a number of current debates about education and virtual technology imply a substantial reduction in the numbers of teachers and other resources required to continue the process of education (see Selwyn 2011).

While all valid points of discussion, these concerns and criticisms nevertheless shy away from challenging some of the more deep-rooted implications of virtual technologies in education – not least their implicit reinforcement of the organization of education along individualized neo-liberal lines. Returning to the main concerns of Chapters 1 and 2, we now need to consider a number of fundamental criticisms of virtual education that centre on the essentially reductionist nature of these technologies. These issues all cast substantial doubt on the claims of enhanced freedom, choice and diversity made for virtual technologies in education. Moreover, they suggest a number of ways in which virtual technologies are linked to the dominant ideological interests outlined in Chapter 2. In brief, these concerns include: the continuities of virtual education with offline concrete forms of education; the reductive nature of virtual education; and the links between virtual education and the deskilling of educational labour. Each of these issues will now be considered in further detail.

I. The Continuities of Virtual Education

Firstly, it can be argued that the various forms of virtual technology just described all tend to replicate (rather than disrupt and alter) offline processes and practices. These continuities are perhaps most obvious with virtual forms of educational provision. 'Virtual schools', 'virtual universities', 'virtual museums' and the like all mark the institutional persistence of their offline equivalents in terms of organization and administration, social relations and culture. Many of these virtual forms even involve faithful imagined renderings of the physical architecture and general appearance of 'real-life' institutions, from the school classroom to the surgical operating theatre. Of course, the same is not necessarily the case with the development of educational provision in virtual worlds such as Second Life. Yet even in these ostensibly 'free-form' environments, one continues to find familiar classroom-like arrangements with rows of seats and desks, whiteboards and teachers at the front of rooms, and all the corresponding tacit conventions one would expect to find in a concrete offline classroom. These continuities are also evident in the individual actions and interactions that are conducted through virtual technologies. Within a virtual learning environment or virtual classroom, for example, learners are usually positioned much in the same way that they would be in any physical form of formal education – that is, as passive consumers of resources and instruction, as individuals who are formally assessed, whose attendance is required and whose collaboration with other learners is expected to follow the largely artificial conventions of 'group work' and seminar-style discussions that remain 'on topic'. It is telling that within even the most supposedly unconstrained virtual educational settings, learners will still often replicate the materialities of off-line learning processes – printing off papers and books, adhering to self-imposed schedules and maintaining strict division between curriculum domains of knowledge. As Mc-Knight (2012, p. 373) observed of the governance structures that tend to be chosen by virtual world communities, "managerialism is the norm". In this sense, virtual education is not so much of an escape from the constraints of traditional education structures, routines and conventions as an entrenchment of them.

That the established traditions and tropes of 'traditional' education remain largely intact and dominant in the educational use of virtual technologies certainly goes against the prevailing rhetoric of freedom and diversity. Indeed, there is very little evidence of a prominent 'long tail' of esoteric, niche and outré educational provision being made available to potential consumers in virtual form. Rather, it could be observed that virtual technologies support 'more of the same' educational provision. As such, virtual technologies appear to be doing little to challenge or disrupt what David Tyack and William Tobin (1995, p. 454) refer to as the basic 'grammar' of formal education – that is, the combination of material artefacts and social relations "designed to instruct, socialize and discipline" learners and therefore providing the dominant underpinning "structural framework of pedagogical practice" (Brehony 2002, p. 178). This grammar of formal education includes the persistent structures and rules that divide time and space, classify students and allocate them to groups, and splinter knowledge into 'subjects'. Indeed it is notable how many of the virtual forms of educational provision outlined in this chapter echo the almost subconscious way that rules and approved 'ways of being' are internalized, adhered to and often reproduced by those who work within concrete educational institutions – not least the principles of standardization, order and hierarchization.

These observations chime with general criticisms that computer-based virtuality tends towards replication, standardization and homogenization. As Murphy (2012, p. 133) reasons, most virtual technologies tend to be immaterial expressions of material practices and processes – "an intensification of the old" rather than the purveyors of anything 'new'. Critics such as Campanelli (2010, p. 13) therefore see virtual technologies as little more than the mirroring of reality in a more visible data-driven form – at best leading to "the progressive aestheticization of reality" rather than offering any genuinely alternate arrangements. Thus despite the rhetoric of change and opportunity, virtual technologies could be seen as representing "a parallel reality that overlaps and replaces physical reality . . . Life happens in an unrelenting visibility and – mostly thanks to digital media – in a perfect (numeric) transcription" (Campanelli 2010, p. 60). It is important to note that this replication and continuity are often evident at an individual as well as institutional level. Indeed, some critics have noted how virtual technologies tend to *preclude* a plurality and fluidity of self-presentation and identity formation. Rather, it has been observed that when interacting through virtual technologies people are generally compelled to be themselves. Thus it could be argued that in many virtual environments a tendency remains to be overpresent and 'overreal' (i.e., to behave and present oneself in ways that reaffirm one's presence and participation). As Lovink (2011, p. 13) concludes, "The idea that the virtual liberates you from your old self has collapsed. There is no alternative identity".

These points raise a significant challenge to the notion of virtual technologies as somehow enhancing individual freedoms. In this sense, people tend to replicate rather than deviate from their offline identities when using virtual technologies – especially in terms of gender, race and social class – often replicating crude forms of 'cybertype' that do little to challenge offline norms and stereotypes (Nakamura 2002). For example, many of the social, cultural and political dimensions of being physically disabled are not simply bypassed by learning online (Lewthwaite 2011). As Friesen (2008, n.p.) concludes, "It is not possible to simply construct an online identity or persona *ex nihilo* or from scratch". Thus the ability of virtual technologies to alter or overcome the offline restrictions and conventions of identity can therefore be challenged seriously. Indeed, faced with a virtual indeterminacy it would appear that people often tend to revert to what they know. Thus in a virtual world such as Second Life,

> [A]ble to do or create anything (there aren't even laws of gravity), the majority of users end up with avatars that are sexier versions of themselves walking around shopping, gambling, fixing up their houses, and trying to meet people ("meet" can be read euphemistically here). It's not only boring – it's stifling as it confronts users with their lack of skills and imagination . . . The paradox: cyberspace is not virtual enough.
>
> *(Dean 2010, p. 7)*

Thus in contrast to the transformatory claims outlined at the beginning of this chapter, the realities of virtual technology use in education need to be understood in terms of continuity with the traditional, offline, concrete forms of education that both preceded and continue alongside them. Woolgar's (2002) mantra of 'the more virtual the more real' is certainly relevant here – reminding us that engagement in virtual activities usually stimulates more engagement with the 'real-life' activities that they replicate. For example, the 'convenience' of virtual teleworking usually is associated in practice with more physical travelling in the 'real' world. It may therefore make more sense to see virtuality – as Jordan (1999) suggested – as the reinvention of familiar physical realities and spaces in digital online settings, rather than any radical break with what went before.

II. The Restrictions of Virtual Education

Of course this is not to claim that virtual technologies support *exactly* the same types of education as their offline concrete forms. Instead, all of the forms of virtual education outlined in this chapter can be seen as reduced, simplified versions of what are complex educational processes and practices. However, this distillation is not necessarily for the better. For example, the clean lines of the virtual classroom and virtual school omit a wealth of detail that otherwise gives character, vitality and meaning to a real-life 'messy' classroom. Virtual learning environments often offer abstracted icon-based representations of the core activities of learning and teaching, omitting all manner of informal and tacit processes and practices. Any computer-based simulation, however sophisticated, can appear lacking in emotional depth and 'dead-eyed' when set against the realities of the setting it seeks to simulate. In short, it could be argued that virtual technologies tend to offer abstracted, decontextualized and ultimately diminished replications of educational processes and practices. As Alexander Galloway (2012, p. 78) asks of virtual technologies, "Are some things unrepresentable?"

At its heart, then, any form of virtual education needs to be understood as a simulation of a physical, concrete form of education, with all of the reductions and restrictions that simulation entails. Indeed, Edward Castronova (2006) proposed the description of 'synthetic' rather than 'virtual' as a means of acknowledging the essentially replicated form of virtual worlds and virtual environments. Although these technologies do combine impressive amounts of audio, gestural and haptic information, they are largely visual in nature – offering what Castells (1996) terms 'symbolic environments' that are based predominantly around the image. In this sense, virtual technologies could be seen as presenting necessarily abbreviated and simplified versions of the complex processes and practices that they seek to represent and simulate. Brian Massumi (2002), for example, dismisses the forms of virtuality supported by digital technologies as artificial 'sweeping gestures' that bypass the sensations, movement and affect of the processes that they seek to replicate while systematizing the possible number of predefined outcomes. Other critics have described these technologies as presenting a 'simulacrum' of an object (Murphy 2012), undermined by their tendency to reduce complexity to the level of "something already known" (Krapp 2011, p. 2).

In this sense, virtual technologies could be said to involve a number of limitations, restrictions and omissions. Firstly, virtual technologies often appear to present unrealistically straightforward and unproblematic versions of educational processes and practices. As Bauman (2010, p. 15) observes, "The main attraction of the virtual world derives from the absence of the contradictions and cross-purposes that haunt offline life". Virtual technologies could also be said to present users with limited forms of choice and action. As Campanelli (2010, p. 92) notes, despite the 'founding myth' of interactivity, virtual technologies are capable at best only of offering the user an "infinite number of finite options". All these technologies – from the most sophisticated immersive simulation to the most expansive virtual world – are predicated upon designer-created hierarchies of 'choice'. The restricted, 'scripted' nature of any virtual technology is therefore in-fluenced by how application developers and designers have configured the tech-nology for the imagined 'ideal' users. As Campanelli (2010, p. 94) writes, this can leave a virtual technology as a frustratingly 'castrated form' for all but the most unremarkable of users:

> Designers impose a one-size-fits-all model upon what is, in fact, a chaotic mass of non-aggregated users. The search for formal standardization and the effort towards the homogenization of interfaces have produced 'castrating forms', which bridle the individual's creativity as they interact with differ-ent interfaces. No matter how efficient the navigation, where is the pleasure in visiting websites that look like each other and that work in the same predictable way?

Seen in this light, it could be argued that virtual technologies tend to support enclosed rather than open forms of action, thereby positioning individuals into "pre-defined relationships and structures, which are reproduced and reinforced through even the most trivial statements and actions" (Friesen 2008, p. 10). This is often evident in the way in which virtual learning environments position indi-viduals in a role of 'the student' (producing work, being assessed and monitored) or 'the tutor' (providing resources, grading assignments, monitoring participa-tion). These roles and the 'scripts' that are associated with them tend to be laden with unequal distributions of power and control. As Friesen (2008, p. 10) writes, once 'positioned' in these roles, "individual identity is to some extent defined by them".

All these issues therefore highlight the generally abstracted and decontextual-ized nature of engaging with education through virtual technologies. In this sense, parallels can be drawn between virtual spaces and Marc Augé's (1995) notion of the 'nonplace' – that is, places of transience that do not hold enough significance to be regarded as real-life, sustained, meaningful 'places'. Augé focused on loca-tions such as the airport terminal, supermarket, hotel room and motorway as some of the primary nonplaces of modern times, yet the argument could be made for the virtual educational spaces described earlier as having similar transient, decontextualized characteristics. Here, then, all individuals (be they learners or teachers) are assumed to be 'average', divested of their real identities and back-grounds, on the assumption that their needs can be catered to through a process of mass customization. Whereas these virtual spaces may claim connections with concrete equivalents in the offline world, they are not integrated with the history of these predecessor places but simply seek to appropriate their memory. As such, many of the virtual forms reviewed in this chapter could be seen as little more than educational encounters with the (old) life sucked out of them. It is of little surprise, therefore, that these are abstractions of existing educational forms that more often than not descend into 'banal utopias, clichés' (Augé 1995, p. 95).

III. The Reduction of Education Along Data-driven Lines

A significant element of this reduction of education to its core constituent elements is the recasting of 'virtual' education along more business-orientated 'data-driven' lines. This, of course, is not a unique characteristic of digital education. Most contemporary educational systems are now seen as being based around the creation and use of data that support the organization of relations through communication and information. For example, many forms of formal education are predicted around well-established systems of self-evaluation, development planning and performance. Schools, for instance, are largely predicated upon data-driven processes of internal school management, teachers' performance management, target setting and pupil tracking. The intentions of this amplification of data-work within the organization and management of education are deliberate – not least the intentional move towards what Jenny Ozga terms 'governing education through data' and the shift from centralized governance to individual self-regulation:

> Data production and management were and are essential to the new governance turn; constant comparison is its symbolic feature, as well as a distinctive mode of operation . . . The shift to governance is, in fact, heavily dependent on knowledge and information, which play a pivotal role both in the pervasiveness of governance and in allowing the development of its dispersed, distributed and disaggregated form.
>
> *(Ozga 2009, p. 150)*

Of key interest here is the obvious role of technologies such as virtual learning environments as systems underlying this production and management of educational data. For example, in terms of supporting a data-driven 'audit culture', many of the virtual technologies described in this chapter (with their emphasis on the digital capture, manipulation and representation of data) could be seen as key elements of the "active surveillance of people through the documents and databases they produce" (Apple 2010b, p. 179). This links the use of virtual educational technologies with a range of wider concerns relating to surveillance – most notably Foucauldian concepts of governmentality and disciplinary power. Here, then, the panoptic qualities of digital technologies such as databases raise a range of issues relating to the self-conduct (or, in Foucauldian terms, 'techniques of the self') of individual subjects, who regulate their behaviour according to internalized social norms.

Above all, it could be argued that the entrepreneurial rhetoric of a 'bottom-up' individualized empowerment and/or freeing-up of individual action is not readily apparent in the ways in which many of the virtual technologies described in this chapter tend to be used. Their emancipatory potential notwithstanding, these are often manifest as systems that are built around what Foucault terms a 'cellular individualization', involving the observation of a mass of individuals, the subsequent hierarchization and judgements made about these individuals and – most notably – the construction of 'administrative identities' of individuals as an 'effective' teacher, student and so on. As such, the disciplinary character of these digital technologies is apparent throughout the use of these technologies – with these systems supporting what Hoffman (2010) identifies as the aim of maximizing the utility as well as the docility of individual bodies. Indeed, there are a number of ways in which virtual technologies could be said to make individuals accountable for their actions – particularly in terms of placing teachers and learners under a managerial and bureaucratic accountability to the demands of higher authorities. As such these technologies cannot be seen as heralding any notable emergence of 'posthierarchical relationships' (Zuboff 1988) or interactions that are especially 'interactive' in the usual sense of the word – that is, where "the viewer has the power to be an active participant in the unfolding of [the] flow of [an] event, influencing or modifying its form" (Lovejoy 2004, p. 167). At best, the interactivity of virtual learning environments and their like is best described as involving top-down impositions and "false modes of active engagement" (Fuery 2008, p. 33).

This is illustrated in the use of many of these virtual technologies to extend the 'politics of representation' within educational institutions – not least in terms of the consequences of how individuals (re)present themselves online, coupled with what is also recorded about that individual by others online (Fuery 2008). For example, one of the main functions of virtual learning environments is to collate and intensify personal data into publicly accessible profiles. These profiles often have the disempowering effect of displacing people as knowing subjects, and reducing education to a set of digitally based "textually-mediated work processes" (Daniel 2008, p. 253). This leads to virtual learning systems allowing for the implicit (if not explicit) forms of 'predictive surveillance' where data relating to past performance and behaviour is readily available to inform expectations of future behaviours (see Knox 2010). Crucial here are the ways in which these data are connected, aggregated and applied in ways not before possible. For example, teachers' and students' online profiles are often used as a crucial element of the administrative identity of being an 'effective' or 'deviant' teacher or student – labels that are constructed "on the basis of knowledge obtained through observation" (Hoffman 2010, p. 37) rather than direct experiences. This 'dataveillance' functions to decrease the influence of 'human' experience and judgement, with it no longer seeming to matter what a teacher may personally know about a student in the face of his or her 'dashboard' profile and aggregated tally of positive and negative 'events'. As such, there would seem to be little room for 'professional' expertise or interpersonal emotion when faced with such data. In these terms, institutional technologies could be said to be both dehumanizing *and* deprofessionalizing the relationships between people in an educational context – be they students, teachers, administrators or managers.

These latter points highlight the extent to which these technologies exclude a range of qualities from the processes and practices of education. In this respect, it could also be reasoned that what is *not* represented and known within systems of surveillance is equally as important as what is highlighted and recorded (Apple 2010a). The silences of virtual technology systems could be said to be the more 'difficult' aspects of teachers' and students' lives, such as professionalism, emotions, effort and interpersonal relationships. These issues have little or no space to feature in what is being observed and monitored when abstracted forms of virtual education are being engaged in. In this way, the operation of virtual learning environments renders what would usually be considered to be important aspects of educational relations as unimportant or invisible. For example, in terms of the interpersonal relationships between students and teachers or between groups of teachers, it could be argued that online relationships and interactions take the form of a 'contrived collegiality' involving coerced collaboration amongst teachers, managers and administrators (see Grieshaber 2010). These are not spontaneous forms of collaborative collegiality, but interactions between teachers that are coerced, administratively regulated and orientated around the implementation of predetermined outcomes.

IV. Virtual Education and the Deskilling of Educational Labour

Many of these reductive features, it could be argued, relate to the essentially disembodied nature of the teaching and learning process as represented through virtual technologies. All of the technologies outlined in this chapter rely on virtual interactions in lieu of face-to-face commitment and embodied interaction. At best, then, these virtual technologies reconstruct the categories of 'student' and 'tutor' with few of the usual visual or material cues. For example, whereas many virtual technologies seek to replicate a sense of copresence, this does not equate with the total corporeal experience of the real-life classroom. As implied earlier, many commentators celebrate this 'freeing-up' of interaction from the synchronous, embodied forms of face-to-face communication as leading to briefer, multiple forms of encounter. In the eyes of some educational authorities, this diminished role of the teacher is a desirable change – primarily because teachers have 'insufficient understanding' of business needs, and because their present role hinders "internal searches for efficiency" (Levidow 2005, p. 159).

Alongside this disembodiment of teaching and learning, however, is the potential reduction of the role of the teacher to that of initial provider of instruction, and the student to that of consumer. As Les Levidow (2005, p. 158) writes,

The technology can be designed to discipline, deskill and/or displace teachers' labour. This approach changes the role of students, who become consumers of instructional commodities. Student-teacher relationships are reified as relationships between consumers and providers of things. This marginalizes any learning partnership between them as people.

Some commentators have therefore pointed to a number of limiting characteristics that the digital 'automation' of education along these lines infers. For instance, the virtual provision of courses may well make good 'business-sense' for educational institutions eager to reach wider markets of students, but it can have a number of destabilizing implications for the professional status of the teacher. Once a course has been delivered online for the first time, a teacher has little or no intellectual property rights over the future use of that material. Indeed, it is not unknown in higher education settings for academic labour to be outsourced to lower-paid, lower-qualified staff once materials have been captured in virtual form. As was noted earlier, a teacher's virtual work is made more visible and therefore more easily monitored and 'assessed' by their employers. Overall it could be argued that virtual technologies contribute to an 'erosion of academic freedom' (Petrina 2005), and hasten the transformation of university education into what David Noble (2002) characterized unfavourably as a 'digital diploma mill'.

Many of these concerns therefore centre on the role of digital technology in rationalizing and standardizing the job of being a teacher, and therefore contributing to the separation of the 'conception' of teaching from the 'execution' of teaching. While this fragmentation of the teaching process may make technical sense, it can have significant consequences for the teacher. As Apple and Jungck (1990, p. 230) have observed with regard to computers and the school curriculum,

> When complicated jobs are broken down into atomistic elements, the person doing the job loses sight of the whole process and loses control over her or his own labour because someone outside the immediate situation now has greater control over both the planning and what is actually to go on.

While many of these arguments were made in an era of 'stand-alone' computers, much of this 'deskilling' analysis holds true in the present context of virtual learning environments, digital portfolios and shared learning resources. Through these virtual technologies, it could be argued, the work of educators is being restructured in ways that reduce their autonomy, independence and control over their work. Moreover, these technologies can be seen as placing workplace knowledge and control into the hands of administrators and managers. This, David Noble (2002, p. 33) concludes, "robs faculty of their knowledge and skills, their control over their working lives, the product of their labour, and, ultimately, their means of livelihood". Of course, these criticisms of digital education are rooted in previous criticisms of the increased automation of factories and production lines during the twentieth century. For example, in his analysis of the deskilling of factory workers, Harry Braverman (1974) noted how seemingly 'helpful' technologies were used to enhance ways of controlling the workforce. As such, it is important to remember that workplace technologies have long been used to eliminate the need for direct supervision of workers, with management controlling workers by either automating work, or breaking down jobs into fragmented work processes that require little conceptual ability. So too in education, virtual technologies such as the 'virtual learning environment' or the 'virtual school' system can be argued to depend on the deskilling of teachers and their students, engendering a 'tool' mentality towards the mechanisms of teaching and learning (Monahan 2005).

Conclusions

This chapter has gathered together a diverse set of arguments in contrast to the assumptions of freedom, control and choice that are usually associated with virtual technologies in education. In many ways, these counterarguments raise a common concern with the ways in which virtual technologies remain connected to – rather than separate from – the 'real-life' contexts of education, especially in terms of control of education by dominant interests. While virtual technologies can be imagined as functioning as systems for a more democratic, freer, universally accessible form of education, they can also be seen in contrary terms – as a "symbol of control; trails of information, security networks, and so on" (Murphy 2012, p. 138). In particular, as has been suggested throughout this chapter, these virtual technologies could be seen as placing education firmly in the midst of the immaterial 'new' economy – standardizing and commoditizing education, reducing educational processes and relationships to forms that are easily quantifiable and recorded, distancing educational professionals from the process of educational engagement and thereby deprofessionalizing and deskilling the teaching profession. All these concerns suggest that virtual technologies act as powerful determinants of human action, in ways similar to the built environments and structures that they replicate. These concerns also highlight the need to better recognise the correspondences that persist between digital technology and the real-life social, cultural, economic and political contexts of education. Only through heightened awareness of these connections and correspondences can the full nature of virtual education be understood. As Ben Agger (2004, p. 109) reasons,

> Virtuality is neither to be celebrated nor condemned without thinking theoretically, dialectically, about the interaction between the pace and space of social life, on the one hand, and our technologies, on the other.

These are complex issues, yet it is now time to refocus our attention towards other genres of educational technology. Having spent this chapter considering some of the most prevalent and well-established digital forms being used in contemporary education, it is time to focus on an emerging 'type' of educational technology – the much feted area of 'open' technologies. These technologies – including open-source software, open access courses and open educational resources – also promise much in the way of disrupting established patterns of power and control in education, and challenging dominant elite interests. Indeed, as will soon be discussed, these open technologies are seen by many educationalists and technologists as a potential 'game changer' in terms of transforming contemporary education. So what, then, do open technologies offer to education, and why should be we distrustful of *these* seemingly benign developments?

4

DISTRUSTING 'OPEN' TECHNOLOGIES IN EDUCATION

Introduction

'Open' technologies have risen to prominence over the past 10 years, not only within the software programming communities where the concept of 'open-source' originated but also amongst nontechnology communities, such as artists, authors, scientists, scholars and political activists. From alternative cola drinks (such as 'Open Cola') to automobiles (such as the 'C,mm,n' open-source car), the notion of opening up production processes to a mass of user/innovators is seen as chiming with broader contemporary concerns, particularly in terms of the changing nature of expertise, ownership and governance. As Lawrence Lessig (2002, p. 9) observes, digital technology is seen as an integral element of this contemporary 'free culture', thereby allowing "a whole generation to create [and] share that creativity with others".

The 'open' philosophy has certainly been welcomed by technology enthusiasts eager to explore ways of disrupting the dominant concerns of commercial IT production. Open principles and practices are seen as supporting the user-driven production of devices and software which are more efficiently, expertly and elegantly designed. Although gaining in significance across many areas of society, open-source software has found particular support of late from sections of the educational technology community which have long bemoaned the lack of 'fit' between commercially produced IT products and the needs of students and teachers. Indeed, the educational potential of open-source software has been portrayed as overcoming many of the issues at the heart of the enduring patterns of ineffectual use of digital technologies within educational institutions. As such, it is argued that open software and digital content offer "new approaches to teaching and learning, specifically enabling personalized learning and enhanced learner voice; enabling knowledge sharing and collaboration between teachers; overcoming structural divides between developers of educational software and its users" (Bacon & Dillon 2006, p. 7). Thus, for many educational and noneducational authors alike, open-source software has assumed "an aura of unstoppability" (Shirky 1999), with some privileging it as "an extension of what we regard as best practice in [education]" (Carmichael & Honour 2002, p. 4).

While not denying the undoubted utility and overall significance of open-source software for computer programmers and software developers, this chapter contends that current struggles and debates over future form(s) of educational technology require a more measured understanding of the sociopolitical nature of 'open' production. Indeed, much of the educational debate can be criticized for positioning 'open' principles as a benign, 'neutral' force for good and, therefore, failing to account for embedded structures and processes of power, authority and governance. If such issues are not considered fully, then it could well be that open products and practices work in ways that actually restrict the more equitable and empowering development of technology use in education. With such concerns in mind, this chapter offers a critical rejoinder to the growing reification of the 'open' philosophy within educational circles. In particular it highlights the ideological agendas which underpin much of the current enthusiasm for the adoption of all things 'open' in education and thereby obscure the likely limitations and unintended consequences of their implementation in educational settings.

Unpacking the Key Features and Underlying Philosophies of 'Open' Technologies

What is now understood popularly as 'open-source' software derives from a succession of prominent projects within programming communities from the 1980s onwards. Indeed, much of the impetus for 'open' products, practices and principles stemmed from a resistance to the increasing dominance of 'proprietary' commercial software production and a corresponding desire to re-establish the experimental, grass-roots ideals of computer programming, which originated in early mainframe computing in the 1950s and 1960s (see Levy 1984). Richard Stallman's free software version of the UNIX operating system (known as 'GNU's Not Unix') is acknowledged as one of the first significant manifestations of open-source principles, prompting the subsequent formation of the free software movement in the 1980s. Stallman's Free Software Foundation was predicated upon the notion that software should be available to all users free of charge and, crucially, free of restrictions on further development and distribution. In emphasising the need for accessible source code (crucially through the counterproprietary notion of 'copyleft' as opposed to copyright) Stallman's model moved beyond the notion of *gratis* software and sought to prevent future closed-source versions of any piece of software. These stipulations all embodied the moral underpinnings of the 'hacker ethic' that frames information sharing as a positive moral good, and positions programmers as bound ethically to share their coding at all times (see Levy 1984; Himanen 2001).

During the 1990s, author/activists such as Bruce Perens and Eric Raymond did much to popularise a more business-driven notion of open-source software inspired by the rise of Linus Tordveld's celebrated 'Linux' operating system. In particular, Raymond's (1998a) influential treatise 'The Cathedral and the Bazaar' made a powerful case for the inefficiencies of a closed, top-down, hierarchal mode of software production (i.e., the 'cathedral', where production is overseen by an elite group of abbots and abbesses) when compared to the efficiency and elegance of mass, non-proprietary modes of production (i.e., the 'bazaar', where many producers coalesce in a free-for-all market situation). These arguments were bolstered by the 'Open Source Definition' proposed by Perens in 1998, which classified open-source as software that is distributed with its source code for no more than the cost of distribution. Moreover, Perens suggested that any user/innovator should then be free to redistribute modified versions of the software under the same terms without royalties or licensing fees to the author. This philosophy has since been extended throughout the 2000s and 2010s into the notion of 'creative commons' – a series of copyright licenses that ensure the right to distribute work at no charge, either in an unchanged *verbatim* form, or in an altered, derivative form.

While the free software and open-source initiatives remain distinct in their compulsion to distribute software free of charge and involvement of commercial organizations, these two sets of practices and protocols have tended to be referred to in conflated terms as 'open'. Thus in most debates the notion of 'open' has come to denote any digital content with accessible source code which is publicly distributed on noncommercial lines, non-proprietary and open to amendment and (re)development. This is often described in terms of a digitally based 'gift economy', where "property is freely given away, there is no accumulation, no money or other medium of exchange, and no exchange value" (Fuchs 2008, p. 162). This philosophy of 'openness' is seen as altering fundamentally the mode of production and consumption, towards a model of commons-based peer production of social and public goods (Benkler 2006). Some authors have talked of processes of 'produsage' and 'prosuming', based around decentralized decision making, individual autonomy in peer production, and the creation of resources that are held collectively by a community that permits sharing of the resources created amongst its members and often beyond the community (Meng & Wu 2013). This sees the encouragement of processes of sharing, such as peer-to-peer collaboration and cocreation – all enabled through 'new architectures of participation' associated with digital technologies (Peters & Roberts 2011).

Educational Interest in 'Open' Products and Practices

This philosophy of the open development of digital technologies has found a ready home in education, which has a long history of 'open' education provision and practice. Indeed, the current enthusiasms for the use of 'open' digital technologies for education and learning can be traced back to the 'open education' movement and its support for the provision of distance education with no barriers to access – not least the establishment in the 1960s of the UK Open University, Canada's Athabasca University and subsequent counterparts around the world. Now the notion of technology-supported 'open' forms of educational provision and practice take at least three distinct forms.

I. Open-source Software

Open-source software and the principles and practices of its production have proved highly attractive to a range of interest groups and actors within education. Indeed, open-source software now commands a prominent place within contemporary computing culture, with most major genres of commercial software mirrored by high-quality open-source applications which have been developed and adopted by open-source communities. Current mainstream open-source packages include the aforementioned Linux operating system, the Android operating system for mobile devices, the Ubuntu suite of desktop applications, the Firefox web browser, the OpenOffice suite of 'Office' applications and the Apache web server. Alongside these general applications are a range of education-specific tools and programmes. In college and university institutions across the world, the Moodle online content management package was developed as an open course alternative to commercial 'virtual learning environments' such as BlackBoard. Moreover, a range of 'niche' educational products are now growing in use in educational settings. Educational open-source communities have thrived through forums such as Schoolforge, FLOSS Posse and FLOSSWorld. Alongside these communities, a range of specific educational open-source products are now used in schools – from the Crocodile Clips physics package to OpenEuclide's geometry software.

The widespread use of open-source software in educational settings is celebrated as a powerful means of circumventing the constraining 'proprietary lock-in' and dependency on major IT suppliers that many educational institutions otherwise experience (Carmichael & Honour 2002). Countries such as Brazil, for example, are aiming to use open-source software to bring computer access to the large proportion of its population who are currently without. As the coordinator of the Brazilian Free Software Project argued, "Every license for Office plus Windows in Brazil – a country in which 22 million people are starving – means we have to export sixty sacks of soya beans" (Marcelo Branco, cited in Anderson 2009, p. 105). Similarly, the 'Deer Leap' school computerization program in Georgia during the 2000s introduced the mandatory use of the Linux operating system throughout the national school system. As Chris Anderson (2009, p. 105) concludes, "From this perspective, free software is not just good for consumers, it is good for the nation".

II. Open Educational Resources

Alongside the development and use of educationally specific open-source software are the production and use of open educational content. One prominent
instance of this is the push for 'open courseware' and 'open educational resources'
within higher education, concerned with making higher educational materials
available online for no cost. The term 'open educational resource' was introduced
in 2002 via a series of UNESCO seminars and publications, promoting what
was described as "the open provision of educational resources, enabled by information and communication technologies, for consultation, use and adaptation
by a community of users for non-commercial purposes" (D'Antoni 2006, n.p.).
The open educational resource (OER) movement supports free access to information in the form of web-based digital resources for learning, teaching and
research. These resources are usually placed in the public domain at no cost for
free use or repurposing by others, and can range from full courses to individual
lessons or sessions. As the Cape Town Open Education Declaration (2007, n.p.)
stated,

> This emerging open education movement combines the established tradi-
> tion of sharing good ideas with fellow educators and the collaborative, in-
> teractive culture of the internet. It is built on the belief that everyone should
> have the freedom to use, customize, improve and redistribute educational
> resources without constraint.

The use of open resources is now a significant element of university education.
Since the introduction of its commitment to 'open courseware' in 2001, it is reckoned that content from almost 80 per cent of courses at the Massachusetts Institute of Technology are available in this free-to-use manner. Similar commitments
can be found in institutions ranging from world-class universities such as Oxford
and Yale to local community colleges. In all these cases, course materials such as
seminar notes, podcasts and videos of lectures are shared online to public users.

The emphasis of open educational resources is not simply to allow teachers and learners to use materials as provided but also to encourage users to alter
and add to these resources as required. The UK Open University's 'OpenLearn'
project provides free access to all of the institution's curriculum materials with
an invitation for teachers and learners to adapt these resources as they see fit.
Other ventures rely on educational content that is created by individuals as well
as institutions. For example, the 'YouTube.Edu' service concentrates on providing educational videos produced by individuals and institutions alike. As Swain
(2009, p. 7) enthuses, "Thousands of hours of material are online for potential
students, or educators looking for inspiration". Enthusiasm is increasing for the
use of open educational resources that are concerned with making educational
materials available and reconfigurable online for no cost. There are now many

examples of these open educational arrangements – from large professional re-
positories to volunteers from China and Taiwan translating open-source materials from North American and European universities into Mandarin Chinese. In
all these instances, high-quality teaching and learning are no longer seen as the
domain of closed educational institutions and professional communities.

III. Open Courses and Delivery of Education

This ethos has been carried forward into the provision of open courses and the
open delivery of sustained educational programmes. There has been growing
interest in established educational institutions offering free online courses and
instruction. Early examples of this included the 'AllLearn' consortium of Oxford, Yale and Stanford Universities offering over 100 online enrichment courses,
followed by Stanford University's 'Introduction to Artificial Intelligence' open
course and the $60 million 'edX' programme run by Harvard and MIT, offering
certified university-level courses. Similar consortia of established universities have
been established to offer online, free access to adjunct educational provisions –
such as the 'OER University' backed by Athabasca, South Queensland and Otaga
Polytechnic – where students can follow courses for free, and pay reduced fees
for formal assessment and credit applicable for recognised qualification from these
institutions. On a more *ad hoc* basis, there are a growing number of 'massively
open online courses' (MOOCs) being run by academics and faculty around the
world. These MOOCs use a combination of online content management systems,
group forums and other content sharing software to facilitate online courses for
large numbers of dispersed students – often involving online lectures from invited
faculty and experts, accompanied by readings and discussions.

Some instances of this open, communal approach involve communities of educators and technologists in developed countries adopting open-source methods to
provide education to more disadvantaged learners. The 'International University
of the People' is one such example – a not-for-profit volunteer university offering courses provided entirely online and largely free of charge. The university is
designed around altruistic social networking principles. Groups of students participate in weekly discussion forums where they can access lecture transcripts and
associated reading material prepared by volunteer professors (often moonlighting
from their 'official' paid university positions elsewhere). Students are also provided
with assignments and discussion questions, which then direct their study for the
week. Students are expected to contribute to discussions and comment on their
peers' ideas. For broader discussions and learning, a university-wide forum of all
the university's teaching faculty and students operates to aid the discussion and
clarification of points not covered in the weekly 'classes'. As well as seeking to expand higher education access to social groups who would otherwise be excluded,
the International University of the People also offers some fundamental conceptual challenges to traditional forms of university education.

Whereas the International University of the People could be characterized as a 'pro-poor' solution, other collaborative open programmes in developing countries have framed disadvantaged users as 'active producers and innovators' (Heeks 2008). One such project was the Open Knowledge Network that ran during the 2000s in countries such as Kenya, Tanzania, Mali, Uganda, Senegal, Zimbabwe and Mozambique. The Open Knowledge Network was promoted as "a human network, which collects, shares and disseminates local knowledge and is supported by flexible technical solutions" (WSIS 2005, n.p.). As Richard Heeks (2008, p. 28) describes, the Open Knowledge Network sought to collect, share and disseminate "relevant local data content focused on livelihood-appropriate issues such as health, education, agriculture, and rights".These projects were usually community-based, with individuals often developing content and information offline, and then using the internet mobile phones and other communication technologies to share with other users. One of the obvious advantages of this user-created content was its relevance and usefulness – not least because content could be produced in a variety of national and local languages.

Support for the Use of Open Technologies and Techniques in Education

The growing use of open technologies in education has been accompanied by numerous justifications and perceived benefits. For many proponents, the educational significance of open products and practices spans far beyond the notion of users consuming free, non-proprietary software packages in a passive manner. Indeed, the perceived collective efficiency of communal content creation and redistribution has helped the notion of 'openness' gain credence both as a technical process *and* as a guiding wider philosophy of empowerment and public good (Von Hippel 2005; May 2006). In particular, open-source and open access movements have prompted a burgeoning belief amongst educational technologists that teachers and students are themselves capable of reshaping digital technology around their own needs and demands. Much is now being made of the capacity of local, 'bespoke' open software and content production to offer "greater choice and control" for educational users (Waring & Maddocks 2005, p. 415), as well as providing opportunities for "customizing to fulfil specific educational needs and for the development of collaborative on-line learning communities" (Carmichael & Honour 2002, p. 47). Instead of altering their practice to fit around the constrained forms of computing offered by 'off-the-shelf' commercial software packages, it is argued that teachers and students are more than capable of assuming control of the means of technological production and developing educational technologies for themselves via open products and practices. As Hamilton and Feenberg (2005, p. 117) contend, "There is now wide latitude for faculty intervention and participation in shaping the terms on which [digital technology] will impact the academic labour process, the division of academic labour, and owner-ship of intellectual resources".

In this sense we are currently witnessing a period of considerable enthusiasm for the increased flexibility and control that 'open' principles are believed to offer educational users. This is particularly the case with regards to the potential for collaborative creation in the direct shaping of applications and content being used in educational settings. Some of this enthusiasm conveys an almost revo-lutionary zeal, with the widespread use of open products in educational settings anticipated as a ready means of challenging the influence of major IT suppliers on educational institutions (Carmichael & Honour 2002). In this way, as Van de Bunt-Kokhuis (2004, p. 269) enthused, open products and practices "might serve to democratize [education] and allow greater grassroots input". Moreover, given the long-established legacy of shared responsibility within education, as well as cultures of peer review and regular revision of knowledge in the light of expe-rience, such arguments often portray education to be an especially conducive setting within which the 'open' ethos can thrive. This has even prompted some authors to argue for the mandated use of open products in educational institutions whereby governments force schools and colleges to adopt open alternatives to commercially available products (Comino & Manenti 2005). As such the notion of 'openness' has moved beyond being a matter of technical interest for program-ming and coding communities to become a prominent and persuasive part of wider debates concerning the future shape and forms of educational provision.

In particular, a frequently voiced set of justifications for 'open' forms of digital technology is framed around the efficient, creative and even elegant process of content production. The open-source 'bazaar' is often portrayed as a highly effi-cient model of innovation, benefiting from ongoing voluntary labour rather than the finite development of a marketable product. It is argued that the "high level of peer review" (Waring & Maddocks 2005, p. 415) associated with open processes allows far greater numbers of users to scrutinise and refine content than would be viable within the economic limitations of commercial production. Moreover, open practices are also seen as reinstating the craft-like qualities of software and content development, encouraging "ardent (if quirky) programmers, capable of brilliant, unorthodox feats of machine manipulation" as opposed to the mundane graft of the commercial programmer (Nissenbaum 2004, p. 196). Thus there is a sense that the 'open' development of technology allows individual program-mers and technologists to regain an importance and prestige within the process of production. This reification of the empowered individual is often expressed in decidedly anticorporate terms (Bezroukov 1999), with open-source software celebrated explicitly by some authors as 'smacking down' transnational IT cor-porations (Kirkpatrick 2004, p. 92). All these arguments feed into a seductive positioning of "engineers as 'elite' actors in a society where social boundaries are drawn primarily in terms of technical expertise" (Lancashire 2001, n.p).

Above and beyond issues of programmer efficiency and prestige, the open philosophy is also associated closely with a powerful sense of increased equity. For some proponents, these sentiments are based on the simple premise that "sharing is better than not sharing" (Streeter 2003, p. 658), thus evoking values of trust, generosity, openness and recourse to a gift-economy model of collaboration. Much of the support for open technologies in education therefore reflects an idea of making education fairer – not least increasing social justice and equalities of opportunity. For many supporters, open-source, open content and open delivery technologies are portrayed in explicitly emancipatory terms. Some commentators associate these technologies with the removal of 'unfreedoms' (Atkins, Brown & Hammond 2007, p. 1) and ensuring "the provision of access to learning opportunities to those who would not otherwise be able to obtain them" (Downes 2010, n.p). In this manner, the moral imperative behind the open educational resource movement is described by many proponents simply as follows: "Making educational resources freely available to all is a fundamental right" (Conole 2012a, p. 2). Indeed, the original UNESCO description of the notion of open educational resources framed the movement in decidedly liberal transformatory terms, expressing the "wish to develop together a universal educational resource available for the whole of humanity . . . they hope that this open resource for the future mobilizes the whole of the worldwide community of educators" (cited in D'Antoni 2008, p. 7). These sentiments can also be found within the rhetoric celebrating the widening of technical expertise and power to the mass of nonexpert computer users. As Lankshear and Knobel (2007, p. 18) enthuse, open-source user/innovators "needn't be experts and most of them are not".

While these notions of gift culture, craft and democratization of expertise may appear idealistic, they all point to a more nuanced association of open products, practices and processes with wider sociopolitical reform – not least the notion of the 'open' exemplifying a fundamentally new postmaterialist mode of industrial organization (Lancashire 2001). This more politicized alignment of openness with a reconfigured economic order is articulated usually in one of two (conflicting) forms. From one perspective, openness has come to act as a talisman for a set of explicit concerns about 'new forms' of property, 'hybrid ownership' and "asserting indigenous people's rights to knowledge and resources" (Amin & Thrift 2005, p. 233). In particular, the apparent flattening of hierarchies of production implicit within 'open' principles appeals to long-standing socialist concerns over achieving collective ownership of the means of production, a return to handicraft and even the reinstatement of the all-round craftworker. For some Left-leaning advocates, therefore, the notion of 'open' taps directly into socialist ideals of collaboration and worker-ownership leading to 'better' outcomes. Richard Sennett (2008), amongst others, has argued passionately for the open-source philosophy as a ready means of imaginatively crafting 'better' products while also reskilling otherwise deskilled workers by devolving control of the means of production. As Coleman (2004, p. 512) concludes somewhat wryly, "Leftist . . . activists adore [the open-source model] for its subversive, anti-capitalist potentialities".

Conversely open software and content has also attracted the support of a neo-liberal and ultralibertarian lobby of predominantly North American commentators, drawn to the individual rather than collective benefits of decoupling technology production from the 'interference' of overarching central organizations. In this sense, open-source software has been enrolled into the wider neo-liberal 'declaration of independence' often foisted onto new media and technology by those on the Right (Fischer 2006). This sense of independence is most often predicated around utilitarian (rather than romantic) notions of individualism and individual gain. Thus the principles of open production are seen as corresponding with neo-liberal views of the desirability of a weak state and diminished public intervention as well as the desirability of citizens to make an individual effort and an individual success of themselves (see March & Olsen 1995). In this sense, open production has been aligned with declarations of 'freedom', 'our American liberal heritage', 'mistrust of centralized authority' and opposition to the 'dry, bureaucratic detail' that typifies centrally controlled processes (Streeter 2003; Coleman 2004; Nissenbaum 2004). This emancipation from the top-down strictures of state, monopolistic corporations and other institutions is seen as fostering a powerful form of individually driven creativity, "not imposed by a transcendent instance from above [but] where itinerant following and group creation prevail over the issuing and obeying of commands" (Harper 2009, p. 136).

A final set of values that underpins current support for educational use of open products draws upon the ways in which individuals work, and therefore, learn together during the production and use of open content. As already described, the ongoing development of open products is seen as operating along communal, collaborative lines, with solutions arising from the distributed intelligence and expertise of participants within communities of users (Kogut & Metiu 2001). Furthermore, it is assumed that individuals who contribute support and advice will themselves learn through the help-giving process (Lakhani & Von Hippel 2003). Thus in educational terms, open artefacts and resources have become something of an icon for the qualities of openness, collaboration, mastery and apprenticeship that are seen by many to lie at the heart of 'effective' learning. Seely-Brown and Adler (2008, p. 32) talk of open educational resources in terms of a new form of learner-driven learning, "creating the conditions for the emergence of new kinds of open participatory learning ecosystems that will support active, passion-based learning: Learning 2.0". In particular, these qualities are presented by some in the learning sciences and educational technology as embodying constructivist and constructionist beliefs concerning sociocultural knowledge building. Thus obvious parallels have been drawn with various forms of collaborative, learner-centred approaches to education, general enthusiasm for peer review and scaffolding of learning and, from an educational technology perspective, a long-standing constructionist belief in children as programmers (see

Papert 1980). Indeed, open principles are argued by some educationalists to be of core relevance "to our understanding of how people learn and produce knowledge; of how communities collaborate and work to solve problems; and of how innovative practices emerge" (Bacon & Dillon 2006, p. 49). As Gráinne Conole (2012b, p. 2) concludes,

> The key characteristics of these new technologies, such as peer critiquing, collective aggregation, personalization, networking and more open practices, generally sit well alongside what constitutes good pedagogy and more learning- and learner-centred approaches such as inquiry-based learning, scenario-based learning, dialogic and reflective learning, and more constructivist and situated pedagogies generally.

Problematizing the Use of Open-source Software in Education

At first glance, the case for the use of open technologies in education appears difficult to challenge. Indeed, aside from opposition from commercial competitors wary of the market interference of freely shared products, there has been remarkably little popular criticism of open forms of educational technology. Besides occasional criticism of the veneer of self-righteousness that can pervade discussions of open products and practices, they remain widely welcomed and promoted within discussions of educational technology. Of course, this is not to argue that these technologies are beyond critique. While open production has proved appealing to a disparate range of interest groups in education, we must be wary of the ideological motivations and political agendas underlying many of the more 'lavish claims' accompanying the rise of 'open' philosophies and principles (Weber 2000).

In this sense, some of the recent educational endorsements of open products and practices clearly follow a well-worn tendency for the romanticizing of any 'new' digital development. Indeed, within the general realm of technology development open production and open access has been presented in emotive, evangelical but ultimately hollow terms of 'revolution' (DiBona, Ockman & Stone 1999), 'crusade' (Williams 2002) and even 'magic' (Raymond 1998b). Yet it would be foolish to dismiss the current promotion of openness within educational circles as merely another instance of new technology 'boosterism' and hyperbole. As just outlined, 'open' philosophies are being championed within the context of education by a broad amalgam of interest groups seeking to reorientate the social relations of education in a variety of (often conflicting) ways. This support ranges from self-serving communities of technologists and programmers, and neo-liberals pursuing a de-schooling agenda, to "disillusioned lefties who have found in the rhetorical activism of [open technology] a new and less troublesome kind of politics" (Harkin 2007, p. 33). This cacophony of wider ideological agendas belies the apparently straightforward case for the implementation of open products

and practices in educational settings. Thus any widespread adoption of open technologies is a matter not only of technical adjustment but also of profound social,
cultural and political importance for future forms of education and, as such, is not
a process to be entered into lightly. Moreover, as we shall now go on to argue, the
current ideologically driven and partisan nature of the debate serves to obscure
a number of compelling reasons to suggest that a reliance on open products and
practices in education may be as problematic (and only partially as effective) as
the current reliance on proprietary products, whatever ideological lens one may
choose to view it through.

While often well intentioned, it could be argued that the prevailing discourses
currently framing open principles within the education community fail to acknowledge and account for the limited and structured nature of the 'open' process
of production. In many ways such misrepresentation of technology is to be expected. As Mansell (2004, p. 97) notes, it is natural for those seeking to introduce
new media into social settings to "concentrate on promoting access with little
regard for the associated structures and processes of power that are embedded
within them". Yet the educational misrepresentation of open products and practices is not borne solely from technological overexuberance. Instead much of the
current enthusiasm for openness is (un)consciously yoked to wider ideological
motivations of re-engineering and reorientating the social relations of educational
technologies and educational institutions. As such, the educational application of
open-source software and open content "beholds a complex political life despite
the lack of political intention" (Coleman 2004, p. 507), which is currently voiced
rarely in debates over future forms of education and technology. As such, it is
important to challenge the ongoing debate concerning openness. With this intention in mind, we now go on to present a brief critical analysis of the supposed
benefits of open production and open access for educational and noneducational
users alike.

I. The Tensions Between Individual Competition and 'Communal' Production

A first obvious disjuncture between the rhetoric and realities of open production in education is the received wisdom that individual user/innovators make
contributions to open projects for altruistic reasons related to the public good of
the endeavour. From the empirical research conducted to date on the processes of
open-source software development it would appear that the motivations of those
involved in open projects are many – from artistic compulsions to create elegant
and beautiful work and opposition to large commercial interests to the less discussed, ego-driven desire to be seen as a good programmer. This latter motivation
has been identified by researchers as being perhaps the most significant, given its
link to underlying driving motivations of career and financial benefit. As Weber
(2000, p. 21) explains,

> Ego gratification is important because it stems from peer recognition. Peer recognition is important because it creates a reputation. A reputation as a great programmer is monetizable – in the form of job offers, privileged access to venture capital, *etc*.

In their investigation of the development of the Apache and Perl applications, for example, Lerner and Tirole (2002) describe how individuals participated in open-source projects only if they expected to derive a net benefit from doing so. Matters of reputation enhancement were seen by 'community' members not necessarily as ends in themselves, but as powerful means to signal individual technical expertise which could later be leveraged to gain privileged (and usually paid) employment. Thus in contrast to the prevailing rhetoric of communal altruism, open production can be seen as an individualistic and self-centred pursuit, with little obligation to contribute above and beyond issues of personal gain. Indeed, open projects cannot be assumed to have a *de facto* collective workshop mentality. Many of the forms of open innovation described in this chapter could alternatively be characterized as largely individualized pursuits rather than the collective cooperation and collaboration that one would find within the configuration of a traditional workshop. As Sennett (2012) observes, the social relations and rituals that characterize a workshop are usually not replicated in open 'collectives'. In this sense, the sustainability and collective benefit of open 'solutions' are questionable as "the majority of participants leave the community once *their* needs are met" (Shah 2006, p. 1000).

II. Power Imbalances Within Open Processes of Production

The notion of open production as a harmoniously inclusive and even nonhierarchical process is also problematic. Indeed, popular portrayals of open-source software and open content within education are based upon the notion that production takes place within democratic cooperatives based on the "collaborative efforts and outcomes of a large number of people working incrementally on a problem or artefact without being organized on either a market-based, managerial or hierarchical model" (Bacon & Dillon 2006, p. 13). Thus one of the central tenets of open technologies is that any individual can contribute and therefore benefit from the production process. As Schoonmaker (2012, p. 508) reasons,

> For example, in large scale peer production projects like the Linux kernel, a kind of 'meritocratic hierarchy' exists . . . Authority in such a hierarchy is based upon the respect that peer producers hold for a leader's contributions, as well as on the leader's powers of persuasion. Since large-scale peer production projects involve interdependent contributions from individuals, these projects are organized to make it possible for individuals to contribute in a wide range of ways, such as coding, writing documentation, and

translation. Individuals with diverse abilities, levels of training, commitment, or availability can thus all participate in the project.

Instead, the realities of open production projects could be said to be based more in rigid hierarchies of privileged and authorized elites of charismatic leaders and core users who oversee and moderate the creative process. For example, it is acknowledged widely that tight ownership and coordination are prerequisites to any successful open-source software project, not least because "an effective open source project takes a lot of work" (O'Reilly 2007). In particular open production communities tend to be organized tightly along the lines of experience and expertise (Berdou 2008). In practice, then, open production tends to be not simply a 'bottom-up' or flattened collective action but a highly coordinated process based around seniority rules, leadership and constraining working practices and rules, as well as sanctioning mechanisms such as shunning and 'flaming' (Weber 2000; Mansell 2006). As Bergquist and Ljungberg (2001, p. 315) observe, the 'pure' efficiency of open-source software is compromised by "power relationships that are expressed as an elitism of the inner circle and exercised as the right to hinder a person in contributing to the common good".

In this sense there is a reluctance throughout much of educational literature to acknowledge that the inclusiveness of open production is tempered by the levels of skill required to participate, just as the production and reproduction of open resources require a similarly high level of professional confidence and aptitude. Although it is often claimed that "user/developers come from all walks of life" (Weber 2000, p. 15), meaningful participation is limited clearly to technically skilled individuals, whether hobbyists, committed hackers or full-time programmers. In contrast to the 'pro-am' free-for-all envisaged by some commentators, communities of open content developers tend instead to be sustained and reproduced over time through the gradual integration of technically proficient new members who are able to progressively construct identities as 'software craftsmen' via specific programming 'rites of passage' (Ducheneaut 2005). Successful participants therefore tend to be those who understand the political nature of software development and progressively enrol a network of similarly skilled allies to support their efforts. It would seem naively optimistic to imagine the open production of software and other content taking place within heterogeneous communities of experts and nonexperts sharing common interests and goals. Indeed, unequal relations of power are not made explicit, or even acknowledged, in most discussions of open technologies (Mansell 2004), and if so, are usually explained away as being a necessary and productive aspect. As Meng and Wu (2013, p. 128) argue,

> Conflicts and hierarchies are rife within these communities as elsewhere, illustrating the dynamics of power relationships within peer production communities. [However] in these communities, power is often understood

to operate as a generative rather than a repressive force that sustains peer production at both the organizational and discursive levels.

III. The Mass Consumption of Openly Produced Products

This notion of unequal participation and power in the peer production of open technologies highlights the discrepancy between elite production and mass consumption of these products and practices. As Bacon and Dillon (2006, p. 49) posit, a key challenge underlying the educational success of open software and open content is the extent to which "learners and teachers want to, or are able to, become involved in co-creating digital resources". It could therefore be argued that only a minority of educators are ever likely to have the requisite resources and interest to engage with open products above the level of merely using products as cursory end users. This lack of engagement with the dynamic coconstruction of open-source products and content was highlighted in Ellen Helsper's review of open software adoption in UK higher education institutions. Here it was found that while use of open platforms and software in higher education was relatively high, the involvement of universities and colleges in the modification or coconstruction of these products was remarkably low. It appears that most educational users turn to open products for economic reasons of saving money in relation to purchasing propriety software (Helsper 2006).

While understandable, this lack of engagement in the productive processes marks a significant diminishment of the supposed benefits of open products, as according to the principles of open production and access, the advantages to be accrued from the coconstruction of effective products require a mass participation in innovation. Yet without the sustained, active involvement of a critical mass of educational contributors it is increasingly likely that open production processes will reposition rather than overcome the existing hegemony of the production of educational content, products and services. As Fischer (2006, p. 141) contends, "The question is, therefore, who will manipulate? Everyone, as a naïve communications democracy utopia would have it? Or the most powerful? Will [open-source software] be the empire of virtue . . . or the empire of force?"

It could therefore be argued that open production is most likely to lead to a two-track system of a minority of involved 'innovator-users' and a majority of uninvolved users. In other words, while all members of the educational community may benefit to some extent from the consumption of 'open' products, those with more technological capital look set to benefit on a far greater scale than those with less technological capital. At best, a turn to open content within educational settings will shift the nexus of power and control away from commercial actors and towards an elite of educational technology actors located within and around educational settings. It is highly unlikely that there will be a noticeable empowerment of a mass of 'ordinary' teachers and students. Indeed, given the integral role that "computer programmers and expert consultants" inhabit within the development of open-source software (Fischer 2006, p. 130), a widespread turn within education towards open products may well lead simply to exaggerated inequality between an empowered educational technology community and their rather less empowered mass of nonexpert colleagues. The concern therefore emerges that for the majority of teachers and learners this will facilitate a comparably 'closed-source' mode of educational technology use as before. Even whether such a 'producer (re)capture' by educational technologists at the expense of commercial firms would result in noticeably better forms of educational technology use in the classroom is a moot point.

IV. The Limited Outcomes of Open Production Processes

This contrast between elite production and mass consumption also raises the issue of the restricted nature of the applications and content that are produced. As has already been argued, the focus of open production projects is seen as limited only by what individual contributors consider to be 'interesting' and/or 'important' problems, rather than being constrained to issues of commercial importance. This is celebrated as imbuing open products with an unconstrained flexibility, as experts "will tend to focus on an immediate and tangible problem (the 'itch') – a problem that they themselves want to solve" (Weber 2000, p. 35). Yet this apparent freedom to be guided only by practical interest, intellectual challenge or perceived importance of the topic lends obvious limitations to the open production process – most notably in areas where there is little expert interest (or 'software love' as Shirky [1999] described it in programming terms). In the production of open-source software, for example, the problems that many programmers would perceive to be important or interesting are predicated upon variations of the 'hacker ethic' and consequent desire to produce 'antiproprietary' projects for which strong, relatively low-cost commercial alternatives already exist. Consequently, other marginal (or less stimulating) projects are unlikely to be pursued – resulting in a situation where "certain useful programs don't get written" (Johnson 2002, p. 637). As Shirky (1999, n.p.) concludes,

> Existing software which is old or broken but has to be updated or fixed won't clear the 'interesting problem' hurdle. Boring software won't acquire enough beta testers. Projects which require treating the user like an idiot (an oxymoron in the open source world, since scratching a personal itch turns the lead developer into User#1) won't attract enough developers to take off. The overlapping categories of old, broken, boring and disdainful of the user's intelligence currently describe a majority of the world's software, an installed base that isn't going away any time soon.

In terms of the production of educational content, it is therefore questionable whether open production will result in a plethora of obscure and niche content in the vein of a rich 'long tail' of minority educational products and services. To date, open educational products and practices have tended to reflect the interests and backgrounds of those educators involved in their establishment – hence the proliferation of courses and content concerned with computer studies, business studies, learning sciences, educational technology and so on. As Jeremy Knox (2012) has argued, such limitations of production and consumption are evident in the emphasis of open educational resources on individual self-direction, autonomy and the simplistic assumption of 'passion-based learning'.

V. Open Production as a Site of Exploitation and Commodification

All of these issues point to the fact that open products are party to many of the limitations of other educational commodities – that is, "as abstracted, intellectual value-in-motion that is to be consumed" (Hall & Hall 2010, n.p.). It is therefore misleading to view open peer production as a wholly altruistic, gift-giving, noncompetitive and noncommodified process. Clearly 'cooperation' within open production communities takes place under a competitive logic between individuals, with exchanges taking place on the basis of personal gain as well as eventual collective benefit. As such, open production could be described as "an entanglement of gifts within the commodity form" (Fuchs 2008, p. 171–172). Alternately, as Mansell and Berdou (2010) describe it, open production is a 'mixed economy' in which features of the exchange economy come to the fore more often than features of the gift economy. Although not being produced by proprietary interests for direct economic gain, open educational resources and other open educational technologies could still be said to be driven by "an agenda of consumption, marketization and commodification" (Hall & Hall 2010, n.p.).

Indeed, despite their countercultural, anti-institutional credentials, there is little sense in assuming open products and practices to be opposed to the dominant economic order of educational provision. In many ways, the open technologies described in this chapter represent a shifting in the economics of education. The involvement of large dominant educational institutions like Harvard, MIT, Stanford and Oxford in the implementation of 'massively open online courses', for example, highlights the continuation of the established educational order. Open technologies could be seen as a ready means of these dominant institutional interests and corporate capital identifying and developing new markets. Open course ventures such as Coursera and edX are clearly based on a 'freemium' model of allowing no-cost access to a basic version of the 'product' (i.e., the course content), while requiring payment for the advanced 'full' version (i.e., the certified degree). These free goods and services are also means of increasing numbers of users that can then be sold to advertisers, with the commodity therefore being the access to users and user data rather than the initial product itself.

As Sharpe (2009) observes, one of the key features of contemporary capitalism is the ability to generate profits from 'free' information. Indeed, the increased involvement of large multinational corporations such as Pearson in open education movements has caused some consternation. As Cormier (2012, n.p.) reasons, this could be seen as little more than a corporate misappropriation of a countercultural ethic (what he derides as putting 'a Deadhead sticker on a Cadillac'), and thereby misappropriating open education as "a new business model – not a new model of learning". As Geert Lovink (2011) has also contended, notions such as Creative Commons, open content, free software and open access do little to challenge or alter the basic revenue model of capitalist society. Indeed, it could be argued that these movements strengthen the hegemony of corporate capitalist interests by appearing to challenge and undermine their dominance while actually reinforcing it:

> The networks of communicative capitalism at the basis of Free Software instead produce inequality, insecurity, and subjection to the conditions and demands of a recalcitrant finance sector. What proffered itself as a vehicle for bringing in something new, something better, becomes the mechanism for further embedding and extending the old, now strengthened by the rhetoric of its own over-coming.
>
> *(Dean 2010, p. 27)*

Seen in these terms, one of the more likely outcomes of the increased use of open products and practices in education is the increased exploitation of individuals. The framing of the individual user of open educational resources and courses as the administrator and accreditor of his or her own learning therefore also enforces the notion of the self-responsibilized and self-disciplining learner. As Jeremy Knox (2012, n.p.) observes, the model of open educational resources "permits particular behaviours and activities that influence and compound the sense of autonomy and empowerment in the production of the self as human capital". More subtly, open models of peer production also involve the exploitation of the individuals that contribute their 'free labour' to the peer production of open educational resources and content. Of course supporters of the open technology movement tend to portray these participants in heroic terms – take Branco's (2006, p. 295) celebration of the "cyber proletarians who make life hell for Bill Gates". However, these contributors could be seen alternatively as part of the huge rise of free labour that has taken place throughout digitally based cultural industries – notably in the reliance within the computer games industry on a 'shadow industry' of games players being involved in finding bugs and other faults, and later encouraged to produce additional user-generated content, modifications and other forms of microdevelopment (Terranova 2004). As Dyer-Witheford and de Peuter (2009, p. 27) conclude, while "initially a subversive threat to corporate control of digital culture, the [IT] industry has increasingly learned to suck up volunteer production as a source of innovation and profit".

Conclusions

Although 'open' technologies are celebrated as a common, fair and counterhegemonic form of digital education, this chapter has developed an argument that they are, in fact, a ready vehicle for individualism, neo-liberalism and new capitalist ideology. These are technologies that embody values of individualism, competition and transient forms of 'collaboration'. Moreover, there are significant inequalities of participation in terms of the production and consumption of open products – seemingly reinforcing inequalities between technological elites and the majority of mainstream consumers of technology. While these products and services may appear to be positioned outside the market economics of conventional educational provision, there is a sense that they continue to be commodified, and subject to an exchange economy rather than a pure gift economy basis. Finally, it can be argued that open technologies are entwined with new capitalist modes of exploitation – not least the exploitation of the free immaterial labour involved in the production and reproduction of open content. In contrast to current enthusiasms, it would therefore seem that there are some significant limitations to the adoption of digitally enabled open products and practices in education. As Rhoads, Brown and Toven-Lindsey (2013, p. 106) conclude,

> Critical questions must be asked about the nature of the [Open Course-ware] movement and its growing appeal. Otherwise, whatever democratic potential it does hold may be easily minimized or eradicated by a variety of power/knowledge inequities operating in antidemocratic ways. This . . . raises critical questions about the Open Courseware movement with regard to the nature of the knowledge being advanced (the problem of epistemology), the conditions of construction and delivery of information and knowledge (the problem of pedagogy), and the potential for certain social actors, institutions, and nations to dominate courseware development and, in essence, further dominate the advance of knowledge (the problem of hegemony). All of these issues point to antidemocratic facets of the Open Courseware movement – a reality that is almost never addressed in the Open Courseware literature.

This disjuncture could be said to stem largely from the fact that many of those arguing for the use of open products and practices in education are presupposing (and indeed hoping for) a fundamental 'domain shift' (Sennett 2008) in the practices of education. As such these arguments are wilfully and provocatively at odds with formal educational contexts, where it can be argued that the likelihood of teachers and learners getting involved in the production of open software or content are curtailed by the realities of institutionalized education – not least issues of time, technical expertise, interest and motivation. Thus it could be argued that openness is not necessarily being promoted for reasons of 'educational fit' or effectiveness. Rather it is based upon a variety of political, social and cultural agendas centred on a desire to reorientate educational institutions and systems and the power relations therein. Although often conflicting in their political and ideological intention, most of these viewpoints are compromised by a shared determinist viewpoint that overlooks the limiting influence that social relations have on open production processes. One emerging contention in this sense is that if such misrepresentative rhetoric is allowed to go unchallenged, then enthusiasm for the 'open' will continue to act only as a distraction to more fundamental problems facing education. With these thoughts in mind, it is now time to turn our attention to another ostensibly 'disruptive' form of digital education that is widely feted in educational technology circles – the use of games and gaming technologies.

5

DISTRUSTING 'GAMES' TECHNOLOGIES IN EDUCATION

Introduction

More than 50 years after the development of rudimentary games of 'Tennis for Two' and 'Spacewar' in research labs of US universities and government organizations, games are now one of the most popular and profitable genres of digital technology. Games have grown to be a mainstream and diverse element of the digital landscape, and are seen increasingly as a source of education as well as entertainment. The term 'digital game' encompasses a range of applications – from relatively simple 'casual' games for smartphones and other mobile devices, and 'social gaming' applications embedded into social networks, to complex 'massively multiplayer' online games and multimillion-dollar blockbuster console games. While traditionally seen as the preserve of male, adolescent users, gaming is now a popular practice across most demographic groups. Studies conducted for the US games industry, for example, suggest that the average games player is 30 years old and has been playing for 12 years. Sixty-eight per cent of game players are aged 18 years or older, with a broadly equal split between men and women. Significantly, it is estimated that over 90 per cent of children and young people play with digital games (ESA 2012).

Mirroring this expansion in users, digital gaming is now a substantial business concern. From a commercial point of view, the games industry is estimated to be worth in excess of $50 billion, with the most popular games being consumed in vast quantities. It is reckoned that over 1 billion copies of the 'Angry Birds' and 100 million copies of the 'Tetris' smartphone games have been downloaded. Similarly, over 40 million copies of the various 'Super Mario Brothers' games have been purchased. As such, games playing is one of the core applications of most digital devices – from the smartphone to the desktop computer and dedicated console. The most successful games are now prominent elements of contemporary popular culture, and the production of digital games is increasingly seen as a serious creative and artistic endeavour. Most importantly, the practice of playing a game is generally associated with a range of potential benefits above and beyond entertainment. All in all, many commentators now see games as an integral element of using digital technology. As Tom Chatfield (2010, p. 28) reasons,

> We are deeply and fundamentally attracted, in fact, to games: those places where efforts and excellence are rewarded, where the challenges and demands are severe, and where success often resembles nothing so much as a distilled version of the worldly virtues of dedicated learning and rigorously coordinated effort.

What Constitutes a Digital Game?

Despite their longevity, the definition of what a digital 'game' is remains a source of considerable disagreement. There are, of course, many different forms of digital game – from simple games of chance, games of skill and role play and strategy games to scenario planning and mimetic play. Games differ not only in their subject and scope but also in terms of their emphasis on chance and strategy, repetitiveness and linearity, time boundedness and whether the player views events from the perspective of 'first person', 'third person' or even 'god'. Games can be played by solitary individuals or by 'multiplayer' groups of thousands of remotely connected people. Amidst this diversity, it is perhaps understandable that digital games continue to suffer from what Waern (2012, n.p.) terms an "everlasting problem of definition". Nevertheless, despite the broad scope of the genre, all games can be said to share some common characteristics. In this sense, Waern (2012) offers two dominant lines of definition – that is, defining digital games as systems or else as forms of human activity. Both these perspectives are worth considering in further detail.

The notion of games as 'systems' reflects the significance of rule-bound actions within any form of digital game. As Zimmerman and Salen (2003, p. 80) note, from this perspective a digital game can be described as "a system in which players engage in an artificial conflict, defined by rules, that results in a quantifiable outcome". The notion of games as an 'activity', on the other hand, implies that it is not the digital game itself that is of primary interest but the act of playing the digital game – something that can vary considerably between different players. For example, the activity of playing digital games can be driven by play motivations that are not bound by shared conventions and rules of the system, but are more exploratory and free-form in nature – what Gaver (2002) terms 'playful interactions'. Thinking beyond the system of the digital game is also evident in the academic trend to focus on the 'narratology' of games – that is, adopting a literary theory approach which positions the digital game as a story and text akin to films, books and television. From this perspective, games can be described as forms of interactive fiction that involve storytelling through the communication of events, settings, characters and perspectives, and therefore constitute an embodied, experiential form of narrative (Carr 2006). While contestable, these descriptions of activity and narrative highlight the importance of the representational dimension of digital games alongside the regulatory dimension.

These differences in definition correspond in part with various understandings of 'play' that can be associated with digital games. Here Caillois' (2001) hierarchical classification of play (from 'paidia' to 'ludus') is often drawn upon. At one extreme, 'paidiac' play can be described as 'spontaneous', 'frolicsome' and 'instinctive' manifestations of the 'play instinct' (Caillois 2001, p. 27). This form of play therefore includes free-form and unscripted amusements, open-ended role playing and fantasy play. In contrast, the conception of 'ludic' play describes more formal instances of play that are bound by rules and conventions, and based upon "the pleasure experienced in solving a problem arbitrarily designed for this purpose" (Caillois 2001, p. 28). Clearly, then, the notion of 'digital games' should not be taken to encompass *all* forms of digital play – especially the purer forms of paidiac play. Thus, as Buckingham (2006, p. 6) acknowledges, "all games must be played, but not all play takes the form of a game". In defining digital games one should therefore accept some degree of pre-agreed form and rule-boundedness. Thinking along these lines, Waern (2012, n.p.) offers a nuanced working definition of digital games as "systems, which have been designed to be played or evolved within a play practice". This definition seems as good as any to take forward into the remainder of this chapter.

The notion of digital games as systems that have evolved from play practices and the activity of play clearly draws on many of the characteristics associated with Caillois' notion of 'ludus'. Indeed, as Juul (2003) reasons, the characteristics that set digital gaming apart from other digital media can be described in largely ludic terms. In particular, digital games can be seen as being based (to some extent) around sets of rules and parameters, as well as corresponding sets of goals and opposing means of preventing players from reaching these goals without some effort. Digital games can also be defined as having varied outcomes which are usually quantifiable and assigned different values. Moreover, digital games require players to invest effort in achieving these desired outcomes and thereby manipulate forms of emotional 'attachment' to succeeding in the game. The embodiment of all these characteristics within a *digital* game therefore sees gaming actions structured by a complex of "protocols, networks, codes and algorithms" designed to represent these characteristics in a computerized form (Krapp 2011, p. 77). Thus at the heart of digital 'gameplay' is the ability of players to 'fit' themselves around the coded contours of the game as programmed into the computer. As Tom Apperley (2009, p. 24) describes,

> Players are insinuated into the rhythm of the game through the process of play; they must 'fit' into the rhythm of the game, not vice versa. . . . To win

you can't just do whatever you want. You have to figure out what will work within the rules of the game. You must learn to predict the consequences of each move, and anticipate the computer's response. Eventually your decisions become intuitive, as smooth and rapid fire as the computer's own machinations. This on-going attuning process of learning to anticipate and respond to the computer's actions begins a rhythm of action and reaction that involves the internalization of the computer's rhythm by the player . . . a 'merging of consciousness', precipitated by thinking like the computer.

As with any computer application, then, digital gaming needs to be understood as an essentially bounded and predefined activity – albeit often one that allows the potential for huge variation of action and engagement. As Grimes and Feenberg (2012) suggest, the 'game world' of any specific digital game is perhaps best understood as structured around a finite set of themes and activities defined by the games designer and developer. While this predesignated architecture demands a precision from the games player, players can still act in a variety of 'playful' ways within their direct interactions with the rules, temporality, sequence and structures of a game. As Newman (2004, p. 92) observes, "Not every player plays a given game in the same way, nor do they necessarily seek the same pleasures from their play". Thus when playing a digital game, individuals can play in a number of different ways. A game can be played simply by 'exploring' and interacting with the game world, or by seeking actively to 'achieve' success through acting on the rules and goals of the game world (Bartle 1997). Alternatively, gameplay can be approached as a means of 'socializing' with other players, or alternatively striving to outperform and fulfil a desire to win at the expense and distress of others (what Bartle describes as displaying a 'killer' mentality). As Aarseth (2005) and others have noted, games can also be played by intentionally modifying or breaking the rules of the game through forms of 'cheating' and 'counterplay'.

These varied forms of interaction coupled with the acceptance of arbitrary rules and conventions reflect the fact that playing a digital game evokes a sense of distinctness and separation from the real world. As Buckingham (2006) observes, one of the defining characteristics of digital games playing is its status as an alternate 'fictional' activity that is set apart from 'ordinary life'. This otherworldliness can be seen in terms of the 'protective frame' that surrounds a person in a playful state of mind – a frame that derives from the 'social contract' that constitutes the act of playing a game (Stenros 2012). Some commentators have gone as far as suggesting the establishment of a 'magic circle' once a game begins to be played (Zimmerman & Salen 2003). The notion of the 'magic circle' sees the act of playing a game located within a 'special place in time and space' where actions are interpreted playfully, the rules of the game have authority and the actions that take place have no direct effect on the everyday world. In this sense, playing a digital game can be seen as a ritualistic endeavour that is socially and mentally divided from ordinary life (Stenros 2012).

The Rise of Educational Interest in Digital Games and Gaming

These characteristics certainly lend digital games an exotic and seductive air when compared to other seemingly more mundane forms of educational technology. The inherent appeal of digital games to educationalists is heightened further by the many benefits that are believed to be inherent in the practice of games playing. For example, alongside increased psychomotor development and hand-eye coordination, a range of cognitive benefits have been perceived in terms of mental agility and neurological capacity. Some commentators have pointed to benefits associated with the increased sociability of game playing and the creative practices that can take place within and around the playing of digital games. In these terms, digital gaming is often associated with a number of emotional and psychological outcomes. For example, games playing is described as evoking a sense of 'hard fun' that derives from the delayed emotional gratification of overcoming challenges and winning battles. Borrowing a concept from the field of positive psychology, games are also associated with an enhanced 'flow' – that is, a sense of intense happiness that can come from the 'immersive power of play' (McGonigal 2011). In all these ways, then, games playing is often described as an intensely stimulating experience.

It is perhaps not surprising that digital games have come to be associated so closely with education. As has already been suggested, learning is seen to be a key element to successfully playing a digital game. As Carr, Oliver and Burn (2010, p. 23) reason, "Learning obviously happens in this game world . . . otherwise players would not progress". Moreover, alongside the implicit learning that takes place within the mastery of any digital game, there is a long history of the development of explicitly 'educational games'. One of the earliest mainstream examples of educational gaming was the 'Oregon Trail' adventure game – originally developed in 1971 and requiring players to re-enact the nineteenth-century North American pioneer trail. Schools have long made use of specifically designed games – most famously the 'Math Blaster' and 'Carmen Sandiego' series of games, which have been regularly revised and reassessed since the early 1980s. Similarly, there is a well-established lineage of educational games for adults, including the popular mental development games such as 'Dr Kawashima's Brain Training' and 'Big Brain Academy'. In workplace settings, there has also been a long-standing use of training games in areas such as aviation, military combat, business and management.

Against this background, there is now considerable interest in digital games as a mainstream form of educational technology. Echoing what was described in Chapter 1 as the 'boosterism' that often surrounds educational technology, there has been a notable tendency for the educational benefits of games to be portrayed in exaggeratedly enthusiastic terms – as a 'panacea for education' (Spring 2012, p. 98), or as "a Holy Grail in the uphill battle to keep kids learning" (Salen 2008, p. 2). As such accolades suggest, digital games are often framed as an otherworldly means of rejuvenating formal educational practices. Thus, as Caroline

Pelletier (2009, p. 84) contends, "a consequence of this is that games and game-play tend to be treated as 'out there', beyond the school gate, in some better, more authentic, more democratic, more meaningful place, other than the current and failing educational regime". This rhetoric clearly requires unpacking – especially in terms of the silences that lie beneath this notion of games as an inherently 'better' means of supporting educational engagement. Looking beyond these heightened expectations, we can therefore identify three recurrent forms of game use in education that are worthy of further discussion: the development of bespoke games for education; the use of commercial games in education; and the rearrangement of education along game-based lines.

I. Developing Games for Education

As just described, there is a long history of games being produced specifically for educational purposes – from simple counting, spelling and math games to more complex and involved adventure and strategy games based around particular elements of school and university curricula, as well as the training needs of business and commerce. While these games are often produced on a commercial basis, the rise of online and smartphone-based games playing has also led to a rise in the production of small-scale casual educational games. Public organizations such as the British Broadcasting Corporation and the US Public Broadcasting Service now produce a variety of free online educational games designed to be used from preschool to high school level. As Joel Spring (2012, p. 81) contends,

> With smart phone apps, children carry the school in their hands. The home is curricularized the child's entire life. Educational apps are marketed as edutainment; learning for adults and fun for kids.

As Spring implies, the development of digital games to be played within educational settings sits alongside an established tradition of the development of digital games aiming to 'curricularize' the home – often referred to as 'edutainment' (i.e., a combination of education and entertainment). Some of these games have proved to be highly popular. For example, one of the most popular computer games in recent times has been 'Dr Kawashima's Brain Training' – a mental agility game for children and adults that has sold tens of millions of copies since its launch in the mid-2000s. With the ever increasing sales of digital devices such as tablet computers to parents anxious to augment their children's formal education, the edutainment software market is now one of the fastest growing sectors of the commercial IT industry.

In contrast to these examples, the genre of 'serious games' (also referred to as 'smart games' or 'game learning') is another form of gaming that has been developed increasingly for educational settings. While a loosely defined term, serious games tend to place less emphasis on the playful and enjoyable elements of digital gaming, and instead make use of games as a method of ongoing train-ing within formal educational institutions and workplace contexts. As Apperley (2009, p. 105–106) describes,

> While diverse, the genre [of serious games] is united by a sense of purpose. Play of serious games has deliberate stakes; it is neither play as an escape from everyday life, nor as the development of ill-defined general skills . . . Serious games propose purposeful play with meaningful outcomes; they aim to bring an issue, or issues, to the players' attention through play. The primary significance of this sub-industry of digital games is that it positions the communication of ideas and persuasion through play as an essential, rather than periphery, design concern.

In many ways, the 'meaningful' element of serious gaming relates to the devel-opment of systems and procedures that are less detached from real-world contexts than is usually the case in digital gaming – as Ian Bogost (2011) puts it, serious games are based around content that is 'beyond entertainment'. The scope of seri-ous games ranges from physical exercise ('exergames') to activist and propaganda games that relate to political issues and debates. Recently, interest in serious games has extended to the increased use of games mechanics within versions of the simulation software reviewed in Chapter 3. This includes the production of highly complex battlefield simulations used by the military and surgical simulations for use by health professionals – all allowing individuals to experience a range of processes and outcomes while 'playing' to gain points and complete against other players. Thus, as Arora (2012, p. 612) concludes,

> play is used to engage in serious endeavours of social transformation and education where conventional strategies have perhaps failed. The sancti-mony of the serious gets webbed with play, and instead of trivializing the goal, it can give it a new lease to life.

II. Using Games in Education

Of course, there has also long been considerable interest in the educational ben-efits of playing commercially produced popular games and, in particular, the ben-efits that can be gained by using such games within formal educational settings. While some commentators argue that any game can be of educational benefit, enthusiasm has tended to be directed towards 'importing' particular genres of games into classrooms and curricula. For instance, much attention has been paid towards the use of 'realistic' simulation games as offering a ready means of sup-porting exploratory spaces for constructivist learning (e.g., Collins & Halverson 2009). These include 'sandbox' games such as 'The Sims' where players control artificial populations, empire-building games such as the 'Civilization' series, city-building games such as 'SimCity' and business and management games such as 'Railroad Tycoon' and 'Rollercoaster Tycoon'. Games of this sort are seen to engender a range of skills, competencies and understandings – in particular supporting constructivist forms of learning through exploration, problem solving, development of complex microworlds and reflection on experience.

There has also been growing educational interest in the use of online 'game worlds' – in particular 'massively multiplayer online role playing games'. As their name suggests, these games put players in control of customized characters within extensive, geographical cohesive environments which are populated by numerous other player-characters. Players then progress through these digitally supported worlds by interacting with others – often forming associations and groups to accomplish necessary tasks. As such, these online game worlds require users to interact consciously with particular structures and constraints while offering multiple modes of participation (Carr, Oliver & Burn 2010). Much of the educational benefit from these games is seen as arising from interactions with other players. Online game worlds will often involve the formation of 'clans' or 'guilds' that involve groups of players within elaborate social protocols and complex divisions of labour. Here experienced players will assist novices by teaching tactics, orientating them to the geography of the game world, upholding codes of behaviour and other forms of 'community'-based learning.

III. Redesigning Education Along Gaming Lines

Thirdly, interest is also growing in the imposition of games design and games mechanics onto real-life contexts and settings, thereby rearranging and reordering educational settings as 'play-driven spaces' (Arora 2012). This sometimes involves the educational application of 'augmented reality' techniques – that is, the addition of computer-generated features (such as graphics, video or sound) – to real-life physical environments. There are a growing number of such applications. For example, Arora (2012) describes the conversion of staircases in a Swedish subway station to depict giant piano keys, thereby encouraging people to walk up and down stairs rather than take escalators. The use of such 'choice architecture' is seen as encouraging 'productive' behaviour change through the introduction of digitally supported play. In more explicitly educational terms, recent developments in mobile technology, wireless connectivity and global positioning systems have supported the development of outdoor role-playing games that respond to learners' physical environments as well as their interactions with other learners who are also playing. Using mobile technologies, for example, different features can be imported into the same environment, so that a classroom becomes a surgical operating theatre, or a small piece of woodland becomes a vast Amazonian rainforest (see Klopfer 2008). It is argued that these forms of 'mobile gaming' can support learning that is both 'social' (meaning that it can involve 'real' social relationships between learners) and 'authentic' (meaning that it relates to actual people, places and events). In Grabinger, Dunlap and Duffield's terms, these technologies can support 'rich environments for active learning' (1996, p. 5).

Another trend is the embedding of game mechanics and "interactive online design that plays on people's competitive instincts" into everyday educational contexts (Quitney & Rainie 2012, p. 1). This 'gamification' of education has been realized in different ways. One recent instance has been the promotion of digital 'badges' that recognise and reward instances of informal learning in noneducational contexts. The use of badges to recognise different instances of alternate learning is seen as motivating informal learning behaviours and encouraging interactions between different individuals and organizations. As the Mozilla (2012, n.p.) 'open badge' project states,

> A 'digital badge' is an online record of achievements, tracking the recipient's communities of interaction that issued the badge and the work completed to get it. Digital badges can support connected learning environments by motivating learning and signalling achievement both within particular communities as well as across communities and institutions.

Alternatively, other educationalists have been involved in the gamification of formal educational practices and processes. Perhaps the most striking example of this has been the development of public high schools in New York and Chicago around game-based 'quest' principles. In this case, the social organization and physical architecture of the school reflect a game-based learning model, with classrooms and curriculum designed to support students within inquiry-based activities of 'questing'. Under these conditions the school curriculum is divided into 'domains', with teaching and learning based around game principles involving secret 'discovery missions', students being 'levelled-up' in academic difficulty and so on. In this sense, gamification can be seen as striving to combine intrinsic motivation, competitive sentiment, performance measurement and metrics with the extrinsic rewards associated with play (Nelson 2012; Williamson 2014). As Salen, Torres, Wolozin, Rufo-Tepper and Shapiro (2011, n.p.) conclude,

> Gaming and game design offer a promising new paradigm for curriculum and learning. The designers of Quest to Learn developed an approach to learning that draws from what games do best: drop kids into inquiry-based, complex problem spaces that are built to help players understand how they are doing, what they need to work on, and where to go next. Content is not treated as dry information but as a living resource; students are encouraged to interact with the larger world in ways that feel relevant, exciting, and empowering.

The Perceived Educational Benefits of Games and Gaming

As all these examples imply, educational efforts to make use of games and gaming are usually motivated by a number of perceived benefits. In an immediate sense, games are described as an inherently enjoyable and 'truly fun' means of stimulating learning (Bell, Smith-Robbins & Withnail 2010). The sense of play as offering "a rupture in the everyday" (Apperley 2009, p. 39) is seen widely as making educational engagement more motivating, engaging and 'relevant' than it otherwise would be through traditional means (Pelletier 2009). As suggested earlier, some commentators justify this appeal in terms of 'hard fun' – that is, giving people 'hard challenging things to do' that are "matched to the individual and to the culture of the times" (Papert 2002, p. 3). In similar terms, games are often justified as a stimulating amalgamation of the 'work' of learning and the 'leisure' of playing – referred to in some quarters as 'weisure' or 'playbour' (the latter term being an equally unwieldy amalgam of 'play' and 'labour'). Thus learning and its assessment are seen as being able to take place in an almost unconscious manner when subsumed within the context of a digital game – what Owston (2009) refers to as educational processes taking place by 'stealth'.

Aside from these motivational benefits, much support for the educational application of digital games relates to perceived links with high-quality learning processes. Indeed, it is believed widely that digital games enhance the processes of learning – be this in behavioural, cognitivist or socio-constructivist terms. Thus as far as enthusiastic proponents of game-based learning are concerned, much can be gained when initially learning to play a game, and then from learning to play a game well (Prensky 2005). For instance, it is argued that the processes of playing a game entail a range of inherent learning outcomes – in Becker's (2011) words, things that one *must* learn before one can play effectively and eventually win or complete the game. In this sense, games clearly involve the development of psychomotor and cognitive skills, alongside complex series of memorization and comprehension, which are developed and achieved through gradated practice and eventual mastery. As Krapp (2011) continues, the design rules of games tend to require the development of a range of additional skills and competencies – not least efficiency and expediency of action, alongside a mastery of interfaces and interactions.

While these skills and competencies are important, many commentators argue that the educational potential of computer games lies in the learning that can occur beyond the learning that is necessary to simply play a game. This is what Becker (2011, p. 4) classifies as 'things we *can* learn', and includes forms of 'collateral learning' (i.e., things that "are not part of the game and that do not impact on our success in the game" [ibid.]) and 'external learning' (i.e., "learning that can impact on our success in the game but that happens entirely outside of the game" [ibid.]). In these terms, games can be seen as supporting a wide range of more sustained and complex forms of learning. The point was illustrated in David Sudnow's (2000) description of his own efforts to learn to play a 'perfect' game on the 1980s' arcade game 'Breakout'. Sudnow equated this task to learning simultaneously to watch a television, operate a typewriter and play a piano. Thus playing any form of computer game could be seen as involving similar combinations of manual dexterity and delicate mental creativity. As Krapp (2011, p. 77) concludes,

The difference between playing a game and playing with a game is crucial to gaming culture: whereas the former teaches one the game through navigating the game's commands and controls, the latter opens up to critical and self-aware exploration. Like learning to swim, gaming means learning to learn and initiates us into training systems, but like learning to read, it does not stop at a literal obedience to the letter.

Thus, akin to learning to read or play the piano, games are seen to correspond with a range of 'higher order' domains of learning. Of all the claims made for the learning potential of digital games, perhaps the most extensively argued has been James Paul Gee's (2003) 36 'learning principles' that he argued underpin the self-directed learning undertaken by game players as they encounter and master a 'good' game. According to Gee, for example, digital games usually demand that players actively and critically engage with the design principles of the game. Gee also sees players as learning from being required to engage with the multiple ways that meanings are signified and conveyed within games – such as images, words, actions, symbols, abstract design and other artefacts. In this sense, much game-based learning can be seen as semiotic and 'multimodal' in nature. Within the context of the game, Gee describes learning as taking place through discovery and interaction with other agents within the game – be it other players (in the case of multiplayer games) or computer-generated characters. In this sense, meaning and knowledge can be seen as distributed across the learner, objects, tools, symbols, technologies and 'material objects' within the game environment. Gee also suggests that learning often occurs through the assumption within the design of many games that players take on and play with a number of new identities.

Gee's arguments are now repeated widely within educational discussions – a popularity that stems, in part, from the commonsensical correspondences between these descriptions of game-based learning and sociocultural views of learning. Indeed, digital games are seen as having a close affinity with the socio-cultural and socio-constructivist philosophies of learning that are central to much educational thinking about technology. From this perspective, learning is seen as arising from not only the game itself but also the practices of 'gaming' that surround it – that is, "the sum total of activities, literacies, knowledge and practices activated in and around any instance of a game" (Salen 2008, p. 9). For example, much interest has been shown in the sociocultural learning potential of participating in 'massively multiplayer online games' such as World of Warcraft. These gaming environments are based on large groups of users encountering, interacting and engaging with other users. These processes often lead to the formation of informal and formal communities where users will work together in groups with hierarchies of expertise and learning. In all these ways, multiplayer online gaming and virtual worlds are seen as supporting the 'social dynamic' that many educationalists believe lies at the heart of effective learning. Thus, as Kurt Squire (2006, p. 22) contends, today's generation of games contain a whole new set of features, making them intriguing suites of learning. Specifically, they are sites where we can look at learning both as (a) interaction in the social and material world, where learners participate in open and closed problem solving; and (b) participation in distributed social organizations such as self-organizing learning communities, which are microcosms for studying the emergence, maintenance, transformation, and even collapse of online affinity groups.

Aside from these situated and highly socialized modes of learning, games are also valued for their capacity to support users in engaging with ideas and knowledge in a more dynamic manner. As Ian Bogost (2011, n.p.) reasons, "Because games are systems, they offer a fundamentally different way of characterizing ideas. They can inspire a different kind of deliberation than we find in other forms of media, one that considers the uncertainty of complex systems instead of embracing simple answers". Thus digital games are seen by some commentators as providing rich, interactive environments within which users can interact with concepts, narratives and knowledge in a manner that is meaningful and relevant to their situation (if only the immediate situation of having to play the game). Thus, as Barab, Gresalfi, Dodge and Ingram-Goble (2010, p. 28) argue, digital games make abstract concepts not only more concrete but also more consequential as players use these concepts to make sense of – and transform – particular narratives and storylines within the game:

> By bounding up disciplinary context within interactive narrative contexts, we have the potential to not only change learners' understanding of the use value of the content but also offer the opportunity for learners to see themselves as capable of meaningfully applying disciplinary content. Many commercial games . . . provide learners with a sense of legitimacy, intentionality, and consequentiality in ways that are difficult to achieve in many school-based lessons.

Criticisms of Digital Games and Education

While much support can be found for the inherently educational nature of digital games, this is an area of educational technology that also attracts a considerable level of controversy. In particular, doubts continue to be raised regarding the empirical rigour of most studies purporting to demonstrate links between gameplay and educational benefit (Egenfeldt-Nielsen 2006). As Owston (2009, p. 106) notes wryly, "There is much more enthusiasm shown in the literature for describing the affordances of games than for conducting research that demonstrates the impact of these affordances on instruction". Interestingly, proponents of educational games are often quick to defend the lack of rigorous positive evidence by acknowledging that not *all* games "are good for all learners and for all learning outcomes" (Van

Eck 2006, p. 18). As such, any lack of rigorous evidence is taken primarily to be evidence of the failings of specific designers and products rather than the general principle of game-based learning. As Marc Prensky (2005, p. 103) reasoned, "Many criticize today's learning games, and there is much to criticize. But if some of these games don't produce learning it is not because they are games, or because the concept of 'game-based learning' is faulty. It's because those particular games are badly designed".

Generally, then, the use of digital games in education has managed to avoid sustained criticism, with many academics prepared to spare gaming the scrutiny that is often directed towards other forms of educational technology. At best, the arguments against digital games in education have tended to be sensationalist and largely unconvincing. For example, opposition continues to be raised against the generally detrimental and 'harmful' nature of many games. For example, digital games have long been the focus for a series of moral panics, much as was the case with previous popular media such as comics, television, cinema and video (Martin 2012). One of the foremost objectives of these criticisms has been to establish evidence of the 'effects' of digital games based on previous assumptions and research on television and video. Thus a series of 'effects' research has "attempt[ed] to link videogame play with horrific events such as shootings and punitive societal decay" (Newman 2004, p. 62).

Similarly, the use of digital games in education has been questioned in terms of the supposed addictive qualities of gaming, associations with short- and long-term repetitive strain injuries (such as the phenomenon of 'Nintendo thumb' during the 1990s and 2000s), desensitization to violence and even possible negative relationships with scholastic performance (Skoric, Teo and Neo 2009). While these arguments retain a credence in popular and political discourse, they certainly conform to the 'doomster' arguments outlined in Chapter 1. Most significantly – and returning to the core theme of this book – these arguments obscure a set of ideological criticisms that should be levelled at digital games. These all relate to the contention that it is a mistake to see digital games as somehow 'apart' or 'separate' from the social, political, cultural and economic contexts of education. Rather than drawing the user into some sort of decontextualized 'play world' or 'magic circle', the playing of games remains embedded firmly in specific contexts and what Sassen (2006) describes as 'cultures of use' of any technology. It can therefore be argued that situating digital games within wider contexts of contemporary education introduces a number of correspondences that are acknowledged rarely in discussions of games as an educational technology. In this sense, four broad sets of objections can be made against the increased use of digital games in education: firstly regarding their rationalization of education; their entrenchment of dominant values and structures; their commodification of learning and education; and their imbrication of education with the interests of capital. These four issues will now be discussed in more detail.

I. Digital Games and the Rationalization of Education

First is the contention that digital games are built around a rationalization of action through closed forms of repetitive 'training' rather than open-ended exploration or discovery. This point echoes Grimes and Feenberg's (2012) analysis of digital gaming as systems of social rationality. Here it is argued that the rule-bound 'system' of any digital game produces an inherent 'institutional order' similar to other systems of social rationality. Thus, "similar to economic markets, legal systems and scientific research, games break loose from the undifferentiated communicative action of 'ordinary' life to impose a rational form on a sector of experience" (Grimes & Feenberg 2012, p. 21). As has been suggested throughout this chapter, the realities of game-based play are often structured and constrained in nature – not least in the underlying demand of any genre for "an 'infantilizing' obedience to rules" (Krapp 2011, p. 81). Thus despite their associations with intense excitement and thrill seeking, games tend to played along rational and repetitive lines, with players adhering to strict rules and developing bounded strategies in order to succeed. As Grimes and Feenberg (2012, pp. 22–23) observe,

> Players and player moves are standardized through the program code (exchange of equivalents); formal rules are established by the game engine and operators as well as the player community (classification and application of rules); and player efforts are optimized and calculated through numeric levelling and points systems that are further reinforced by the status and social capital granted to players of high standing.

In specifically educational terms, then, the argument can be made that the rationalization of action inherent in digital games is at odds with freer, individually determined forms of learning. Indeed, as Tom Apperley (2009, p. 140) contends, the rationalization of learning and education within digital games should be seen more accurately as resulting in a form of 'training' – in other words, while the 'latitude' or 'margin' of free action within games might appear to be considerable, any action is free only with respect to being "free within the limits set by the rules". In order to be successful at playing any computer game, therefore, players must surrender themselves to the demands and expectations of that game – be it in terms of physical movements, postures, gestures and reactions, mental patterns and processes, emotional states or social interactions. The successful player is therefore one who is able to adapt him- or herself to the expectations and requirements of the game. However sophisticated and complex this process of adaptation might be, a player is most accurately described as being trained rather than learning *per se*. This distinction evokes Henri Lefebvre's (1992/2004) distinction between education, learning and training – the latter of which he termed *le dressage*. Lefebvre's description of training in terms of dressage is telling – implying a process of repetition and the individual being 'broken in' like an animal, and therefore being shaped to the accepted values of a wider society or group. Thus, as Ted Friedman continues, digital games involve a similar form of 'breaking in':

> The way computer games teach structures of thought is by getting you to internalise the logic of the program. To win, you can't just do whatever you want. You have to figure out what will work within the rules of the game. You must learn to predict the consequence of each move, and anticipate the computer's response. Eventually, your decisions become intuitive, as smooth and rapid fire as the computer's own machinations.
>
> *(cited in Anderson & Pold 2011, p. 115)*

Of course, the extent to which digital games can be associated with creative, educative practice as opposed to repetitive training depends on the context in which they are being used, as well as the design of the game and the intentions of the player. Many educationalists would acknowledge that the educational games of the 1980s followed rather basic repetitive patterns of behaviourist 'drill and practice' (often referred to in pejorative terms as 'drill and kill'). However, most would consider the sophisticated and expansive games of the 2010s to offer substantially more variety and freedom of action. Yet the counterargument could be made that even the most sophisticated and carefully designed digital games retain an inherent rationalization of action. By its very nature, therefore, digital gameplay is entwined with issues of power and control – not least the capacity of the player to make empowered choices and act in meaningful ways. Apperley (2009, p. 41) suggests that the complex dynamic between the games player and the game being played is "fraught with subtle negotiations of power" which reflect wider societal relationships between individuals and technology in a capitalist society. Parallels can therefore be drawn with Marx's description of the necessary adaption of workers to machines where 'the conditions of work employ the worker'. In this sense, the educational benefits of digital games could be seen to be compromised by an underlying and ongoing tension between the domains of work and leisure, play and labour.

II. Digital Games and the Transmission of Dominant Values

A second criticism relates to the values and ideologies that are often conveyed through games and also associated more subtly with the gaming structure itself. Referring back to the idea of digital games as narrative, it is clear that all games involve an element of storytelling and therefore convey a variety of messages and values within their 'texts'. In one sense, then, many of these values are 'written into' the game by developers and designers both intentionally and unintentionally. Indeed, a common criticism of digital games – especially real-time strategy games and simulation games – is that they convey a limited set of values and interests, particularly with regard to their portrayal of gender, race, age and sexuality. As Dyer-Witheford and de Peuter (2009, p. 228) observe, many games are infused with "banal ideological conventionality" with regard to gender roles, racial profiles and notions of masculinity. Another common critique of digital games is their dominant framing of thought and action within a militaristic ideology of violent competition and conflict, as well as a reliance on tactical and strategic thinking – what Kontour (2012, p. 353) terms "the governmentality of the battlefield space". Much has been made of the origins of computer games in US defence-funded research and the use of digital games as aids for military training. While the influence of these origins on contemporary games is often subtle, it can still be argued that the design of most games continues to demand an obedience to follow orders and acceptance of hierarchy that is decidedly militaristic in nature.

In a general sense, then, it can be argued that the mechanical operation of any digital game demands that players adhere to a rationalised set of assumptions, conventions and dominant values. Many games certainly could be said to indulge and normalise traits of individualism, possessiveness and competition. These criticisms apply to even the most expansive and open forms of game environments that can still be said to convey a sense of absolute worldview. Thus, as Mackenzie Wark (2007, p. 20) reasons, games are not accurate or open-ended representations of the world – instead they are allegories that "encode the abstract principles upon which decisions about the realness of this or that world are decided". These arguments were illustrated in Ted Friedman's (1999) critique of the popular 'Civilization' series of empire-building games. Here Friedman outlined a number of ideological assumptions that underpinned the 'logic of the program', and that had to be successfully internalized by players in order for them to progress successfully and eventually win the game. As Friedman (1999, p. 145) described, these dominant values included an overt emphasis on expansionist competition rather than outright collaboration, reflecting an underpinning assumption that "global coexistence is a matter of winning and losing". Success in the game also rested on overseeing the in-game development of new technologies, reflecting an implicit scientific determinism as well as an ahistorical conceptualization of science, religion and the development of nations. This latter point was reinforced by Galloway's (2006, p. 96) example of the game's insistence on "the founding of a market economy in a place called 'London' in 4000 BC". Moreover, Friedman also points to the game's oversimplification of colonization and imperialism, enforced by its underpinning sense of nationalistic destiny and the stereotyping of homogenous (rather than diverse and hybrid) cultural formations.

These ideological assumptions could be said to be determined largely by the designers, developers and producers of games. However, it can also be argued that the underpinning 'system' of the digital game leads to an imposition of a dominant valuing of algorithmic determination and computational thinking – along the lines of what Galloway (2006) refers to as 'algorithmic culture'. Thus, as Dyer-Witheford and de Peuter (2009, p. 220) reason, "in a sense every game, even apparently very simple ones, is a world. To play is to figure out a universe. To win demands experimentally learning a system, a programmed ecology, or code metabolism whose simple algorithms generate more or less complex events". Thus, despite their apparent complexity, variety and 'artful surfaces' (Wark 2007), this reduction of any form of digital gameplay to interaction with algorithms suggests that the nature of learning that takes place is ultimately reduced to a form of algorithmic mastery. As Galloway (2006, p. 90–91) continues, "To play the game means to play the code of the game. To win means to know the system. And thus to interpret a game means to interpret its algorithm . . . to discover its parallel 'allegorithm'". In this sense, playing a digital game could be seen as little more than a matter of "learning, internalizing and becoming intimate with a massive, multipart, global algorithm" (ibid.).

This suggestion that digital games explicitly condition players to accept an underlying dominant value of algorithmic control – what Bogost (2008) terms 'procedurality' – infers a correspondence between games playing and political control. In this sense a connection can be made between digital games and Deleuze's notion of 'control societies' – the late twentieth-century successors to the modernist 'discipline societies', which rely on systems of 'free-floating control' that are increasingly based around immaterial forms. As Alexander Galloway (2006, p. 90) writes, "video games don't attempt to hide informatics control – they flaunt it". These systems of control implicit within digital games include an emphasis on apparent flexibility in the manner in which the player is able to interact with the variables within a game. For critics such as Galloway, flexibility is a key aspect of informatic control – allowing systems to adjust and compensate for differences in individual actions, albeit via restricted forms of bounded 'menu-driven' choices. This flexibility allows systems to subsume greater numbers of users and eventually to make all equivalent in the form of a mass universal standardization. Thus, it could be argued that digital games convey the dominant values, practices and logics of living within the conditions of a control society and orientating one's action around the requirements of the algorithm.

III. Digital Games and the Commodification of Learning

A further critical caveat to the increased use of digital games in educational settings is the commodification of action inherent in most – if not all – digital games. As has already been noted, most digital games are based around specific 'economies' that offer a balance of rewards and penalties (Buckingham 2006). The introduction of this logic into educational practices, it could be argued, extenuates the framing of learning as a commodity that can be quantifiably valued, competed for and exchanged. In an educational context, therefore, digital games could be seen as introducing "a pedagogical frame which insinuates players into an environment which both links consumption with freedom and choice and naturalizes play as a commodity" (Apperley 2009, p. 48). Of course a logic of reward, measurement and competition is not unique to the use of games in education, but has been a long-standing element of classroom organization and control. Nevertheless, digital games certainly extend and intensify its presence in education, as well as expressing learning in overtly value-based and market-driven terms.

These features are perhaps most evident in the 'gamification' of educational processes, with the emphasis on point scoring, leader boards and badges to structure action and signify progress. While these may appear to be innovative processes, there has been much criticism of these aspects of gamification from within the games community. Bogost (2011), for example, contends that gamification privileges some of the most visible but least important elements of digital games, resulting in the use of 'empty metrics'. Margaret Robertson (2010) has also critiqued what she sees as the reductionist process of regarding all actions with points and increased personal scores – what she characterized as a 'pointsification' of everything. As these comments suggest, gamification could be seen as leading to a degradation of educational interactions through the assigning of meaningless exchange values and the maintenance of a false sense of individual gain rather than collective endeavour:

> Gamification proposes to replace real incentives with fictional ones. Real incentives come at a cost but provide value for both parties based on a relationship of trust. By contrast, pretend incentives reduce or eliminate costs, but in so doing they strip away both value and trust.
>
> *(Bogost 2011, n.p.)*

This commodification of action and interaction is also evident in the increasing privileging of 'symbolic consumerism' within many contemporary forms of digital gaming – that is, the purchasing of virtual goods within games in order to progress. This has long been apparent within multiplayer role-playing games and online game worlds. For example, multiplayer role-playing games "tend to be dominated by market exchange" (Dyer-Witheford & de Peuter 2009, p. 137) with activity centred around the exchange of virtual currencies allowing players to acquire goods, spells, weapons, health and vitality. The significance of 'play money' (Dibbell 2006) to the successful playing of these games has translated into real-life economic activity – not least the practice of virtual game dollars being traded for real-life dollars. The symbolic purchase of digital goods is also a key element of many of the 'social games' played through social networks. Here various forms of playful consumerism are encouraged, as players take the role of 'ludic shoppers' – "mak[ing] real their consumer fantasies through ludic means, by symbolically purchasing items they might not afford in the physical world" (Silva 2012, p. 4). As Silva (2012) suggests rather unconvincingly, the symbolic purchase of virtual goods could be seen to provide specific forms of 'enjoyment' such as the integration of consumption into one's own identity, the classification of one's self in relation to relevant others and the stimulation of strong personal emotions aroused through consumption.

Of course, a strong counterargument can be made that the increased position-ing of digital gameplay within a framework of consumerism and commercial market-driven logic clearly has a bearing on the nature of any educational and learning practices that are being supported through digital games. In particular, this could be seen as subsuming any playful, experimental or creative activities into the system of consumption that lies at the heart of many games, and allow-ing learning to find expression only within monetized and individually com-petitive forms. Indeed, the reality of game-based learning and education within a commodified competitive logic was highlighted in a recent study by Harviainen, Lainema and Saarinen (2012), examining how individuals approached the act of educational gameplay. These findings point towards a diminished set of dispo-sitions and motivations amongst game-based learners. For example, a sense of what the researchers described as 'excessive competitiveness' was found between individuals regardless of any instructions to be noncompetitive. Moreover, the ultimately inconsequential nature of game-based interactions and actions led indi-viduals to hold 'unrealistic' levels of trust in other players coupled with a tendency to take 'unnatural risks'. These behaviours were coupled with a heightened ten-dency for what the authors termed 'outright cheating'. As Harviainen et al. (2012, p. 9) concluded, "there therefore exists the idea that everyone is willing to do what it takes to win, even if the simulation-game is not framed as a competition. This makes dishonesty seem normal".

IV. Digital Games and the Imbrication of Education Into the System of Capital

A final set of critical observations relates to the underlying alignment between the educational application of digital games and the economic needs of capitalism. This further challenges the notion of digital games as somehow being 'apart' from the nondigital 'real world', and locates games playing as situated within dom-inant economic and political contexts of capitalist society. As Dyer-Witheford and de Peuter (2009, p. xxvi) contend, we cannot ignore "the political and eco-nomic contexts of virtual games, skipping lightly over the conditions of paid and unpaid labour in game production, re-inscribing platitudes about the informa-tion age jobs that gamers are training themselves for, and failing to raise awkward questions about the global order for which gamers are now the new model of empowered participants". As this deceptively brief list of issues implies, there are perhaps various ways in which digital games are related to the differential pattern-ing of economic power. As the authors write, "A media that once seemed all fun is increasingly revealing itself as a school for labour, an instrument of rulership, and a laboratory for the fantasies of advanced techno-capital" (ibid., p. xix).

Digital games could be seen as an important site for the increased integration of formal *and* informal education into the labour cycle – not least in terms of providing preparation for the forms of labour most prevalent in the immaterial economy. Indeed, it could be argued that a number of key production processes are extended into educational practice through the use of digital games. On one hand, a regulated sense of play and playfulness is seen as an increasingly important creative disposition and skill to be displayed in the immaterial workplace. As Nelson (2012) observes, the increased use of games in education has parallels with the trends in 1990s' and 2000s' American corporate culture towards the 'gameful workplace' and the reimagining of the workplace as a more fun and playful (and therefore more efficient and harmonious) setting (Nelson 2012). Conversely, games also relate directly to what Krapp (2011) terms the ability to adjust to 'the grind' of productive modes of gameplay, characterized by competitiveness, repetition and persistence, multitasking, problem solving and contingency planning.

Digital gameplay can also be seen as a constant process of dense information processing, thereby preparing players for similar forms of informational and symbolic labour. As Garite (2003, n.p.) observes, "When we strip away the particulars of content, gaming is essentially an aestheticized mode of information processing, and therefore the digital economy's ideal form of leisure". When transferred into educational contexts, digital games can be seen as supporting the development of a number of flexible dispositions, subjectivities and identities appropriate for the immaterial workplace. In this sense, the requirement of games players to assume the identities of "citizen-soldiers, free-agent workers, cyborg adventurers, and corporate criminals" (Dyer-Witheford & de Peuter 2009, p. xxix) could be seen largely as preparation for later work roles and neo-liberal dispositions, rather than completely fantastical role play. As Galloway (2012, p. 44) observed of World of Warcraft, "At root, the game is not simply a fantasy landscape of dragons and epic weapons but a factory floor, an information-age sweatshop, custom tailored in every detail for cooperative ludic labour". In all these ways, then, the use of digital games in educational contexts can be seen as entwined with the needs and expectations of the digital workplace. As Apperley (2009, p. 48) concludes,

> This eurhythmia between work and play foregrounds the role of digital game play as a site of training for work in the knowledge economy, not necessarily in direct application, but in terms of approach, attitude, initiative and procedure.

Conclusions

This chapter has considered how a powerful orthodoxy has developed around the use of digital games in education, framing these technologies as 'bringing in' dynamic learning practices and dispositions from outside of traditional educational contexts. Games playing is clearly a form of digital technology use that is appealing to educationalists in a variety of ways. Indeed, the prospect of better aligning educational engagement with characteristics of 'fun' and 'flow' has proved understandably seductive within educational contexts. Yet, as this chapter has suggested, there are a number of reasons to distrust the increased use of digital games in education. In particular it can be argued that even the most complex digital games act to reduce individual action to a limited set of predetermined possibilities. Most learning that takes place within a digital game might be more accurately described as supporting repetitive adjustments to the rules, rhythms and expectations of the game design, rather than genuinely educational engagement.

Moreover, there are good grounds to conclude that "the work of video games [is to] define and reconstitute players as subjects of ideology" (Garite 2003, n.p.). As this chapter has contended, digital games could be said to rationalise the actions of games players around a diminished set of values and imperatives that promote competitive and commodified behaviour, the primacy of the self-directed and self-driven individual working within dense informatics environments and algorithmic structures. These tendencies of control and rationalization therefore support the wider argument that "in their structure and content, computer games are a capitalist and deeply conservative form of culture" (Stallabrass 1996, p. 107). Alternatively, as Galloway (2006, p. 91) puts it, "video games are, at their structural core, in direct synchronization with the political realities of the informatics age". To argue that digital games constitute forms of educational engagement that are simply more 'fun' and 'enjoyable' is to overlook their inherent connection with dominant forms of ideological control.

Of course, these limitations have not gone completely unrecognised by some critical games scholars – yet it remains rare for sustained challenges to the educational use of digital games to be made along these lines. Some critically minded authors point to the educational potential that exists around nonconventional modes of playing against the expectations and requirements of digital games. As Apperley (2009) concludes, there are a variety of forms of resistant behaviour that can be directed against the rationalization and control associated with conventional forms of gameplay that could be seen to have educational merit. The practice of 'machinima' (the act of creating three-dimensional animations in real time using computer games) and other forms of digital game art have also been welcomed by some critical scholars as progressive reconfigurations of the nature and form of digital gaming. Similarly, the transgressive act of modifying digital games (the practice of 'modding') is seen as a potentially productive means of reasserting the power of the games player and going some ways towards counteracting the dominant ideologies and values inherent in games design. From another perspective, Bogost (2008) points to the development of activist games that can support players in interrogating dominant values and ideologies. Yet, as seductive as these alternative digital games practices might be in the eyes of critical scholars, they do little to redress the economic rationalization and disempowerment that characterizes the majority of games players' experiences of digital games. Even in their most sophisticated 'high art' and 'high technology' forms, it could be contended that digital games do little more than "broker high neoliberalism" (Miller 2011, p. 236). In this sense, the use of digital games in education is decidedly less 'other-worldly' and straightforwardly 'fun' than it might first appear.

6

DISTRUSTING 'SOCIAL' TECHNOLOGIES IN EDUCATION

Introduction

Just as games and gaming are an important part of the relatively short history of digital technology, the rise of 'social media' has been a key recent aspect of technological development. While it is important to acknowledge that "the web has always been social" (Halpin & Tuffield 2010, n.p.), the internet has certainly undergone an intensified 'social turn' over the past 10 years, to the point where social media are an integral element of how digital technologies are now encountered and used by many people. As Vincent Miller (2011, p. 208) describes it, the development of digital media and technology during the 2000s can be seen as "a kind of social 'big bang' leading to an expanded social universe". Tellingly, the notion of 'social' media is now a prevailing element of commercial IT industry activities. As Facebook founder Mark Zuckerberg (2010, n.p.) boasted at the turn of the decade, "We are building toward a web where the default is social". Social media, it would seem, now lie at the heart of how digital technology is used across many aspects of contemporary society and, it follows, require sustained critical attention from the educational community.

Unpacking the Key Features and Underlying Philosophies of Social Media

The general idea of 'social media' has certainly permeated the popular consciousness over the past five years or so. Even the most casual of internet users will be now aware of 'social network' sites and 'blogs', maybe even 'wikis' and 'virtual worlds'. It is also likely that most internet non-users will be aware of these developments, with traditional forms of print and broadcast media now making sustained reference to – and use of – social media applications such as Facebook, Twitter, YouTube and Wikipedia. In fact, since being declared *Time* magazine's 'Person of the Year' at the end of 2006, social media have come to dominate the ways in which digital technology is now framed and understood around the world.

Of course, as with many digital technology developments, the constituent elements of social media are evolving continually. Indeed, as the 2000s progressed, social media often appeared to be an area of digital media that was changing pace faster than most – with seemingly dominant mass-use applications falling quickly out of favour, only to be replaced by what appeared to be even more dominant successors. Who in 2005 would have predicted the rapid decline of Myspace? Conversely, who now would be confident enough to assume the continued success of currently popular applications such as Twitter and Facebook, or their recent counterparts such as Instagram or Pinterest? It is also important to recognise the distinct geographical and cultural variations within the global adoption of social media. For example, whereas people in North America may well be logging on to Facebook and Twitter, Chinese users are more likely to be accessing sites such as QZone and Weibo. Social media is certainly a fast-changing, ever-evolving and ever-fragmenting area of the digital landscape.

This mercurial nature notwithstanding, a common set of principles and underlying philosophies can nevertheless be said to define social media. As such, social media can be understood as internet applications that rely on openly shared digital content that is authored, critiqued and reconfigured by a mass of users. Social media applications, therefore, are those that allow users to engage in a number of specific online activities: conversing and interacting with others; creating, editing and sharing textual, visual and audio content; and categorizing, labelling and recommending existing forms of content. Perhaps the key underlying characteristics of any social media practice are that of 'mass socialization' and 'mass participation' – that is, harnessing the power of the collective actions of online user communities rather than the disparate efforts of individuals, with internet-based actions therefore being "driven by social connections and user participation" (Song 2010, p. 249).

The growth of social media along these lines has transformed the ways in which the internet is experienced by most 'end users'. Now the internet no longer functions primarily as a one-way, linear delivery system where a mass of individuals each independently downloads data, information and other resources that have been produced by a relatively small number of elite content providers. Instead, the internet is seen as now driven by (and to some extent determined through) the activities of its mass of users – what has been described as 'many-to-many' rather than 'one-to-many' transmission (O'Reilly 2005). The 'social media' era of internet use is therefore understood as being arranged along substantially different lines than the preceding 'cyberspace' era of the 1990s and 2000s. For example, in contrast to the 'broadcast' mode of information exchange that characterized internet use during the 1990s and early 2000s, the web applications of the past 10 years are seen as relying on openly shared digital content that is authored, critiqued and reconfigured by a mass of users. In this sense, YouTube does not simply represent a website where an individual user can access and watch videos. Instead, YouTube is a site where people share video content with others, form like-minded groups, communicate with others, comment on and react to others' work, and re-create and re-edit existing work. As such, the significance of a social media application such as YouTube stems from its function as a social and participatory space, reflecting the growing importance that is being placed on interaction between and within groups of internet users.

The implications of this user-led, collective ethos are conveyed in the language used to describe social media applications. For example, social media use is often described in terms of 'collaboration', 'creativity' and 'conviviality'. Social media applications are seen as 'open' rather than 'closed', 'bottom-up' rather than 'top-down'. Individual social media users are no longer simply passive recipients of content, but involved in the mutual 'cocreation' of online content and activities. As the hybrid labels of 'prosumer' and 'produser' imply, the agency of individuals who engage with social media is seen as moving between categories of being a 'producer' or 'consumer', and 'amateur' or 'professional'. Indeed, social media are seen as reducing authoritarian control and, instead, democratising production and consumption processes. This is not to say that social media are simply more active versions of previously passive forms of internet use. As Felicia Song (2010, p. 253) observes, users' engagement with social media now "often involves complex dynamics concerning authority, expertise, and individualism". This can be seen in many of the activities and practices that now surround the use of online content. Social media users are described as going online to 'share' and 'rate', 'mash up' and 'remix', 'friend' and 'trend'. In many ways these are all activities that can be described as 'archival processing' – that is, "sharing content, making connections, ranking cultural artefacts and producing digital content" (Gehl 2012, p. 1228).

The ways in which the internet is now encountered and experienced are therefore very different to that of 10 years earlier. This explains, at least in part, the enthusiasm during the mid-2000s for the 'Web 2.0' label to emphasise the significant 'step-change' and 'upheaval' in the ways that the internet was being experienced by users of social media applications and tools (Crook 2012). Of course, as many computer scientists were quick to point out at the time, most of the apparently 'new' characteristics of 'web 2.0' had been in existence long before the advent of Facebook, Twitter or even the first social network sites such as SixDegrees. Indeed, internet applications since the early 1970s had been allowing users to exchange messages with each other, maintain personal profiles, curate lists of 'friends' and write blog-like journal entries. Yet, while the technical necessity of rebranding and reversioning the internet '2.0' was been rightly questioned and has now fallen out of favour, the current generation of social media applications is undeniably distinct from earlier forms of internet use – if only in terms of the scale of their use. Indeed, contemporary social media are used by hundreds of millions of users (in the case of Facebook a figure that surpassed one billion accounts in 2012). As such, the social media of the 2010s can be said to now boast a sufficient critical mass of users *and* applications to be of genuine collective benefit and social significance. As Christakis and Fowler (2009, p. 30) conclude, "As part of a social network, we transcend ourselves for good or ill, and become a part of something much larger".

This latter quotation goes some way to capturing the underlying principles and values that many commentators see as marking the significance of the recent turn towards social media. These can be described as centred on the values of informality, individuality *and* collectivism. In this first instance, much of the perceived technical and social significance of social media tools and applications stems from their informality – that is, the seemingly routine and mundane 'personal' activities that social media applications and tools support users in doing. In particular, social media have proved to be the key means of supporting and facilitating what could be described colloquially as the 'nuts and bolts' of social life. This includes various forms of social interaction, presentation of self and social grooming – what Mimi Ito et al. (2009) describe as 'hanging out' and 'messing around'. Of course, despite their initial appearance it would be a mistake to dismiss the apparent mundanity of these social media–based practices as inconsequential and trivial. Instead it is precisely these mundane aspects of social media–based activity – what Shirky (2008, p. 86) terms "the ordinary stuff of life" – that underlie its influence on society. Indeed, through social media these activities, processes and practices are now played out on a "more open, personalized, participative and social" scale than was ever possible before (Ravenscroft 2009, p. 1).

This significance of the informal and the personal aspects of social media–based activity corresponds with the individualism *and* communitarianism of action that social media are believed to support and stimulate. On the one hand, much of the significance of social media is seen as stemming from being individually driven and individually empowering. For example, the notion of 'DIY' (do-it-yourself) is seen as a key philosophy of social media use, reflecting the ability of these applications and tools to decentralise power to the individual user. Yet this individualism is understood to be of most value in a collective, cumulative sense – that is, as the actions of individuals are aggregated and amplified into groups and 'communities' of users. One prominent justification offered in support of this collective significance of social media is Yochai Benkler's (2006) explanation of the 'wealth of networks'. In this sense social media are seen as enabling particularly powerful forms of market-led social production and sharing of information and content. Thus, depending on your point of view, the power of social media can be seen as centring either on a communal form of individualization or on distinctly individualized forms of community. Either way, as Song (2010, p. 268) reminds us, social media need to be seen as supporting "structural spaces that are in dialectical relationship with the normative cultural ideals about community and individualism".

The Rise of Educational Interest in Social Media

As these brief outlines imply, the significance of social media does not lie in the technical capabilities and functions of specific tools and applications. Instead, the significance of the notion of 'social media' lies primarily in its resonance with a set of wider contemporary societal concerns and cultural ideals. Indeed, the ideals of collaboration, sharing, individualism and collective empowerment associated with social media chime with a range of recent social, political, cultural and economic developments. As such, the character of social media is aligned with a number of issues central to how the character of society is seen by many people as being reformed and recast. Thus much of the appeal and allure of social media derives from its mirroring of much of what we believe contemporary social life to be becoming. For example, the hyperconnected, instantaneous, individualized and promiscuous nature of social media could certainly be argued to mirror ongoing shifts towards what has been variously described as the network society, liquid age or post/late modern society. Social media can be seen as fitting perfectly with the fluid concerns of the current post-industrial era, and associated recasting of the hierarchical and fixed boundaries and structures of the twentieth-century late industrial era. Indeed, the prominence of social media in popular consciousness is now intertwined with many of the dominant societal concerns of recent times. These range from the most prosaic of issues (such as the role of social media in perpetrating celebrity culture) to the most politically significant of issues (such as the role of social media in mobilizing popular revolts within countries such as Egypt and Libya). In both these extremes, social media can be seen as both driven by and itself driving wider contemporary societal and cultural change.

Thus to return to the specific question of this book, the *educational* significance of social media should be seen as similarly corresponding with a range of wider contemporary concerns, hopes and fears over the changing nature of educational provision and practice in contemporary society. Indeed, the promises of educational improvement and transformation associated with different social media practices have, in the minds of many educational technologists, coalesced into a powerful overall imperative for change. This imperative can be said to be based largely around a perceived set of educational benefits that derive from the common characteristics and principles associated with social media use – most notably principles of community, collaboration, sharing and an overall freeing-up and democratization of action. While the applications and tools may themselves be diverse in form and function, many educational technologists have been enthused by the implications for education practice and provision arising from a general 'spirit' of social media use in education settings.

Forms of Social Media Use in Education

Social media tools and applications are now prominent aspects of digital technology use across all sectors and forms of educational activity. Numerous examples of social media use can now be found in the day-to-day activities of schools, colleges, universities and other formal educational settings. Many institutions are striving to develop ways of using popular forms of social media to support these 'new forms of learning' – such as using Facebook as an alternative 'learning management system', using virtual worlds such as Second Life as alternative learning spaces, and allowing students to communicate in class via microblogging services such as Twitter (see Wang, Woo, Quek, Yang & Liu 2012; Elansky, Mislan & Elavsky 2011; Conole & Alevizou 2010).

There is growing support for redesigning the nature of educational institutions along social media–led lines. From what can be termed a 'reschooling' perspective, many educators maintain that the hyperindividualized and informalized excesses of social media can be tamed to support the provision of what Goodyear and Ellis (2008) term 'serious student-centred learning' within the institutionalized boundaries of schools, colleges and universities. Of course, even the most structured implementation of social media in formal classroom settings implies a degree of 'user-driven' education – that is, allowing learners to take more active roles in what they learn as well as how and when they learn it. Nevertheless, many educators believe that traditional educational institutions are fully capable of accommodating (and consequently benefiting from) these shifts in emphases. Some commentators have therefore begun to talk of how best to redesign education provision along more fluid and collaborative lines in order to exploit the educational potentials of social media. Persuasive arguments have been advanced for the technological (re)engagement and (re)empowerment of learners through the establishment of 'school 2.0', 'education 2.0', 'pedagogy 2.0' and even 'lifelong learning 2.0' (Rosenfeld 2007; Wang & Chern 2008; Lee & McLoughlin 2010). Demands continue to be made for the radical rethinking of the processes and practices of contemporary education institutions – as evident in calls for the introduction of 'remix curricula' and 'pedagogical mash-ups' (e.g., Fisher & Baird 2009). For better or worse, the concept of social media has had a pronounced influence on the ways in which educational institutions have been (re)imagined and (re)approached by education commentators and stakeholders over the past 10 years or so.

One of the prevailing aspects of social media use in education is therefore seen as an inherent imperative for change. However, rather than simply integrating existing social media into and around educational institutions, it is beginning increasingly to be argued that social media conveys an imperative for more radical change. As Tapscott and Williams (2010, p. 10) contend with respect to the use of social media in higher education,

> Change is required in two vast and interwoven domains that permeate the deep structures and operating model of the university: (1) the value created for the main customers of the university (the students); and (2) the model of production for how that value is created. First we need to toss out the old industrial model of pedagogy (how learning is accomplished) and replace it with a new model called collaborative learning. Second we need an entirely new *modus operandi* for how the subject matter, course materials,

texts, written and spoken word, and other media (the content of higher education) are created.

In this sense, many educators see social media as supporting the negation of institutionally provided learning altogether. At present, a number of high-profile and well-supported trends in social media–supported learning are positioned defiantly outside of the formal education system. Much has been made, for example, of the growth of social media platforms where communities of learners can access professional-grade learning content and courseware such as YouTubeEDU, iTunes. U, TED-Ed and Academic Earth. While many prestigious educational institutions and educators are involved in the provision of this content, at present many of these spaces are, at best, analogous to more formal modes of institutionalized education provision and based, instead, around altruistic social networking principles.

Of course, as has been implied earlier, many other educationalists see social media as leading to more radical rearrangements of educational provision. From this 'deschooling' perspective, therefore, comes a more radical set of understandings. Here commentators see social media as offering opportunities for the complete redesign and reorientation of education provision. Social media are therefore seen as a means to infuse educational provision with the vibrancy and fluidity that can be found within the 'virtual adolescent cultures' of social media as opposed to less dynamic 'formal school settings' (Schuck & Aubusson 2010). Growing numbers of educationalists are now predicting the diminishment or even complete disappearance of the educational institution in favour of technology-supported collective learning (Downes 2010). As Russell Francis (2010, p. 7) reasons with regard to elite forms of higher education provision, "We have indeed entered a period of profound and historic change in the culture of higher education that requires us to reconceptualise how, why, where and with whom learning takes place". Similar arguments have been made for the reconstitution of most other forms of compulsory and postcompulsory education. Social media, it would appear, have proved to be a ready platform upon which to reimagine totally the nature and form of most educational processes and practices.

Perceived Benefits of Social Media in Education

There are, of course, a number of obvious connections between the principles of social media use and current understandings of desirable forms of learning. In this sense, much attention has been paid to the personalized and socially situated forms of learning that can accrue from social media activities. For example, the participatory experiences implicit in the online coconstruction of content are seen as mirroring current assumptions amongst educational experts that learning is an inherently social process that best takes place within interactions between groups of learners involved in the creation as well as consumption of knowledge (e.g., Lameras, Paraskakis & Levy 2009). For many educational technologists, therefore, social media are imbued with a range of inherently educational characteristics, supporting idealized teaching and learning practices such as inquiry learning, communities of practice and the multimodal nature of intelligence (Crook 2012). Often these benefits of cooperative and collaborative forms of learning are contrasted against the deficiencies of 'transmission' models of instruction (C. Jones 2011).

In particular, the framing of social media use around participatory and collaborative group activity is seen as fitting well with contemporary constructivist and sociocultural accounts where knowledge is constructed actively by learners within supportive communal social settings. Social media applications are therefore seen as having many of the constituent characteristics of constructivist learning environments, not least supporting actions that are active, collaborative, conversational, complex and reflective (cf. Jonassen 1999). A central aspect of social constructivist models is that learning often takes place outside of formally structured educational provision – therefore mirroring the informal nature of much social media use. Mimi Ito and colleagues, for example, identified a set of different genres of social media–based participation, all of which can be said to involve elements of learning. For instance, at a basic level is the popular practice of using social media to simply 'hang out' with others (see Ito et al. 2009). Often these forms of 'hanging out' can spill over into the more focused engagement of what Ito terms 'messing around' – that is, activities that are interest-driven and more centred on peer sociability, perhaps involving fortuitous searching, experimentation and playing with resources. Sometimes these instances of messing around can lead to the more intense commitment of what Ito terms 'geeking out'. These are seen as bouts of concentrated and intense participation within defined communities of like-minded and similarly interested individuals driven by common and often specialized interests.

All these latter examples imply significant changes in the nature of individuals' relationships with information and knowledge through social media. Indeed it has been argued that social media support forms of knowledge consumption and knowledge construction that are very different to the epistemological principles of formal education and individualized instruction. These differences are encapsulated, for example, in Thomas and Seely-Brown's (2011) celebration of a digitally enhanced 'new culture of learning' – that is, learning that is based around principles of collective exploration, play and innovation rather than individualized instruction. The changing relationships that social media users appear to have with information have even prompted some educationalists to fundamentally reassess the nature of learning. Take, for instance, the increasingly popular notion of 'connectivism' – that is, the idea that social media–based learning centres now have the ability to access and use distributed information on a 'just-in-time' basis. From this perspective, learning can be seen as an individual's ability to connect to specialized information nodes and sources as and when required. Thus being 'knowledgeable' can be seen as the ability to nurture and maintain these connections (see Chatti, Amine & Quix 2010). As George Siemens (2004, n.p.) puts it, learning can therefore be conceived in terms of the "capacity to know more" via social media rather than a reliance on the individual accumulation and cognitive retention of prior knowledge in terms of "what is currently known".

Aside from the learning benefits of social media use, it is now argued that social media tools offer improved means of engaging different types of individuals in education and learning. Often these benefits are portrayed in distinct generational terms, with commentators pointing to incoming cohorts of younger learners who have been "born into a world woven from cabled, wired or wireless connectivity" (Bauman 2010, p. 7). For many educators, therefore, the increased presence of social media in educational settings is seen as enabling educational institutions to (re)connect with individuals who are "used to networking; its members work collaboratively, they execute several tasks simultaneously, and they use the web to acquire knowledge" (Ulbrich, Jahnke & Mortensson 2010, p. i). As Mason and Rennie (2007, p. 199) conclude, "Shared community spaces and intergroup communications are a massive part of what excites young people and therefore should contribute to [their] persistence and motivation to learn".

These expectations of enhanced motivation and interest are often accompanied by a belief that social media can enhance equality of educational opportunity and outcome. As Solomon and Schrum (2007, p. 8) reasoned soon after the mainstream emergence of Facebook and Wikipedia, "Everyone can participate thanks to social networking and collaborative tools and the abundance of web 2.0 sites . . . The web is no longer a one-way street where someone controls the content. Anyone can control content in a web 2.0 world". This sentiment anticipates the belief that now persists amongst many educators that social media allow learners to engage in learning activities that are more individually meaningful and more publicly significant than was possible before. As Willinsky reasons with regards to participatory engagement with an application such as Wikipedia,

> Today a student who makes the slightest correction to a Wikipedia article is contributing more to the state of public knowledge, in a matter of minutes, than I was able to do over the course of my entire grade school education, such as it was.
>
> *(2009, p. xiii)*

Statements such as these echo wider presumptions of an enhanced alignment between the provision of educational opportunities and the lifestyles of digitally attuned and digitally active learners. These alignments are seen as taking a number of forms, all allowing learning to be better integrated with the increased situating of individuals' everyday lives within online contexts. As such, learning can be more easily assimilated into what some commentators refer to as the 'networked self' (Papacharissi 2010). Key here is the more flexible, fluid and accelerated ways of being that social media provide for users. As such, many people see social media as associated with enhanced social autonomy – with social media users now accustomed to having increased control over the nature and form of what they do, as well as where, when and how they do it. Indeed, social media users are described as having an enhanced capacity to self-organize and provide for themselves. As Tapscott and Williams (2010, p. 52) conclude, these individuals "are not content to be passive consumers, and increasingly satisfy their desire for choice, convenience, customization, and control by designing, producing, and distributing products themselves".

Popular Criticisms of Social Media in Education

Despite their high profile, social media have attracted a number of counterclaims and criticisms from those arguing against their educational and intellectual merits. These criticisms range from the heightened educational disengagement, alienation and disconnection of social media–using students to the detrimental effect that social media tools may have on 'traditional' skills and literacies. Early fears abounded within some sections of the education community that social media tools could contribute to the intellectual and scholarly de-powering of a 'Google generation' of learners incapable of independent critical thought, and generally hasten what Ziegler (2007, p. 69) termed "the mis-education of Generation M".

For instance, in contrast to the popular positioning of social media applications such as social networking applications as exciting educational tools, some initial critics viewed them as distracting learners from their studies. As Cassidy (2006, n.p.) bemoaned, tools such as blogs and social networking applications could be said to serve merely "the essential purpose (for young people without jobs, families, and other social responsibilities) of seeing and being seen ... [tapping into] the apparently timeless appeal to young people of just 'hanging out'". In this vein concerns were also raised over the contribution of social media tools to a distantiating of students from the offline realities of their formal education studies. As Bugeja (2006, n.p.) complained, students' use of social media while physically at school or university could be seen as a potential 'misuse' of resources, with the educational institution in effect assisting students to disengage with their studies:

> Information in the classroom was supposed to bridge digital divides and enhance student research. Increasingly, however, our networks are being used to entertain members of 'the Facebook Generation' who text-message during class, talk on their cell phones during labs, and listen to iPods rather than guest speakers in the wireless lecture hall.

Aside from augmenting alienation and disengagement, other commentators have pointed towards the contribution of social media use to "the development of a culture of disrespect" (Ziegler 2007) between students and formal education providers. News media report regularly on instances of school and university students being sanctioned for 'inappropriate' use of social media in ways that denigrate their educational institutions and/or teachers. In this sense concerns have been raised over the realignment of power within the learner/teacher relationship that social media technologies appear to foster, as apparent in websites such as 'Ratemyprofessor' and 'Ratemyteachers', or students posting candid mobile phone video excerpts of their teachers on video-sharing sites such as YouTube. While some commentators welcome the empowering nature of these technology practices, others in the educational establishment portray it in negative terms – what a UK education minister termed at the time 'the sinister downside' of modern technology (A. Johnson 2007).

Arguments Against the Use of Social Media in Education

As these latter examples suggest, social media is currently the focus for a number of long-running educational debates and controversies – not least the devaluing of state-provided education and erosion of public values and the continued viability of schooling. Social media therefore leave educational technologists facing new variations on some long-standing questions – not least whether the rise to prominence of these technologies can recast education and learning in more dynamic, desirable and democratic terms, or else is set to hasten the 'dumbing-down' of education and 'turning-off' of learners. Returning to the central themes of this book in terms of power, politics and ideological interests, however, there are a range of more substantial issues to also consider in assessing the educational value of social media.

I. The Limits of Individual 'Participation'

First is the contention that the majority of interactions with social media are not especially 'participatory' in nature. While undoubtedly of personal significance for the individuals who are involved directly, much of the activity and content supported by social media remain "the ordinary stuff of life" rather than anything more powerful in terms of participatory forms of learning or knowledge creation (Shirky 2008). Although these ordinary activities and processes may well be essential aspects of social life, it would be a mistake to consider them of direct 'educational' significance along commonsensical lines of 'everything is education' or 'everything is learning'. Informal learning is not simply 'incidental' learning that takes place as a matter of course throughout our daily lives. The informal learning that educators are most concerned with when celebrating the educational potential of social media is learning with intent and purpose – the processes that Mimi Ito identifies as the relatively rare instances of 'geeking out' that lie beyond the act of simply 'hanging out' or 'messing around' online. Of course, social media are well capable of supporting specific instances of intentional, intensified, self-directed learning. Yet, as Ito's research itself implies, these occasional instances of 'geeking out' are located within far more frequent engagement in activities that could not be considered educationally productive. Thus it would be a mistake to conflate all social media use as educationally related or educationally productive. The acts of 'hanging out' and 'messing around' are not to be confused with – but may well be important prerequisites of – the processes of educational engagement. Moreover, it would be a mistake to assume that bouts of educational engagement result as a matter of course from these noneducational practices and activities. When individuals do enter the stage of 'geeking out' – and can therefore be said to be genuinely learning through social media – then this is dependent on a range of social factors, rather than any specific inherent quality of social media itself.

These points relate to a fundamental contradiction in popular understandings of the educational potential of social media – that is, the shortfall between the rhetoric of mass socialization and active community-led action and the rather more individualized and passive realities of social media engagement by many users. Although growing numbers of educationalists and technologists view the participatory practices associated with social media use as leading to social forms of learning, there is currently little evidence that the majority of individuals use social media applications in especially participatory, interactive or even sociable ways. For example, despite their undoubted potential for communal activity, the most commonly used social media tools tend to be appropriated for the one-way passive consumption of content. This is readily apparent in the ways that the majority of individuals engage with YouTube or Wikipedia to access existing content – approaching such applications in a 'take-it-or-leave-it' manner rather than the intended spirit of 'make-it-and-leave-it'. In this sense the majority of social media users are more accurately described as recipients rather than participants.

Indeed, internet usage statistics suggest that most social media applications rely on content (re)creation by a small proportion of users. For example, Wikipedia continues to depend heavily on a 'small core' of a few thousand 'highly active participants' (predominantly older, educated, North American males) who write and edit entries that are then consumed by an audience of millions of users (Leadbeater 2008, p. 15). Recent studies continue to find that only 'a few' college-level students demonstrated in-depth knowledge or familiarity with Wikipedia editing processes (Menchen-Trevino & Hargittai 2011). Similarly, it is reckoned that three quarters of the 'tweets' on Twitter originate from just 5 per cent of the accounts, with nearly one quarter of tweets coming from automated bots and feeds, and "social media marketers far much more active than overall users" (Dean 2010, p. 99). Even the most generous of empirical studies confirm the presence of such imbalances within patterns of popular social media use and engagement. According to Van Dijck (2009), for example, it is possible to identify different levels of participation amongst social media users. Using categories from market research studies of social media use, these participatory states can be said to include the following:

- *Active creators*: People actually producing and uploading content such as blogs, videos or photos
- *Critics*: People who provide ratings or evaluations

- *Collectors*: Those who curate recommended links on social bookmarking services which can be shared with other users
- *Joiners*: People who join social networking sites such as Facebook without necessarily contributing substantive content
- *Passive spectators*: People performing activities such as reading blogs or watching peer-generated video
- *Inactives*

Surveys and studies consistently report that the majority of social media users are positioned in what Van Dijck describes as the passive or inactive categories – a trend that certainly challenges the rhetoric of a 'produsage generation' of individuals all learning through the cocreation and sharing of their own knowledge. At best, then, most social media 'users' would appear responsible mainly for the creation and sharing of personal 'profiles' and other personal information. In terms of the substantive creation of content, it would appear that the 'open' philosophy that lies at the heart of the social media ethos encourages a majority of people to choose to 'free-ride' on the efforts of a minority. This reflects what economists term the 'logic of collective action' (Olson 1971). Put simply, this is the logic that not every individual needs to join a group in order to benefit from its collective action. As Mark Considine (2005, p. 199) describes, "If the benefit to be achieved cannot be localized to those responsible for achieving it, then it will be in the rational self-interest of the majority not to participate, and simply to let others put themselves out to press the case for change". Again, the idea that some people will contribute – and therefore benefit – more than others is an accepted facet of the networked 'market' principles that underpin the logic of most social media action. Yet these inequalities are often overlooked or distorted in the framing of social media within educational debate as fully participative, democratic spaces where all contribute and benefit accordingly.

Of course, for many social media advocates these patterns of minority activity and mass nonparticipation can be rationalized as 'a predictable imbalance' that actually serves to drive social media communities towards more efficient and improved outcomes (e.g., Shirky 2008). Yet such imbalances certainly contradict the central tenets of the *educational* expectations of mass participatory learning and sociocultural 'authentic' exchange. As such, it is clearly unrealistic to assume that the groups and networks of individuals supported through social media are comparable to the 'learning communities' or 'communities of practice' imagined by educational proponents of social media. Instead, these are looser, less committed and less obliged groupings of individuals. Most participants in social media groupings are perhaps best classified as temporary clusters of individuals built around communal preferences in consumption or lifestyle rather than involving 'real' action or meaningful, sustained engagement.

Of course, some social media communities are undoubtedly productive for the minority of individuals who are most involved. For example, the core community

of Wikipedia editors would seem to fit the description of an educationally beneficial 'ethos-action community' (Pentzold 2010). Yet communities such as these
are rarely spontaneous, fully inclusive or even fully participatory. While Wikipedia
may be experienced as a thriving community by one small group of 'insiders', it is
much more often experienced as a distant repository by another larger group of
'outsiders'. Any consideration of the educational qualities of social media therefore needs to recognise the transitory and contingent nature of online actions that
are not underpinned by any lasting shared bond, obligation or lasting reciprocity.
At best, then, social media could be described as what Bauman (2001, p. 50) describes as 'peg' communities – that is, "a momentary gathering around a nail on
which many solitary individuals hang their solitary individual fears". In all these
ways, it is difficult to marry the indifference or disconnection that characterizes the reality of much social media use with more interactive, communal-based
rhetoric of social media–based learning.

The suggestion that online collectives do not equate with conventional notions of community has been raised by many commentators over the past 20 years.
Indeed, the notion of what Castells (2001) termed 'networked individualism'
has long been criticized as lacking the durability and obligation of 'traditional'
face-to-face communities. As Bauman (2011, p. 92) observes, "Internet communities . . . are composed and decomposed, enlarged or cut down to size, by the
multiple acts of individual decisions and impulses to 'connect' and 'disconnect'.
They are therefore eminently changeable, fragile and incurably fissiparous". All
these fragilities appear to be replicated – if not amplified – through social media.
This point was made by Eli Pariser (2011, p. 21), drawing upon Puttnam's notion
of 'bonding' social capital between already existing groups as opposed to 'bridging' social capital between different elements of communities: "We're getting a
lot of bonding but very little bridging". Pariser sees this discrepancy as significant,
reasoning that 'bridging' capital is an essential component of "creat[ing] our sense
of the 'public' – the space where we address the problems that transcend our narrow self-interests" (ibid.). At best, then, social media can be seen as contributing
to a limiting rather than broadening of horizons – what some technologists refer
to a process of 'hiving' towards the similar.

Allied to all these latter points is the dominant shaping of social media along
individualized, market-driven and ultimately consumerist lines. Indeed, rather
than functioning as sites of mass productivity and volunteerism, social tools and
applications are first and foremost "mirrors of contemporary individualism" (Song
2008, n.p.). In this sense, social media participation and productive activity can
be seen as being led less by altruism than by individual gain. Social media should
therefore be understood as operating along a market-led logic of individual (non)
participation rather than a collectivist logic of communal benefit. This logic
of (non)participation is reflected in Brabham's (2010) study of participation in
'crowdsourcing' applications, which suggests five dominant motivating factors for
individuals who took part in such activities. All but one of these factors were

focused on individual gain – with the most popular motivations including the 'addiction' to approaching oneself as a meaningful actor and perceiving participation as an opportunity to make money, develop one's creative skills or seek freelance work.

II. The Tendency to Consume Rather Than Produce

The tendency for nonparticipatory and nonproductive engagement with social media is perhaps unsurprising when one considers the role that social media play in supporting and strengthening the pattern and dynamics of consumerism and consumption. The rhetoric of 'produsers' and 'prosumers' should not distract from the fact that social media use remains focused within the prevailing logic of the consumer society. As such, social media do not alter the fact that we live "in a society in which consumers, not producers, are cast as the driving force of economic prosperity" (Bauman 2001, p. 74). Thus, despite the rhetoric of well-meaning technologists and educationalists, the blurring of boundaries between production and consumption that lies at the heart of most conceptions of social media is not necessarily accurate. The individual user of any social media application will still remain primarily a consumer. Moreover, the overall logic of the consumer relies on the individual being in an ambivalent state of always wanting to consume more.

This is not to say that social media do not encourage production. Indeed, it could be argued that some degree of production is an essential part of using social media. As Mandiberg (2012, p. 1) reasons, "From the audience's perspective, in order to experience the site you have to become a media producer". That said, it could be argued that social media encourage individual users to produce content only along bounded lines. More specifically, it can be argued that social media encourage individual users to produce only content that is of productive value. This then brings us to the fact that social media are, of course, linked closely with commercial and corporate interests. Significantly, social media are often not sites of direct profit making – these are not products that are directly 'sold' to consumers. Instead, as Richard Sennett (2012, p. 144) observes, the 'economic undertow' of many social media applications "is less transparent". The main commercial profit to be made from social media lies not in the direct selling of services or advertising potential but in the commercial exploitation of users' sociality – what Minna Ruckenstein terms the capitalist commodification of user-generated content, where social media allow for the exploitation of the unpaid labour of individual social media users – "the intertwining of economic profit-making with individual creativity" (Ruckenstein 2011, p. 1060). Indeed, the real exchange value of social media use can be seen as lying in the ability of elite interests to assume a 'curatorial role" (Gehl 2012) over individually created data. Thus beneath the surface veneer of "immediacy, social connection and instant access to information" lie the less obvious "rationalized storage of vast amounts of data" and the obvious "long-term archival potential" for the commercial control and exploitation of these data and information (ibid., p. 1229). In whatever form, then, the logic of capitalism remains intact.

Social media can therefore be seen as constructing the user as a form of 'free labour' that can be readily exploited – encouraging users to participate in unpaid work during the course of their use of such tools and applications. Some commentators have equated this with Dallas Smythe's (1977) theory of 'the audience commodity' with regard to the exploitation of viewers of broadcast media. In this sense, social media can be said to rely on the active participation of a mass audience of users ('audience work') to increase the value of its advertising revenues, as well as to produce content and sustain services on an unpaid basis. One obvious outcome of this work is the commercial exploitation of data relating to individual users' activities, preferences and other personal background information. As Mager (2012, p. 772) describes, "Based on users' search history, locations and search terms, search engines develop highly detailed 'user profiles' capturing desires and intentions of individuals and groups of users". These profiles can then be sold to marketers and advertisers, thereby making money through a 'service-for-profile' model (Elmer 2004), where the price for individuals being able to access seemingly 'free' services is the collation and exploitation of personal information. Other forms of exploitable labour are the commercial reuse of user-generated content, as can be seen in the use of 'citizen journalism' by media companies, the formation of 'brand communities' on social networking sites or the archiving of photographic images on applications such as Instagram for later possible commercial gain. As Blank and Reisdorf (2012, p. 541) conclude, all of these practices have seen a shift in the locus of capital "from mass production to production by the masses".

III. The Commodification of Behaviour

Beyond motivations of profit seeking, educationalists need to be aware of the less obvious – but not less intrusive – commodification of action that many social media tools engender. As Arvidsson and Colleoni (2012, p. 135) reason, social media are not based around the direct buying and selling of commodities, but the value that can be created through the initiation of "webs of affective relations, and value realization as linked to a reputation-based financial economy". These economies can take different forms. For instance, Gerlitz and Helmond (2010) describe the 'like economy' of social media – similar to the 'link economy' of web pages and search engines, but with value predicted upon the quantification of user engagement through the results of various options to 'like', 'retweet', 'resend', 'recommend' or 'bookmark'. The building of social media around these user displays of affective reaction therefore "allow[s] for transforming intensive social and affective dynamics into comparable metrics and thus add[s] a social and personal qualification to the hit economy" (Gerlitz & Helmond 2010, p. 3). Social media could therefore be said to constitute a form of what Jenkins (2006) describes as an 'affective economy', where the main criterion of value is what Negri (1999) termed 'affective self-valorisation'. In other words, these are spaces where individuals infuse their communicative and affective interactions with messages about their consumption and their selves.

From a more individually focused perspective, concerns are beginning to be raised as to how social media bound individuals' actions within an 'attention economy' (cf. Simon 1971), compelling users to concentrate on a commoditized promotion of self in pursuit of competitive status-driven and reputation-driven advantage. Many social media tools and applications certainly encourage a focus on presentation of self, as well as the maintenance of personal status, favour and online reputation. These concerns could be seen as shaping user behaviour and action towards a commodified promotion of self and exchange of personal 'microdetails' in pursuit of competitive advantage and digital 'one-upmanship' over others. As Geert Lovink (2011, p. 101) observes, social media therefore serve to "validate and celebrate the personal, individual and singular. They mobilise the personal as celebrity, championing the individual". As A. Cox (2008, p. 506) also notes,

> Users' behaviour combines quite conscious altruistic appearing behaviour whose purpose is gaining attention with a cloying language of community and positivity. In this way, the users' consumption of the site leads them to commodify their own behaviour, in ways which coincide with commercial purposes. Much of this behaviour . . . seems quite solipsistic.

It has therefore been argued that the 'very structure' of social media applications "tends to create normativity" (D. Miller 2011, p. 186) – shaping and controlling users' actions in ways that are more "subtle, seductive and indirect" than has previously been the case with earlier forms of internet applications (Ruckenstein 2011). For example, social media could be said to engender a particular type of 'sociability' – a safe, nonthreatening exchange where everyone is obliged to 'join' and 'participate' but where actual actions and knowledge are highly conformist and consensual. As such, the 'like-mindedness', 'homogeneity', 'cultural consensus' and 'conformist collectivism' (Ashton 2011) that can be observed in much social media use are best understood as necessary elements of this attention economy. As Campanelli (2010, p. 29) observes, "Rather than freely and effectively expressing their thoughts, many users seem concerned only to conform as closely as possible to the 'aesthetic canons' that rule specific forums. Thus dialogue becomes increasingly ritualized, and composed solely of mantra and cliché". This also leads to a minority of people engaging in contrary, extreme asocial behaviours of 'flaming' or 'trolling' – what Coleman (2012) describes as "acts of transgression and spectacle". As Campanelli continues, "The only escape from these ritualized, shallow and pointless exchanges, it seems, are personal insults, vilification and politically incorrect statements" (2010, p. 29). This also explains popular forms of shared distractions such as cat pictures, jokes and viral round robins that "provide momentary, even fleeting, changes and intensities, interruptions and divergences" (Dean 2010, p. 116). As such social media may be best understood not as a place to get things done, but rather as a place to be seen as getting things done.

This is not to say that such actions are worthless or without merit. Similar to our analysis in the previous chapter, the argument can also be made that these social media provide a powerful means of individuals 'learning to labour' within the new capitalist economy. As Cote and Pybus (2011) argue, users of Facebook, Twitter and similar applications learn quickly to develop a 'networked subjectivity' required to survive and thrive as a productive worker and consumer in the immaterial economy. Through social networking sites, for example, users are learning a range of workplace skills – "skills necessary for professional success" (Gregg 2011, p. 10). These include the ability to "integrat[e] oneself into networks" (Boltanski & Chiapello 1999/2005) and the "codified intimacy" of the "bourgeois business culture" where there is a deliberately "blurry line between professional and personal etiquette" (Gregg 2011, p. 6). These tools therefore provide a valuable 'apprenticeship':

> The new social and communicative practices underlying social networks like Facebook are hallmarks of immaterial labour 2.0. In turn, both are integral to cognitive capitalism. In short, youth and adults, young and old are learning techniques and practice that are necessary for the transformation and continued growth of capitalist relations.
>
> *(Cote & Pybus 2011, p. 186)*

However, this is not to suggest that the majority of social media actions and activities should be seen as individually empowering and beneficial. Instead it is important to understand social media use (and social media users) in terms of the power relations that are at play within these online activities. In this sense, the majority of social media–based actions should not be seen as potentially 'free' forms of participation. Instead, as Beer (2009) notes, social media–based participation embeds users within pre-existing relations of power, rather than liberating or empowering them. Social media–based actions are structured heavily by implicit and explicit hierarchies and rules of engagement, and are replete with power plays between users, media providers and commercial interests. In this sense, these forms of participation should not be seen as forms of freedom from power, but rather as forms of subjugation to power. As Brian Massumi concludes,

> Among the most invidious regimes of power are the ones that impose an imperative to participate, particularly if the imperative is to 'truly' or 'authentically' express yourself. You are constantly interpolated. You are under orders to be yourself – for the system. You have to reveal yourself for who you are. In fact, you become who you are in expressing yourself. You are viscerally exposed, like a prodded sea cucumber that spits its guts.
>
> *(cited in Mulder 2007, p. 77)*

Conclusions

An important point that underpins all of these latter criticisms is that while bounded and disempowering modes of action and types of activity are understandable (and even obvious) in terms of the everyday context of social media use, they go against much of the rhetoric of social media as expressed by educationalists and educators. As such, social media can be seen as mitigating many 'educational' qualities and characteristics, not least supporting individuals in questioning information and knowledge, or engaging in sustained criticism, debate and disagreement in a constructive manner. In terms of the use of information, for example, social media are more likely to encourage a reproduction of a market-like 'herd mentality' – supporting 'information cascades' where users are most likely to "tak[e] information shortcuts by assuming that what everyone else is doing must be right" (Dean 2010, p. 106). This disjuncture can also be seen in terms of the personal interactions and relationships that education and learning require. As Friesen and Lowe (2012, p. 191) reason, the commercialized conviviality of 'liking', 'friending', 'confirming' and so on are not to be conflated with genuine instances of learning – "Facebook is consistently structured to support certain modalities of interaction and attention and to exclude others such as traditional educational interaction where teacher-student relations could rarely be defined as synonymous with friendship". As such, social media are configured (in a technical *and* social sense) for modes of restricted communication and exchange that go against the improved forms of educational engagement outlined earlier. Indeed, it could be argued that these technologies are serving to prepare learners for life in an individualized, commodified, market-driven society. As Nick Couldry (2010, p. 82) concludes, through social media "neoliberal logic can now rely on a pedagogic machine installed deep within the dynamics of contemporary media culture".

Of course, many of these latter points should come as little cause for surprise. These characteristics of social media are not unique to social media *per se* – rather they are characteristics of contemporary society at large. As many social theorists have noted, this is a time of 'hyperconsumerism' which is characterized by self-interest, 'weak ties' and "fleeting forms of association" (Sennett 1998, p. 24). A tendency to seek the company of those similar to ourselves (what Bauman terms 'mixophobia') is a feature of many contemporary offline communities – from fears over stranger-danger to our increasing predication for gated communities. The notion of the 'like' and 'attention' economies reflects the shift of capitalism towards what Illouz (2007) terms an 'emotional culture' – built around the blurring of the private and the public sphere. These tropes, it could be argued, constitute the sociality of our times, whether it is mediated online *or* offline. Indeed, it appears that individuals' engagements in the 'community' activities that take place in offline 'real-world' contexts are similarly restricted and bounded. For example, official statistics continue to show that a minority of the adult population are responsible for the majority of community volunteering, engagement in charitable activities and donations of charitable gifts (see Staetsky 2009). That social media appear to replicate – rather than radically disrupt – these general societal patterns is not wholly unexpected. After, why would we expect social media to be able to recreate forms of collectivism, communality and a public sphere "that perhaps never was" (Papacharissi 2002, p. 23)?

What *is* surprising, however, is why so many people should be so convinced that social media are capable of leading to radically different social arrangements and social relations – especially in educational contexts. In this sense, more attention needs to be paid to the wilful misunderstanding on the part of some educationalists with regard to the redemptive power of social media. For whatever reason, many educational technologists appear unwilling or unable to see the recent social turn within digital technology for what it is – that is, an extension of capitalist relations and contemporary consumer society. This, then, has fuelled a distinct romanticization of social media along misleadingly empowering and emancipatory lines. So why then, do we persist with the notion that social media are a necessary addition to educational provision? Certainly social media pander to the social-constructivist sympathies of many educationalists, appearing to operate along many of the principles seen as characterizing 'good' learning. Clearly, social media also appeal to many of the concerns of critical educators – offering a means through which learners can be set free from the structures and boundaries of institutional control.

A further imperative for the increased use of social media in education and learning is economic rather than educational, with many of the activities and roles that are seen as inherent in social media–based learning – that is, knowledge creation, knowledge sharing, creativity, group work, cooperation, problem solving, emotional engagement – being precisely the roles and competencies that are seen as necessities within the neo-liberal workplace. As such social media use can quite reasonably be justified as supporting the emerging forms of contemporary 'fast capitalism' and the required 'twenty-first-century' skill sets and competencies. In this sense, social media – as with many of the digital technologies discussed over the past four chapters – can be said to bring a number of ideological values and agendas into contemporary education. With this thought in mind, it is now time to bring our attention back to the 'bigger picture' of these different technologies in education. How should we best make sense of what has been argued against these various genres of digital technology? Most importantly, how can we make productive use of our growing distrust of contemporary forms of educational technology?

7

EDUCATIONAL TECHNOLOGY

Continuities, Contradictions and Conflicts

Introduction

These four different 'genres' of technology use provide clear illustrations of the ideological nature of educational technology. Virtual, open, games and social technologies are all sites for the 'working out' of values associated with libertarianism, neo-liberalism and the needs of the 'new' economy – giving these ideologies symbolic form as well as grounding them in new sets of educational processes, practices and relationships. These are all educational technologies that constitute a powerful cultural support system for wider ideological agendas. From this perspective, it makes little sense to pursue specific debates over the 'rights' or 'wrongs' of particular technologies in education (e.g., the value of providing 'an iPad for every student', or the mass provision of higher education through 'MOOCs'). These are all proxy battles for much broader struggles over the nature, form and function of education in the early twenty-first century. As has been suggested throughout this book, educational technology continues to be enmeshed with long-running conflicts concerning the role of education in contemporary society – that is, tensions between market and state; private and public good; and the primacy of individual as opposed to collective interests. Of course, the relationships between these wider ideological conflicts and educational technology are not wholly deterministic. The forms of digital technology just described in this book are not straightforward manifestations of wider ideological values and agendas. Instead, the ideological nature of these educational technologies needs to be understood in less direct and more nuanced ways.

The ideological nature of these educational technologies is not always easy to discern. Of course, the fact that it is difficult to recognise these agendas and interests is itself an indication of the ideological nature of educational technology.

The general sense of digital technologies being inherently 'beneficial' is a dominant position within the field of education and, it follows, a difficult orthodoxy to challenge. There are many influential interest groups seeking to promote and protect these assumptions as commonsensical and maintain what Freeden (2003, p. 108) terms "the impenetrable and non-transparent shield of self-evidence". That said, the past four chapters have gone some way towards deconstructing and looking beyond this fuzziness of definition and multifaceted appeal to various interests and agendas that these digital technologies exhibit. In particular, an obvious conclusion that emerges is the close links between these technologies and established economic interests. All these technologies could be said to orientate educational provision and practice towards a set of underpinning conditions where primacy of individual action and market forces is aligned with a set of skills, behaviours and dispositions linked with the demands of the new economy. Indeed, in many ways it is difficult to look beyond the influence of the imperatives of contemporary capitalism on these forms of educational technology. In particular, the immaterial forms of digital education reviewed over the past four chapters all have clear links with the needs of immaterial labour – that is, the need for self-directing, self-disciplined and routinized workers who are comfortable working with (and within) informatic and algorithmic environments. In this sense, digital education could be seen as pre-empting the organization and exploitation of future immaterial workforces.

From this perspective, the ideological function of these contemporary forms of educational technology could be seen as nothing new *per se*. It could be concluded that besides superficial differences in physical form and appearance, the forms of digital technology considered in this book represent simply the latest means of maintaining the capitalist order. While the specific characteristics may have changed, the dominant 'frame of meaning' (Collins & Pinch 1982) of these forms of education can be seen to continue on from the earlier forms of education that they seek to replace – that is, the establishment of educational arrangements that primarily benefit elite economic interests at the expense of the majority. As such, the allegedly 'new' features of contemporary digital education could be said to be rooted in the long-established logics of accumulation, not least the overwhelming imperative of capital and the maintenance of the rate of profit.

Yet these enduring continuities should not be allowed to obscure what is 'new' or 'different' about these recent forms of digital education. For instance, while old models of power appear to remain intact it would appear that there are also a number of new forms of power relation emerging from the increased use of these technologies in education – what Matthewman (2011, p. 60) describes as "new practices, new observations, new organizations and new knowledge". Certainly these digital technologies appear to support an accelerated dematerialization of ideology, marking the intensification but also the further displacement and normalization of values of individualization, marketization and new capitalism in educational contexts. These digital technologies can be understood as acting as fluid spaces where ideologically driven activities and practices can be continu-ally 'tamed', legitimated and normalised in ways that are unencumbered by the material and cultural structures of 'traditional' physical educational institutions. These digital technologies therefore offer a highly flexible means of embedding dominant ideologies as "rationality in everyday social organization and imagina-tion" (Couldry 2010, p. 5).

All these observations suggest that there is much here to be challenged and critiqued – not least in terms of further exploring the obvious contradictions and 'cracks' within the apparent hegemony of educational technology. The remainder of this chapter therefore attempts to develop an immanent critique that explores the differences between what is claimed within prevailing commonsensical ideas about educational technology and what has become evident from this book's analysis of the same technologies. In other words, the chapter seeks to contest the 'pretention' of educational technology to "correspond to reality" (Adorno 1981, p. 32). Hopefully, this will provide solid grounds for challenging the current forms of technology use that are found in contemporary education.

Unpacking the Core Values of Educational Technology

First, it is necessary to acknowledge the common values and beliefs that could be said to underpin the different forms of educational technology featured in this book. Perhaps most prominent have been values relating to the individualization of practice and action. All these digital technologies could be said to increase the responsibility of the individual in terms of the task of making choices with regard to education, as well as dealing with the consequences of choice. All these technologies also demand increased levels of self-dependence and entrepreneurial thinking on the part of the individual, with educational success dependent primar-ily on the individual's ability to self-direct his or her ongoing engagement with learning through various preferred forms of digital technology. In this sense, all of the digital technologies considered over the past four chapters reinforce many of the individualized behaviours and dispositions that are 'highly valued commodi-ties' within contemporary forms of capitalism – for example, self-directed 'entre-preneurial' behaviour, conviviality and communicative skills, openness, curiosity, reflexivity and so on (see Boltanski & Chiapello 1999/2005). In addition, these technologies act to displace formal educational authorities from being involved directly in acts of educational provision and consumption, at best repositioning the state as capable only of "steering from a distance" (Allen 2011, p. 378).

Alongside this individualization of action is an increased informalization of education, with digital technology reconfiguring the "extent and strictness of the social rituals which bind the behaviour of people" in their dealings with education and learning (Misztal 2000, p. 8). In this way, all the forms of digital technologies reviewed in this book support forms of learning that could be said to be indeterminate, fragmented, uncertain and risky. As was apparent throughout the past four chapters, this informality is usually assumed to work in favour of the individual and at the expense of self-interested formal institutions. While this might well be the case in some instances, these characteristics of informalization and anti-institutionalism also favour a number of needs of the 'new economy'. Thus unwittingly or not, digital education provides a ready means through which new economic rationalities are internalized as norms and values by individuals, groups and institutions. Indeed, from the 1970s onwards, capitalism has adapted through the development of networked forms of (dis)organization, based on employees' enhanced autonomy and initiative as well as the establishment of other 'freedoms'. Now in the 2010s, increasing numbers of work practices are based explicitly around networked principles that are seemingly informal, open and 'crowd-based'. Many of the forms of educational technology reviewed in this book therefore clearly support the increased foregrounding of these practices and activities within education.

Another value underpinning the digital technologies reviewed in this book is the promotion of free-market values and sensibilities as a preferred mechanism of educational organization. On one hand, the past four chapters have documented the technology-supported promotion of rational market exchange as a dominant framework for organizing and regulating educational interaction and exchange. Indeed, many of the forms of digital education reviewed in this book could be said to both reflect and reinforce "insurgent market fundamentalism in public life" (Means 2011, p. 224). From the 'bazaar' ethos of open-source production and consumption to the 'attention economy' of social media use, many current forms of educational technology appear to be imbued with market values of competitiveness, unregulated exchange, low barriers to entry and the primacy of individual choice. On the other hand, many of these technologies also support the overt monetization of education provision within commercial marketplaces. As we saw in Chapter 3, the 'virtualization' of educational processes facilitates their production in forms that are easily replicated and sold for profit. Indeed, one should not overlook the role of all these forms of technology in reconfiguring education into primarily economic forms, and therefore merging education with the circuits of capitalism in a number of subtle ways. This reflects what Freedman (2012, p. 84) describes as "the structural need of capitalism to monetise, and incorporate within a system of market exchange, even those practices – like blogging, commenting, and reviewing – that spring from non-commercial urges".

One of the major outcomes of this privileging of market organization within digital education is the increased diversion of education into a commodity state – that is, framing educational processes and practices into the 'market form' of something that has calculable and quantifiable value, and that is therefore exchangeable (Appadurai 2005). It seems clear that one of the consequences of these digital technologies is the reconfiguration of educational practices and relations into forms that can be quantified and exchanged. For example, Chapter 3 illustrated how 'virtual' technologies permit the intensification of capital accumulation in education by fragmenting various educational services and aspects of educational work into commodity-like units and tasks. As Vincent Mosco (2004, p. 135) argues, this commodification is greatly facilitated by digital "opportunities to measure and monitor, package and repackage". As we saw in Chapters 3, 4 and 6, the virtualization, open exchange and social (co)production of education processes ably support all of these processes.

Similarly, the forms of peer production inherent in many open technologies and social media use could be seen as extending what Boltanski and Chiapello (1999/2005) term 'the commodification of the human' within educational contexts. As with all forms of commodification, these digital processes and practices involve framing what were previously social relationships into primarily exchange relationships between providers and consumers. Thus, as we saw in Chapter 6's discussion of social media, there is a tendency within many of these digital contexts for individuals to have to 'sell themselves' to others through the commodification of their public actions and appearances. Social media use therefore involves a pedagogical dimension of immaterial labour where individual users learn to affect "a kind of online personal brand management in a network comprised by multiple lines of valorisation" (Cote & Pybus 2011, p. 95). Extending Smythe's (1977) notion of the 'audience commodity', it could be argued that virtual, open, games and social technologies all act to extend increasing amounts of the 24-hour day into 'work time' that can be potentially monopolised by educational providers.

This latter point raises the increased valuing of privatization throughout the digitalization of education. As all of the past four chapters demonstrate, digital education is often associated with the reframing and repositioning of the public service of education into the domain of private interests. These privatizations are manifest in at least two distinct ways. Firstly, digital technologies are implicated in what Richard Hatcher (2000) calls the 'endogenous privatization' of education – that is, strengthening the notion of internal markets based around increased choice and diversity of provision, alongside competitive forms of consumption. In this sense, the plurality of educational provision supported by virtual, open, games and social technologies contributes to the shifting of educational activities "closer to those of the private sector or even move[s] them fully into that sector" (Crouch 2011, p. 71). On the other hand, all these digital technologies are also implicated in what Hatcher terms 'exogenous privatization' – that is, enhancing and extending the importance of nonstate and private actors as educational providers. Indeed, one of the clear outcomes of the digitizations of education described in this book is the reconstitution of education into forms that are reducible, quantifiable and ultimately contractible to various actors outside of the educational community (Maguire, Perryman, Ball & Braun 2011). It is unsurprising that a number of powerful private concerns have featured throughout this book's discussions – from the multibillion-dollar concerns of Pearson and News Corporation to a range of more locally focused business interests. Thus regardless of their origins, these educational technologies are clearly linked with the increased "dominance of public life by the giant corporation" (Crouch 2011, p. viii). As the recent analysis by Picciano and Spring (2013) demonstrates in great detail, digital technologies are now a key vehicle for the profit-driven interests of the 'educational-industrial complex'.

Unpacking the Correspondences of Technology Use in Education

While it is relatively straightforward to identify and describe the values implicit within much digital technology use in education, developing a good understanding of their implication and importance is more complex. So what does it mean that digital technology use in education appears to be shaped in the ways just described? Here we need to be careful to avoid reaching oversimplified, crude conclusions that merely replicate the 'booster' or 'doomster' lines described at the beginning of the book. Instead, it is important to remain mindful that the relationships between educational technology and the reproduction of these ideologies are clearly complex. As such it makes little sense to settle for overly simplistic functionalist conclusions that, for example, see all uses of technology in education linked inevitably with serving the interests of capital, or leading to the entrenchment of neo-liberal values in wider society. There is a great degree of diversity within these dominant ideologies, as well as a number of competing influences, and many different instances of disruption and resistance (Graefe 2005). Thus, rather than making any sweeping pronouncements, it is prudent at this point to highlight a number of distinct and dominant interactions between digital education and the general reproduction of capital that are worthy of further consideration.

I. Digital Technology and the Recontextualization of Education

A prominent theme emerging from the past four chapters is the role of digital technologies in reorienting educational processes and practices away from the traditional 'real-world' contexts of education such as the classroom, school, university and other institutionalized forms of engagement. All the technologies reviewed in this book are clearly implicated in reconfigurations of educational organization – from the 'gamification' of school to the provision of 'massively open online courses'. These are fundamental changes that involve the reframing of education around virtual forms and algorithmic structures, often under the guise of innovation, experimentation and flexibility. One of the key claims of 'relocating' educational processes and practices into 'the digital ether' is that the social is somehow neutralized or rendered unimportant through the imagined "special effect of technological procedures" (Lovink 2011, p. 6) – what is often popularly perceived as a de-contextualization of education. At first glance many of the digital technologies reviewed in the past four chapters do appear to have successfully stripped away many aspects of 'education' that do not relate directly to the enhancement of learning and the support of learners. Indeed, all these technologies appear to foreground and prioritize 'learning' as the central concern of educational endeavours, positioning individual users in the role of 'participants' and therefore reflecting the recent 'learnification' of education – where "everything there is to say about education" is translated into terms of learning and learners (Biesta, cited in J. Knox 2012).

Of course – as we have seen – this apparent *de*-contextualization serves to mask what is more accurately described as a *re*-contextualization of education. Thus, these apparently decontextualized forms of digital education actually involve the replacement of one set of structures and boundaries with another. In particular, it could be observed that all the forms of digital technology discussed in this book reframe educational concerns along less collective lines – weakening "the basis for people's ability to enrol [in education] on collective perspectives, and pursue what was recognized as the common good" (Boltanski & Chiapello 1999/2005, p. 532). Unencumbered by the need to learn with those in one's immediate context or locality, these digital technologies certainly make it easier to interact and learn with other people of one's choosing. Yet, as the example of social media illustrates, this often results in the situating of education within "communities of like-mindedness" (Bishop 2009), where differences between individual and collective interests are narrowed substantially. Certainly, the 'communities' of learners established through these digital technologies differ considerably in terms of social solidarity, underlying structures of power, political implications, and ability to support "the social bases of discursive publics that engage people across lines of basic difference in collective identities" (Calhoun 1998, pp. 374–375).

II. Digital Technology and the Framing of Education as a Competitive Process

This shift towards forms of educational engagement that are less collective and less obligated corresponds with the tendency of many digital technologies to frame learning as a competitive endeavour. Of course, the competitive nature of digital education is often well hidden within the outwardly supportive, open and communal appearance of many of the digital practices discussed in this book. In theory, these are technologies that allow individuals to learn harmoniously alongside others, "each involved in personal formative cycles, occupied in unison within individual feedback-action loops. They learn to become industrious self-improvers, accepting and implementing external goals" (Allen 2011, p. 378). Yet, although a sense of achievement at the expense of others may not be immediately apparent, "competition is humanized and disguised and therefore intensified by this formative technology" (ibid.).

Thus while not appearing overtly competitive, much technology-based learning could be said to be driven by processes of personal ambition and a belief in the individual as agent of his or her own destiny. As has been observed repeatedly throughout this book, from an individual's point of view it may often make little sense to act collectively when learning with digital technology. Any group behaviours therefore tend to involve limited forms of collectivism that remain motivated by personal gain. At best, these actions can be seen as constituting forms of cooperation rather than collaboration for genuine communal benefit. As Zymunt Bauman (2011, p. 17) describes,

> Left increasingly to their own resources and acumen, individuals are expected to devise individual solutions to socially generated problems, and to do it individually, using their individual skills and individually possessed assets. Such an expectation sets individuals in mutual competition, and renders communal solidarity ... to be perceived as by and large irrelevant, if not downright counterproductive.

Many forms of digital education can therefore be said to be built around a decreased obligation to others, an enhanced logic of competition and a diminished sense of solidarity and togetherness. As such, when learning through digital technologies there is often more incentive for individuals to be primarily self-concerned, 'rationally selfish' and motivated by "the drive to better their own condition" (Hind 2010, p. 140) rather than being primarily concerned with the condition of others. Thus, as Fuller (2011, p. 111) observes, the primary locus of concern "shift[s] from matters that affect us collectively to those that affect us differentially". Under these conditions, then, there is arguably little 'added value' in pursuing any sustained form of genuine solidarity with others who are worse off. At best, "taking public action or contributing to a common good becomes an act of personal expression and recognition or self-validation" (Bennett & Segerberg 2012, p. 752), rather than a basic public duty or civic expectation.

The framing of digital education as a competitive and essentially self-centred endeavour could also be said to heighten the responsibility that is placed on the individual for his or her relative 'success' or 'failure' – "turning the blame away from the institutions and onto the inadequacy of the self" (Bauman 2001, p. 5). There are a number of reasons that this situation might be seen as educationally disadvantageous. For example, in terms of increasing inequalities, a heighted sense of personal risk makes it easier for those who have the resources required to take the risk. Moreover, it could be argued that digital technologies make the risks and uncertainties of educational engagement a distinctly public matter while privatizing any eventual rewards. This is rarely an equitable process – leading less 'successful' individuals towards public forms of self-censure, self-disparagement and self-selective disengagement (contributing to the formation of what Bauman terms 'the scapegoated self'). There is also a sense that these individually accountable digital forms of educational participation become a performative process, with being seen to engage successfully with education perhaps more important than any longer-term outcomes. Referring back to the arguments made in Chapter 6 regarding the attention economy of social media, learners may well be compelled into 'performing' exaggerated or distorted versions of their self on the digital stage (Nygren & Gidlund 2012), even if many individuals may not be in full control of the 'self' that they are able to present when learning online.

III. Digital Technology and the Total Pedagogization of Society

The digital technologies reviewed in this book could also be said to correspond with an increased expansion of education into unfamiliar areas of society and social life – leading to an 'always-on' state of potential educational engagement. Indeed, the notion of ubiquity lies at the heart of the ideological promises of digital education. As was suggested in the opening chapter, one of the core promises of digital education has long been 'anytime, anyplace, any pace' learning. Thus it is understandable that the digital technologies reviewed over the past four chapters all support the expansion of education and learning into domestic, community and work settings. There are clear parallels here with what Basil Bernstein (2001) identified as the 'total pedagogization of society' – that is, a modern society that ensures that pedagogy is integrated into all possible spheres of life. Indeed, the technologies reviewed in this book all support an enhanced pedagogization of previously nonpedagogized areas of social life. For example, we have seen how virtual learning environments support the extension of schoolwork into home settings, how mobile games support learning in a variety of physical locations, and how the attachment of 'badges' turns everyday online activities and practices into potential episodes of credentialized learning. In all these cases, digital technologies are facilitating educational engagement regardless of place, space or setting.

While these forms of 'always-on' access to education are usually presented as extending individual choice, for many people these technologies might simply exacerbate forms of individual exploitation. The notion of always available educational participation echoes the notion of the 'social factory' – that is, the expansion of work beyond the places where the production process traditionally takes place (such as the factory or the office) into the places of wider society (such as the home and local community). In this sense, one of the requirements of the new economy is the breaking down and eroding of previously clear distinctions between formal and informal labour, and between production and consumption (Tronti 2012). This raises the concern of digital technology augmenting the exploitation of individuals who feel increasingly compelled to engage with education regardless of appropriateness or potential detriment to other areas of life. Through digital technologies this compulsion may take a number of different forms. For instance, school students may find the family becoming reframed as a site of increased engagement of schoolwork while outside of school – further increasing what Beck-Gernsheim (1998) describes as the 'pressure' placed upon the contemporary family to educate. Similarly, adults may find digital technologies further integrating the social relations of learning and consumption, and reducing the available time for what Andre Gorz (2001) refers to as 'time for living'.

IV. Digital Technology and the Dehumanization of Education

These latter points lead on to the correspondences between digital technology and the altered emotional aspects of learning and educational engagement. In particular, the disembodied and dematerialized forms of technology-based education described over the past four chapters could all be said to involve the experiencing of education on less intimate grounds. Joel Spring (2012), for example, argues that the increased use of technology in education encourages the formation of a 'digital mindset', where most elements of the education system are visualized in terms of being composed of data rather than personal relations. In this sense, we should not overlook the capacity of these digital technologies to 'quantify and instrumentalize' educational relations (Gregg 2011). As the examples of the virtual learning environment, virtual classroom and MOOC all demonstrate, digital technologies can easily be used to frame the relationships between teachers and students in terms of finite services or contracts rather than sustained human interaction.

Of course, all the digital forms of education outlined in this book need to be contextualized within broader historical shifts from the dominance of direct social relationships towards indirect social relationships. As Craig Calhoun (1998) has noted, this has been hastened by the increasing societal dominance of large-scale markets, impersonal data-driven administrative organizations, transportation and communication technologies. As Calhoun (1992, pp. 211–212) implies, all forms of digital technology act to remediate and reconstitute the nature and form of interpersonal human relations within education – "indirect relationships do not eliminate direct ones, but they change both their meaning and their sociological significance". In this sense one of the potential outcomes of the generally disembodied nature of digital education is that of displacing the substantive social relationships and social practices that traditionally have been seen to constitute education. A strong argument can therefore be made that in "the absence of a binding framework such as the face-to-face", education is experienced in diminished terms of disembodied information transfer rather than "embodied understanding" (Cooper 2002, p. 38).

Overall, then, all these shifts could be said to contribute to a cumulative 'emptying' of the overall educational experience. For example, it could be argued that many of the digital technologies reviewed in this book atomise educational processes and practices into series of discrete tasks, thereby "enclosing people in an entirely commoditized expression of the work to be done" (Menzies 1998, p. 92). From this perspective, the partial, segmented, task-orientated, fragmented and discontinuous nature of digital education could be said to rarely "add up to any meaningful totality" (Bauman 2001, p. 93). Digital education can therefore be seen as a form of 'spiritual alienation' – that is, alienation at the level of meaning, where 'conditions of good work' become detached from the 'conditions of good character' (Sennett 2012).

The Contradictions and Conflicts of Educational Technology

Regardless of whether one agrees with all of these contentions, the contemporary orthodoxy of digital education clearly disguises a number of significant conflicts and tensions. Of course, these apparent contradictions should not be assumed automatically to be cause for concern. There are, after all, many people who will be advantaged by more elitist, competitive, omnipresent and de-emotionalized forms of educational engagement. The outcomes detailed earlier should not be simply opposed without good reason. Similarly, it could be argued that these are all shifts and alterations that at least need to be 'got on with' or 'worked around' rather than rejected out of hand. Indeed, it would be wrong to judge any of the correspondences just outlined as inherently 'undesirable' for their own sake, or to dismiss any of the actors involved in operationalizing these changes as unknowing and unaware. As Jodi Dean (2002, p. 5) reflects, "People know very well what they are doing, but they do it nevertheless" (in contrast to Marx's original observation that "they aren't aware of it, but they do it"). From this perspective, we need to move away from the notion that these correspondences between digital technology and the changing nature of education have occurred as a result of a mass false consciousness on the part of the majority of people working within education. Instead, as Lefebvre (1981/2007) reasons,

> there is no such thing as false consciousness – everyone has an intellectualized understanding of what they are doing, but these understandings are shaped by the material conditions in which they operate and live. As such we can only make judgement over what is good sense and what is bad sense – in my case from a socially concerned perspective. Every position has an element of good sense, even amongst the dominant and oppressive groups.

Therefore, the reaction that any reader will have to the reconfigurations and rearrangements of digital education just described will clearly depend on his or her prevailing circumstances and conditions, as well as – at a more fundamental level – his or her moral values. As such, any discussion of the arguments just presented in this chapter can never be completely disinterested or value-free. It is appropriate that the remainder of this book considers the apparent outcomes and correspondences of digital education in terms of its own explicit values – that is, the critical concerns of social justice, inequality and the collective public good. If digital education is problematized in *these* terms, then there is much in what has just been described to distrust – not least the clear inequalities and power imbalances inherent in these technologies' deployment in education, and the wider corrosion of meaning that they appear to be associated with. These contradictions will now be explored in further detail.

I. Educational Technology and Issues of Inequality

One of the issues recurring throughout this book has been the role of digital technologies in supporting the reproduction of educational inequalities between individuals and social groups, often in subtle ways. This certainly contradicts the democratic discourses that have surrounded digital education over the past 30 years and more. For example, Chapter 3 outlined how the virtual provision of education tends to be characterized by asymmetrical access, differential engagement and differential outcomes between learners. Similarly, the participatory promises of the educational use of social media obscure the differential levels of 'connection' within networks of peer production and consumption – not least the relatively impoverished and disempowered positions of being outside the core producer groups. These inequalities are also evident in the 'nondecisions' that people make because of educational technology – that is, the actions that some people are dissuaded or distracted from doing. As such, we need to consider the activities and practices that no longer happen or are less likely to happen as a result of technology-based education.

Some of these inequalities are associated with the marketization of education through digital technology. As was argued earlier, the expansion of educational provision in 'virtual' form often aligns education with commercial practices and market logics of online commerce. For example, individuals are now often faced with differentiated forms of digital educational opportunities in terms of whether they are able to pay, and then how much they are prepared to pay. This model of 'freemium' provision masks the difference between basic 'free' forms of educational engagement and 'premium' forms of enhanced engagement that must be paid for. One such example of the educational inequalities inherent in this model is the limited access to social advantage that can be gained from basic forms of online education. It could be argued that most of the advantages to be gained from taking a full programme of 'traditional' study at an elite university such as MIT or Harvard are not accessible through their online counterparts – especially as experienced in the 'free' forms of the 'massively open' edX and Coursera digital programmes. Instead, the full 'value' of these prestigious institutions can be gained only through their 'premium' physical forms, where one can access "face to face connections, personal relationships and physical presence [that] can be forms of privilege . . . Privilege and propinquity, presence and access go together – the principle of the old-boy network" (Sennett 2012, p. 146).

Of course, inequality of outcome is an underpinning feature of market forces – it is an accepted and expected part of neo-liberal thinking that some people will benefit at the expense of others. It is therefore unsurprising that meri-tocratic assumptions of 'winners' and 'losers' run throughout most forms of digital education and thereby become "internalized into the practices of aspiring social subjects" (Allen 2011, p. 376). Of course, as with most aspects of ideology, issues of difference and inequality are rarely (if ever) acknowledged within discussions of education and digital technology. Indeed, issues of inequality, injustice and un-fairness are notable silences within the commonsensical orthodoxy of education and technology. As was observed at the beginning of this book, digital technology tends to be assumed as more neutral, more democratic and simply 'fairer' than tra-ditional educational arrangements. This could be seen as reflecting a wider trend within global consumer culture to homogenize within a neutrality-seeking view of the world that "everybody is basically the same" (Sennett 2012, p. 8). Yet, rather than denying the differences inherent in educational technology use, it surely makes more sense to concentrate on identifying and challenging them. The inequalities of education and digital technology therefore demand sustained attention and action.

These correspondences between digital technologies and educational inequal-ities mark one of the most disingenuous aspects of the popular discourses and commonsensical assumptions that surround educational technology. As has been noted throughout this book, one of the hegemonic effects of digital technolo-gies is that they support a sense of individuals being in control of their actions, thereby reinforcing the classical liberal view of sovereign individuals making un-constrained, informed choices. Of course, in reality this ability to make uncon-strained choices and to be in control of constructing one's existence is a highly privileged position. Beck and Beck-Gernsheim (2002) point to the empowered condition of 'individuation' which is experienced only by an elite of self-sustained and self-propelled individuals, as opposed to a majority of merely 'individualized' individuals who have little option but to act as if their individuation has been attained. Similarly, Bauman differentiates between individuals *de facto* (i.e., the minority condition of people living as individuals by choice) as opposed to the majority of individuals *de jure* (i.e., the majority condition of living as an indi-vidual by decree). Put simply, then, the conditions under which people become individualized and the subsequent consequences of this individualization can be seen to vary considerably according to one's background and biography. For the most part, the rhetoric of a generation of hyperindividualized and hyperem-powered digital learners is disingenuous – obscuring the reality that most individ-uals are faced with an inability to move freely or to choose and ignore selectively. As Bauman (2011, p. 101) continues,

> For most of us, our assumed power to get things done seems suspect – fully, or at least in large part, a fiction. Most of us lack the resources needed to raise ourselves from the status of 'individuals by decree' to the rank of 'individu-als de facto'. We lack both the needed knowledge and the required potency.

The apparent 'successes' of individual learners thriving through personalized and individualized forms of digital education must therefore be seen as exceptions to the rule, rather than broadly generalizable and replicable trends. While *some* people are clearly able to thrive when set free from the traditional collective and communal institutions of education, many other people are not. Despite rhetoric to the contrary, the educational opportunities that digital technologies offer should not be seen as wholly 'free' choices. Digital education does not offer a 'level playing field' of roughly equal educational opportunities. Instead, as has been argued throughout this book, some individuals and groups are clearly able to be more proactive, productive and successful when learning with digital technologies, while others are left more vulnerable. Therefore, the outcomes and opportunities offered by digital technologies are as much socially structured as they are individually driven. In other words, the likelihood of gaining advantage from digital education is clearly related to the resources that social groups command, therefore pointing towards the role of digital technology in the perpetuation of accumulated advantage and the reproduction of inequalities in education. As McCarthy (2011, p. 303) concludes,

> These discourses position the individuals as the locus of success or failure: based on their self-discipline, hard-work, ambition, personality and efforts, they will either fail or succeed procuring for their well-being. . . . Missing in these discourses is any consideration of the differential and inequitable positions of subjects in terms of economic, social and cultural capital, age, gender, class, race, ethnicity and sexual orientation. These discourses are based in the assumption that all subjects are equally positioned to identify, mobilise, and create productive or successful choices.

II. Educational Technology and Issues of Power

These latter points highlight the importance of power in making sense of digital technology use. Digital education should therefore be seen as a significant carrier, conveyor and creator of power relations – that is, a key means through which power is substantiated (see Foucault 1979). Some of the key contradictions that run throughout contemporary forms of digital education include imbalances of what people have the capacity to do (and not do) through digital education, what is permitted and what is prevented. Digital technologies should therefore be understood as an important means through which power is now exacerbated in education. Most significantly, we have seen many examples of how these digitally mediated power relations are distributed unequally. While popular assumptions persist that digital technology can have a 'centrifugal' effect on relations of authority and control within education, much of what we have seen throughout this book would suggest that it is mainly 'centripetal' – that is, leading to a centralization of power rather than a more democratic redistribution of power to those previously less powerful. Indeed, it could be argued that the increased use of digital technology in education serves mainly to increase the ability of dominant powerful groups to control the actions of others. This control is achieved primarily by influencing, shaping or even determining the majority's wants, preferences and expectations of what is possible and what is preferable. As Lukes (1974/2005, p. 155) describes,

> Power can be deployed to block or impair its subjects' capacity to reason well, not least by instilling and sustaining misleading or illusory ideas of what is 'natural' and what sort of life their distinctive 'nature' dictates, and, in general, by stunting or blunting their capacity for rational judgment. Power can induce or encourage failures of rationality.

Seen in these terms, it is clearly misleading to continue to frame digital technology as unproblematically increasing the power of all individuals to act along broadly equal lines. Instead, as Holloway (2002, p. 28) reminds us, any increase in power is embedded in the fragmentation of social relations – "our capacity to do is always an interlacing of our activity with the previous or present activity of others. Our capacity to do is always the result of the doing of others". As an ideological form, digital education is more accurately seen as a site of ongoing conflict between people seeking or holding 'power over' the actions of those whom 'power is done to'. In this sense, the politics of digital education are, as Tim Jordan (1999, p. 211) describes it, "an elaborate dance between individual empowerment and elite domination". Crucially, many of the forms of digital technology outlined in this book could be seen as supporting the maintenance of existing patterns of domination through the largely nonconflictual manufacturing of individual "consent to their own subordination" (Delgado 1993, p. 674). Indeed, as Lukes (1974/2005) reminds us, the most effective forms of hegemonic power are often those that individuals perceive as enabling changes that are in their interests. Much of what has been described in the past four chapters points to the role of digital education in supporting the exercise of disciplinary power by enmeshing individuals into politically compliant and economically productive roles which they nevertheless perceive as individually beneficial. Key here, then, is the extent to which digital technologies function as a means to restrict the power of less dominant social groups – that is, the extent to which digital technologies are explicitly disempowering and restrictive for all but an elite minority.

Indeed, the social groups that appear to benefit most from the use of digital technology in education appear to reflect the interests of many of the privileged actors outlined in Chapter 2 – that is, the technological elite, the new-economy entrepreneurs, the creative capitalist classes and their like. It could be argued that digital technologies serve to further distinctly middle-class, consumerist, 'new economic' norms. It is reasonable to conclude, therefore, that digital education is similarly "embedded into the antagonisms of capitalist society . . . a class-structured, segmented, stratified social space" (Fuchs 2008, p. 346). As such, discourses of providing *all* individuals with the skills, competences and aptitudes to thrive in the new economy are clearly disingenuous. It makes little sense for elite interests to support the development of a majority of empowered, innovative, entrepreneurial, self-directed and creatively disruptive individuals. While these qualities are certainly required of elite segments of the workforce, the logic of domination implies a need for the majority of people remaining digitally docile, subordinate and ultimately exploited by dominant interests. As Alex Means (2011, p. 225) contends,

> This tension can be explained at least partially by raising the question of whether the political elite does in fact desire a highly educated and creative workforce at all – preferring instead a small and manageable core of highly skilled workers. There is certainly a broad spectrum of evidence regarding deepening social stratification and insecurity across educational and employment sectors to support this conclusion.

III. Educational Technology and the Corrosion of Values

As implied before, some of the key tensions evident within contemporary forms of educational technology relate to what is lost and displaced as well as what is retained or added. In this sense, a final set of critical issues relates to the subtle devaluation of the 'character' of education – a less tangible notion than inequality or power, but nonetheless important. As has been noted from the beginning of this book, a key aspect of ideology is the struggle over meaning that is embedded into objects, institutions, practices, social interactions and everyday life. In this sense, the digital technologies reviewed over the past four chapters could all be said to convey and enforce a limited set of meanings relating to the nature and form of educational 'work' (be it learning or teaching), and shifting understandings of the human relationships that underpin this work.

This line of critique therefore echoes the criticism that neo-liberal and market-led ideologies serve to reduce – if not negate – moral and ethical argument from public life. As Sandel (2012) contends, the privileging and promoting of values of individualism and marketization have the effect of 'crowding out' nonmarket and nonindividualistic norms. The promotion of these ideologies through digital education could therefore be seen as having a profound influence on "the ways in which we think about what we do, and . . . our social relations with others" (Ball 2012, p. 18). Indeed, throughout the various 'genres' of digital education examined in this book, little concern is apparent for the values of public good or collectivism. Instead, the 'regimes of value' (Appadurai 2005) that are most prominent in many of these instances of digital education centre on issues of status, attention, reputation and other forms of individual gain – all enforcing a sense of self-preoccupation and indifference to the claims of the community. Conversely, it can be noted that digital education is associated with an increased 'cheapening' of the institutional provision of education, and a corresponding devaluing of people's judgements about this provision. An awkward yet important question that therefore presents itself is the extent to which digital education is 'hollowing out' the meaning(s) of education and learning "in any human sense of the word" (Cooper 2002, p. 28).

In addition to these concerns, it could be argued that digital education is characterized by a number of subtle changes at the level of social relations. For example, personal values of time, duty of care, scholarship or family might be said to count for little within models of digital education that are based on speed, replicability and temporality. This loss of 'coherence' between educational labour and the rest of people's lives could be seen as part of the wider 'corrosion of character' that typifies contemporary life. Indeed, Sennett (2012) argues that decreasing the significance of institutions like the school within contemporary society runs the risk of 'deskilling' people in practising and developing the skills of cooperation, empathy, consideration and dialogue. It could be argued that the current turn towards digital education provision does little to guard against an increased conformity, narcissism and withdrawal from civic participation. Similarly, the current digital education landscape could be seen as doing little to challenge wider shifts in society towards an unwillingness to cooperate and deal with complexity and difference (Sennett 2012).

This alignment of digital education with wider societal shifts towards the corrosion of collective concerns within contemporary society raises a number of important issues. As we have seen, one of the core contradictions of the individualized and marketized forms of digital education is their profoundly 'antisocial' nature – paradoxically "bringing about the 'disorganization' of the community whose empowerment is being sought" (Holmwood 2011, p. 20). These are forms of education that are profoundly socially precarious and unstable. One of the defining moral and ethical shifts of the digital turn within education could therefore be argued to be a declining concern for the common good. As Bauman (2001, p. 49) continues,

> Setting people free may make them indifferent. The individual is the citizen's worst enemy . . . the individual tends to be lukewarm, sceptical or wary of the 'common good', of the 'good society' or 'just society'. What is the sense of common interests unless they let each individual satisfy his or her own?

At best, then, contemporary forms of educational technology could be seen as infusing spaces traditionally intended for the maintenance of public education and the common good with individualized discourses – what Bauman terms "the concerns and preoccupations of individuals *qua* individuals" (ibid.). Tellingly, many of the forms of educational technology reviewed over the past four chapters maintain an illusion that learning is taking place on a collective, communal basis while at the same time promising highly individualized forms of 'engagement', 'participation' and 'empowerment'. As Maraizzi (2011, p. 123) observes, one of the key paradoxes of these types of neo-liberal ideology is their ability to "make of individualism a collective value producing a feeling of supra-personal belonging". Yet if education is viewed in terms of the individual and his or her maximized consumption of education, then the argument can be made that educational actions are made *less* meaningful in a moral or ethical sense. In particular, the potential of education to have any collective, communal meaning is dramatically reduced and degraded, as are the socially redistributive qualities of education. As Christian Fuchs (2008, p. 149) concludes, notions of digital participation and digital cooperation tend to be understood in a very limited sense within ideologies of neo-liberalism and new capitalism "because they leave the asymmetrically, exclusive, non-participatory, non-cooperative distribution of economic property untouched".

Conclusions

This chapter's criticisms of the devaluing and diminishing of education through technological means are clearly contentious. As such, it is likely that some readers will find themselves in strong disagreement with many of the arguments that have developed over the course of this chapter, let alone over the course of this book. Yet even a reaction of intense disagreement is more welcome than indifference or uninterest. One of the key aims of this book has been to make education and digital technology a site of informed controversy rather than uninformed consensus. Whatever one's reactions to the points raised in this chapter, it should be clear that there is much to argue about here. Some of the critiques developed so far in this book may be contestable, yet all point to the need for extended debate over the less obvious consequences of the digital turn within education. A number of important questions therefore remain with regard to what is being lost, as well as what is being gained through the increased centring of education around digital technologies. Above all, it is important to remain mindful that these are complex issues – the controversies of educational technology are certainly not simple technical questions with simple technical answers.

This then brings us to the 'business end' of these arguments and contentions. In blunt terms we now need to face the questions of 'so what?': What does it really mean to be living with and working around these digital forms of educational engagement? What can really be done to ameliorate some of the most undesirable excesses? In short, are there really any alternatives to the dominant forms of educational technology that currently exist? What cracks can be identified in the apparent hegemony of education and technology? These questions certainly fit with the 'pessimistic' approach as laid out at the beginning of this book. Here we argued that it is perfectly acceptable – if not downright sensible – to reject the dominant positive assumption in contemporary Western thought that "there *must* be an answer to our fundamental questions, even if we have not found it yet, and that this answer will deliver us from suffering" (Dienstag 2006, p. 34). If nothing else, this book has been successful in expecting nothing from the current arrangements of education and digital technology, and 'calling attention' to the generally unsatisfactory situation that surrounds contemporary forms of educational technology.

Yet these questions also direct us to now devote time to the second part of being purposively pessimistic – that is, as reflected in the notion of being "a pessimist because of intelligence, but an optimist because of will" (Gramsci 1929/1994, p. 299). To repeat the argument that was developed in Chapter 1, this should be a pessimism that recognises the usefulness of starting from a position that acknowledges the parameters and boundaries of any technological endeavour, and has realistic expectations of the political struggles and conflicts that surround any social change. Yet this realist, informed critical knowledge should *then* be used to go on to inform political action that is more idealistic, progressive and reformist in tone. Thus, while pessimistic educational technologists recognise that they may well be defeated in their ultimate ambitions, they should be in no way defeatist in their actions. In this spirit, therefore, we now need to consider the opportunities that might be available to us for change. This provides the focus for the final chapter.

8

EDUCATIONAL TECHNOLOGY

Is There an Alternative?

Introduction

Despite its critical demeanour, readers can be forgiven for expecting this book to conclude on a reasonably positive note. It is generally not acceptable for authors writing on 'applied' social science topics to maintain a *completely* bleak outlook. Instead, there is a tacit presumption on the part of readers, publishers and authors that the final chapter of even the most scathing critique will rally itself with a concluding call to arms, 'manifesto for change' or 10-point 'agenda for action'. Larry Cuban (2011, p. 51) refers to this as the 'last chapter problem', where a deliberately developed critique then needs abruptly to be "capped with a polished set of policy recommendations". Yet, as has been reiterated across the past seven chapters, there are rarely any neat solutions to educational problems, and there are certainly very few neat solutions that involve the unproblematic use of digital technology as a 'technical fix'. This lack of neat solutions is furthered by the nature of ideology itself. As Alexander Galloway (2012, p. vii) reminds us,

> Ideology is not something that can be solved like a puzzle or cured like a disease . . . instead ideology is better understood as a problematic, that is to say a conceptual interface in which theoretical problems arise and are generated and sustained precisely as problems in themselves.

This final chapter will not pretend that there are ready answers to the conditions described throughout this book. It will recognise, however, that there are perhaps some opportunities and spaces where educational technology might be made more of an overt struggle than is currently the case. If nothing else, it will recognise the need for more carefully considered and clearly articulated debates about education and technology. This final chapter is therefore offered in a spirit of acknowledging that the hegemony of educational technology might not be wholly changed, but that it might well be challenged more effectively. As Paul Virilio contends, there are many ways of 'refusing to collaborate' with the oppressive modes of technology use that pervade contemporary society (cited in Dumoucel 2011).

Of course, rousing such an oppositional spirit amongst educationalists and technologists is no easy task. On one hand, it is understandably difficult to be motivated to look beyond the conditions described in this book. After all, what has been detailed over the past seven chapters is simply how things in education and technology *are*. This is not to say that there is a mass denial of these issues amongst those who are currently most involved in educational technologies. On the contrary, many people in education undoubtedly have a nagging sense that things are not quite right with education and technology. Yet, as with many things in life, it is far easier to simply get on with the day-to-day minutiae of educational technology rather than stopping to reflect upon the bigger picture. Indeed, many people – if they had time to think about it – would be well able to criticize their technology use in education along similar lines to those explored in this book. The nature of ideology, however, is that for the most part people do not do this. As Jodi Dean (2010, p. 5) observes, "Ideology is what we do, even when we know better". This inertia is not driven by the wholesale internalization of dominant values, yet reflects what Fernia (1981, p. 39) describes as "an uneasy feeling that the *status quo*, while shamefully iniquitous, is nevertheless the only viable form of society". Any 'acceptance' of the current state of educational technology as described in this book is therefore best understood as a 'fragmented' consciousness – based on begrudging resignation rather than outright consent. Thus in exploring alternative opportunities we need first to be clear about the latent potential that exists within the educational community for such resistance. As Boltanski and Chiapello (1999/2005, p. xx) reason, there are good grounds for

> credit[ing] people with genuine critical capacities . . . people are able by themselves to measure the discrepancy between discourses and what they experience, to the point where capitalism must, in a way, offer – in practice – reasons for accepting its discourse.

Of course, as this quotation implies, the hegemony of educational technology is not something that can be wholly rejected, opposed outright or changed. As such, perhaps the most straightforward and quickest conclusion to reach is that we learn to live with the ideological functions of educational technology – albeit in a more aware and knowing manner. This is certainly a tempting conclusion to draw. After all, much of what has been described in this book simply reflects a set of wider conditions that characterize the general nature of contemporary capitalism. Digital education is by no means the only area of society that is unequal and unfair. Indeed, education as a whole has long existed under wider conditions of oppression and exploitation, been framed within privileged, middle-class sensibilities and skills, and located within wider correspondences with the needs of the economy. Now, it could be concluded that digital technologies are merely one element of the current intensification and acceleration of these conditions. As such, the weight of history could well be taken to suggest that there is little of substance that can be done to counter the forms of educational technology that we currently have before us.

However, very few people would wish to surrender themselves so readily to such a resigned position. It is sensible, therefore, to attempt to look beyond the presumption that educational technology is a battle that is already long lost. Indeed, it could be reasoned that adopting a stance of weary resignation or uncomfortable compliance would mark the ultimate triumph of educational technology as ideology. The ideological shaping of educational technology along individualistic, neo-liberal and new capitalist lines constructs a 'preferred' response within individuals of being "dutiful, compliant . . . and uncritical of the circumstances and conditions around [them]" (Smyth 2011, p. 29). Indeed, ideology relies on ambivalence and cynicism in order to function – what Žižek (in Žižek & Daly 2004) terms 'the cynical functioning of ideology' that encourages a state of indifference and inaction despite what people believe to be true. Supporters of the dominance of global capital have long relied on the disempowering discourse of 'There Is No Alternative', thereby encouraging the perception that there is nothing that can be done but adapt to dominant political ideologies. Thus it makes little sense to completely absent oneself from challenging the conditions laid out in this book. Resistance to these conditions may well be possible, although it is unlikely to be easy. As Michael Apple (1979, p. 161) concludes,

> Certainly, we must be honest about the ways power, knowledge, and interest are interrelated and made manifest, about how hegemony is economically and culturally maintained. But we also must remember that the very sense of personal and collective futility that may come from such honesty is itself an aspect of an effective dominant culture. As an ideological form, it can lead us away from concrete action on the conditions which deny us 'the values we most prize'.

Doing *Something* about Education and Technology

Clearly, then, attempts should be made to challenge the current orthodoxy of educational technology. Everything that has been discussed in this book suggests that there is no sense in waiting for things to eventually 'come good' of their accord. Instead, by continuing to engage uncritically with digital education in its present dominant forms "we build [a] trap that captures us" within the increasing dominance of these ideologies (Dean 2012, p. 124). The remainder of this chapter therefore concerns itself with the task of considering how education and technology might be made a site of deliberate conflict and struggle. These suggestions, it is hoped, might go some way to developing a counterrationality to the dominant ideologies of individualism, neo-liberalism and new capitalism. Of course the changes that most obviously come to mind are too far-reaching to be of any immediate practical use. In *theory*, of course, much of what this book has highlighted would be most efficiently negated by the dismantling of state-corporate power, the debunking of market economics and the cessation of the 'new spirit of capitalism'. On one hand, then, the obvious logical conclusion that this book leads to is the wholesale resistance and unyielding refusal to accept the terms of contemporary capitalist society.

Yet, while many readers may have sympathy with a radical rejection of the new capitalist order, there is a need to maintain an appropriately modest and realistic tone to our conclusions. As such, this chapter will restrict itself to developing a set of pragmatic, achievable and grounded interventions that centre on the actions and practices of people working within the area of educational technology. Indeed, some critical analyses tend to portray the general population (the 'multitude') either as being passive dopes *or* active insurgents in the face of hegemony. An alternate conclusion to draw, however, involves neither wholly accepting *nor* wholly resisting current conditions. Instead, we should acknowledge the limits of our abilities to engineer radical change and look towards likely ways of working around and subverting the worst aspects of educational technology as and when is possible. As Colin Crouch (2011, p. xi) reasons, "Very few people are ever in a position to change to world, and among those few are many who would change it for the worse. There is a far, far, bigger audience of people who have to cope as best they can with the world they find".

However modest these ambitions may be, they need to start from a point of consciously beginning to think beyond ideology – developing alternative forms of understanding that can then begin to point towards concrete possibilities for action. In this sense, it is important to encourage the understanding of the hegemony of libertarianism, neo-liberalism and new capitalism as 'bounded discourses' – that is, "terms whose limitations we can think and live beyond" (Couldry 2010, p. 6). This involves engaging with the politics of the ideological construction of digital education and beginning to think otherwise. As Burnett, Senker and Walker (2009, p. 7) reason, "While it is *difficult* to become disbelieving of dominant ideologies, it is not *impossible*". This book has already made progress along these lines by contrasting the rhetoric and received wisdoms of the dominant ideologies of digital education against the realities of the social conditions that most people actually experience 'on the ground'. Having recognised these contradictions, we should be in a good position to identify the spaces and gaps in which alternative conceptions of digital education may develop.

In particular, one of the key spaces for conflict is redressing the entrenched inequalities of education and technology. It has become increasingly evident throughout this book that, despite rhetoric to the contrary, digital education is a space where power and control are hierarchized and distributed unevenly between individuals and dominant interests. Indeed, many forms of educational technology would appear to be bound up with political and economic power, and the interests of 'expert' groups. As such, many forms of educational technology would appear to ultimately support the domination of a minority of elite interests. One obvious area for change is supporting the wider collective self-determination of those groups who are currently less empowered and less engaged by the use of digital technologies in education. Thus, rather than continuing to delegate power to industry, experts and other vested elite interests, it makes more sense to consider ways that less powerful and privileged interests might assume more responsibility for the collective self-determination of what digital education is, and in whose interests it works. This implies a more democratic approach to the governance of digital education and the decision making that surrounds it, as well as the development of public lay-expertise and interest in the area.

Towards a New Set of Values for Education and Technology

These potential interventions are clearly connected with the wider issue of imbuing future forms of educational technology with new values and sensibilities. Much of what has been critiqued in this book relates to an obvious 'crisis of values' that surrounds contemporary forms of educational technology. Having spent so much time describing the nature of this crisis, there is a need to set about articulating alternative sets of values. As was also the case with Chapter 7, then, it makes no sense for this chapter to maintain a false sense of somehow being 'value-neutral' in its conclusions. Thus, in line with the concerns of critical theory, we should now be in a position to offer perspectives and alternatives for educational technology that might serve genuinely progressive social needs. Of course, any attempt to think 'otherwise' about education and technology along these critical lines needs to be realistic and grounded in achievable aspirations. Care therefore needs to be taken to offer only what Grace (1994, p. 57) describes as 'complex hope' – that is, recommendations that "recognize the historical and structural difficulties which have to be overcome". So what, then, are these 'complex' hopes and values that might be more desirable and acceptable than those found within current constructions of educational technology? Based on our previous discussions and analyses, we can offer the following suggestions for the revaluing of education and technology.

I. Establishing a Collective Sense of Educational Technology

Firstly, much of what has been critiqued in this book relates to tensions between collective and individual interests. The past seven chapters have detailed the limitations of framing digital technology use in education along individualized lines. Of course, this is not a problem that is unique to the educational use of digital technology. As Maraizzi (2011, p. 41) observes, digital technologies throughout most areas of society tend to "complicate the institutional passage between individual and collective interests . . . everyone tends to represent him or herself; all that is needed to protect one's own interests is the understanding of the communicative techniques within the working-productive process". Thus one of the primary values that is missing from current configurations of educational technology is a belief that the collective good is as important (if not more important) than individual rights. Yet, as has been inferred throughout this book, there is no such thing as an 'individual act', especially for those who are less able to exercise their right to choose. Instead, as John Holloway (2002, p. 26) argues,

> doing is inherently social. What I do is always part of a social flow of doing, in which the precondition of my doing is the doing (or having-done) of others, in which the doing of others provides the means of my doing. Doing in inherently plural, collective, choral, communal. This does not mean that all doing is (or indeed should be) undertaken collectively. It means rather it is difficult to conceive of a doing that does not have the doing of other as a precondition.

Seen from this perspective, it seems sensible to argue that the products, processes and practices of educational technology are better imbued with a social-democratic sensibility that frames digital education in terms of the common good, democracy, public life and long-term 'social connectedness' in human society (Olssen 2010). These collective values might include issues of commitment, loyalty, solidarity, trust, mutual obligation and dignity; a concern with equality and redistribution; and overall interest in improving the human condition. Digital technology use should also be imbued with what Baier (1986) terms a 'principle of fairness' according to which individuals are obligated to contribute in relation to what they receive. This suggests arrangements of educational technology that are communally orientated around shared resources and shared modes of engagement that are "consistent with the development of more egalitarian social relations" and respectful of difference and diversity (Harvey 2010, p. 126).

This is not to argue for a complete denial of the presence of the individual within educational technology – simply for the curtailing of the worst excesses of the self-serving, privatized forms of 'hyperindividualism' that are fostered currently by digital products, processes and practices. As such, we are not arguing completely against the significance of the individual *per se*, but for a better life for all individuals within a collective context. Indeed, it can be argued that genuine individual benefit depends upon a sustained sense of collectivism. This could suggest the rearrangement of educational technology along the lines of what Mark Olssen (2009) terms 'thin communitarianism'. This organizational form offers a working balance between collective politics and individual aspirations and development. In brief, thin communitarianism contends that social, political, economic and cultural arrangements need to build around an overt acceptance of the "interdependence between all things as well as the social and historical character of existence" (Olssen 2009, p. 2). Reorganizing educational technology along these lines would not demand a uniform consensus and homogeneity of action *per se*. Instead, thin communitarian arrangements would still allow for novelty, individuality, creativity and variety, while retaining a commitment to the public structuring of 'social goods' such as education.

How these principles might be enacted in practice will be considered in later sections. Yet, for the time being, a strong argument can be made for reconceptualizing our interest in education and technology in ways that can be beneficial to individuals *and* the collective. This involves seeking to raise the moral and political primacy of the needs of the collective, with the group rather than the individual being seen as the leading agent of change. This approach would require a mass awareness that no one is alone in their plight (Fuller 2011), and the establishment of collective democratic means of deciding policy, the allocation of resources and the allocation of work. There would also need to be a pronounced cultural shift amongst currently successful individuals to sacrifice some excesses of their privileged digital existences in the educational sphere, in order to allow the common pursuit of more equitable forms of engagement. In other words, people should engage in digital technology with an implicit "willingness to submerge individual wants, needs, and desires in the cause of some more general struggle for, say, social equality" (Harvey 2005, p. 41).

II. Rethinking the Position of Market Values Within Educational Technology

These proposals certainly imply a rethinking of the dominant roles currently afforded to market values within digital education. As has already been noted, the primacy of markets in shaping the nature and form of digital education can be seen as compounding and exacerbating inequalities between individuals and social groups, as well as altering the moral character of educational processes and practices. Of course, the dominance of market values within educational technology provision has resulted undoubtedly in the 'efficient' production of many forms of educational provision, and advantaged many 'consumers' of education. Yet market values have also undoubtedly had a distorting influence on the underpinning character of digital education – reducing individual actions towards those that are most easily commodified, supporting competitive practices over cooperative practices, and self-interest over collective development. While these characteristics of uncertainty, risk, good fortune and greed might be appropriate for other areas of digital activity, it should be contended that education (as one of the most vital elements of influencing individual life-chances) is too important an area of society to be left wholly to the distortions of the 'market'. As implied in Olssen's description of thin communitarianism, digital education should be seen as an important social good. In this way, the provision of digital education should still be considered as a civic duty and public responsibility first and foremost, rather than an instrument of profit maximization. Otherwise, as Rose (2005, p. 481) warns, the continued application of market rhetoric and market-like structures to social goods such as education "coarsens our understanding of these matters, leading us into mistakes, loosening our moral grasp, and undermining our ties to others".

A key question that arises from these contentions is whether technology-based markets are the best mechanisms for organizing the production and distribution of education. Of course, there are many variations of 'the market'. Persuasive arguments can be made that the theoretical notion of the 'pure' market mechanism has been an acceptable and deep-rooted feature of social life throughout human history. As Amartya Sen (1999, p. 6) reasons, "To be generically against markets would be almost as odd as being generically against conversations between people (even though some conversations are clearly foul and cause problems for others – or even for the conversationalists themselves)". Approached in these terms, the unfairness and corrosiveness of many of the markets that can be currently found in existence within digital education stem from their practical enactment along 'impure' lines. As Sen (1999, p. 142) continues,

> The market mechanism, which arouses passion in favour as well as against, is a basic arrangement through which people can interact with each other and undertake mutually advantageous activities. In this light, it is very hard indeed to see how any reasonable critic could be against the market mechanism, as such. The problems that arise spring typically from other sources – not from the existence of markets *per se* and include such concerns as inadequate preparedness to make use of market transactions, unconstrained concealment of information or unregulated use of activities that allow the powerful to capitalise on their asymmetrical advantage. These have to be dealt with not by suppressing the markets, but by allowing them to function better and with greater fairness, and with adequate supplementation. The overall achievements of the market are deeply contingent on political and social arrangements.

In this sense, it is reasonable to seek to problematize the types of unsupervised consumer markets that digital technologies appear to readily support and propagate within education. This is not to argue against market forces *per se*, but against the particular type of neo-liberal, commodity-focused markets that increasingly typify educational technology use. Thus rather than denying the existence of market values altogether within the exchanges and interactions implicit in any form of digital education, it might be more realistic to suggest simply the development of more bounded, supervised forms of exchange. As Sen (1999, p. 120) reasons, "The role that markets play must depend not only on what they can do, but also on what they are allowed to do". It seems sensible, therefore, to suggest that more effort is made to reorganize digital education beyond the contemporary consumer market model, and towards ways that better support the generation of equality and reduce the need for competitive behaviours between individuals. This suggestion is made partly in the belief that most individuals are capable of behaving in ways that move "beyond narrowly defined self-interest" (ibid., p. 250). Yet self-regulation by itself is unlikely to be enough, and there is a need to explore ways of "supplementing the market mechanism by other institutional activities" (ibid., p. 128). As Olssen (2009, p. 2) puts it, this suggests the establishment of digital education as "a public space where market exchanges are controlled within a political realm".

III. Establishing a Public Sense of Educational Technology

These latter points relate to a third overarching concern with the public good and a revitalized ethos of public education. As the past seven chapters have demonstrated, contemporary forms of digital education often appear to be positioned in overt opposition to public educational institutions. At best, digital education is infused with a sense that the ideals of public service can be best achieved through the 'bottom-up' efforts of individual citizens and local civic groupings. At worse, forms of digital education are used to explicitly devalue and undermine institutionally organized education. In either form, contemporary educational technology has become infused with the sense that individuals are primarily responsible for their own determination, and that the commons of society (such as knowledge, education, culture) are open for exploitation by private interests. This book has spent much time detailing the inequitable and undesirable outcomes that result when these assumptions are put into practice. From this perspective, then, it seems sensible to suggest that powerful checks and balances are put into place to counter the ideologically driven construction of digital education as a largely private matter. Instead, greater concern needs to be shown within the provision of digital education towards the establishment and protection of collective freedoms and universal rights. As we have seen, these outcomes are as unlikely to arise from the 'organic' development of informal activist movements as they are to arise from the logic of capital. Instead, as Christian Fuchs (2008) reasons, 'real counter power' can perhaps come only from the revitalization of well-resourced, durable, powerful, permanent public institutions. In particular, this suggests a revitalization of the power of government intervention for solving social problems. As Zygmunt Bauman (2012a, p. 79) concludes, "The inequality of educational opportunities is a matter than can be confronted wholesale only by state politics".

What is being argued for here, then, is the development of public forms of educational technology governance that are achieved by placing control of the political, economic and legal institutions of educational technology into the hands of a state that is acting on behalf of society. While not a perfect solution, it seems sensible to argue that the primacy of political control over the means and distribution of digital resources in education should lie neither with individuals *nor* with the market. Instead it seems sensible to argue that educational technology should be a collectively controlled and publicly owned affair. A strong case, therefore, can be made for educational technology benefiting from "the strength of public institutions and a sense of public interest" (Crouch 2011, p. 69), and the encouragement of forms of educational technology that are public, universal, compulsory and free. Digital technology should therefore be seen as an opportunity to continue (rather than abandon) the collective, common public educational project. As John Holmwood (2011, p. 11) concludes, "Public [education] matters to everyone, we contend, because it is a condition of citizenship and full participation in economic, cultural and political life. Whatever diminishes it, diminishes our life in common".

The privileging of these values therefore suggests using digital technologies to support the ideals of public, collective education, rather than propagate the market-led ideals of competition and meritocracy. Looking back to the ideals of the comprehensive schooling movement in post-war Britain, for example, suggests using digital technology to promote values of equality of opportunity and capacity to participate. It also suggests using digital technology to foster a sense of the educational benefits of collective action – that is, that people "however diverse, learn best when they learn together, sharing each other's insight and experience, absorbing knowledge and recreating knowledge as they collaborate, in the company of their teachers in a common pursuit" (Brighouse 2003, p. 3). These principles of collective responsibility and obligation should therefore be prioritized within future forms of digital education, so that education is positioned as an area of certainty rather than risk, and an area that is free from the encroachment of commercial values. In this sense, forms of educational technology can be encouraged that offer respite from the inequalities of other contexts – both online and offline. It is this book's contention that, if functioning properly, the state might well be the best institution to achieve these aims.

Towards a New Set of Arrangements for Education and Technology

As has been noted throughout this book, the ultimate aim of any critical analysis of ideology is to at least consider the possibilities for change – however remote or difficult these might be in practice. As Geert Lovink (2011, p. 69) reasons, academic critics of digital media "must progress beyond *ideologiekritik* and discourse analysis. The goal of 'technology' criticism is to hard-wire self-reflexivity into the feedback loop to change the architecture". Yet successfully 'hardwiring' the adjustments and changes just discussed into contemporary forms of education and the prevailing circuits of contemporary capitalism is an undeniably daunting task. There are no easy, short-term responses to the issues raised so far in this chapter. Much of what has been suggested over the past dozen pages or so relates to the positioning of digital education within a set of profound cultural shifts in the nature of early twenty-first-century society. For instance, the idea of repositioning digital education as a collective, public good overseen by the state rather than market values is an obviously grand ambition in a society where markets, individualism and private interests are predominant. Repositioning digital education along more equitable lines is also a profoundly difficult task to take on. Yet if we confine ourselves to considering the conditions necessary for the very beginnings of initiating such changes then the following simple but realistic shifts might be proposed:

- the stimulation of vigorous ongoing public debate about education and digital technology – leading to the framing of digital education as a public controversy, and allowing digital education to be challenged, contested, problematized and de-reified;
- the establishment of modest forms of enhanced state governance and regulation of educational technology, with the state supporting the identification, development and enactment of alternatives to ideologically driven forms of digital education;
- more rigorous and far-reaching academic problematizing of digital education, involving the pursuit of academic writing and research that is better able to demonstrate the links between the various types of dominance and inequality inherent in digital education.

The nature of these changes can now be considered in further detail.

I. Repositioning Educational Technology as a Site of Public Controversy

One activity underpinning all of the changes raised in this chapter so far is that of dialogue. Indeed, much of what has just been argued for relates to the establishment of educational technology as what Raymond Williams (1958) termed a 'full democratic process'. In this sense, a crucial first step in reconstituting educational technology along collectively fairer and equitable lines is recognising educational technology as a contested public space. As Bauman (2001, p. 201) contends, "Democracy is, indeed, the practice of continuous translation between the public and the private; of reforging private problems into public issues and recasting public well-being into private projects and tasks". It therefore seems sensible to suggest that many of the inequalities and injustices associated with contemporary forms of digital education might be redressed through open discussion, open argument and critical scrutiny of the forms of educational technology that we currently have, and those that we want. The tactic here, then, is not to ignore the vested interests and agendas that dominate the current shaping of educational technology, but to contest them through open argument. By publicly exposing the contradictions, deficiencies and failed rhetoric of educational technology then the greater chance there might be for the interests of the currently 'underserved' majority to hold sway over the interests of a 'superserved' elite. These debates should publicize, politicize and problematize the forms of educational technology described in this book, in a manner that provokes a mass interest in educational technology as a public issue.

Of course, mass public engagement with any issue cannot be imposed but must be encouraged and nurtured through publicity. This itself is not an easy task, especially given the long-standing impoverished condition of public discourse and debate with regard to digital technology and education. One of the long-standing ideological features of educational technology is its framing as a topic which people are conditioned to not think deeply about. This occurs either because of an assumed lack of access to 'expert' knowledge, perceptions of the inevitable direction of technological development and 'progress', or simply the apparent ubiquity of digital technology use throughout everyday life. At best, users are flattered into thinking that digital education gives them enhanced agency and control to the extent that there is little need to question the wider arrangements of digital education beyond one's immediate direct experience. As such, public awareness of educational technology has long been shaped disproportionately by elite interests such as professional technologists, the IT industry and other corporate actors. As should by now be clear, this 'education-industrial complex' has considerable leverage and influence over the ongoing pursuit of educational technology, bolstered by a persistent public indifference towards the subject (see Picciano & Spring 2013).

This current 'crisis of publicity' (Hind 2010) might be countered by the sustained inclusion of *all* interests and stakeholders in the circuits of debate and influence that surround educational technology. First and foremost, this would involve the more prominent inclusion of 'ordinary' but often marginalized users and nonusers of digital education – that is, students, parents, employers, teachers and other "groups of concerned citizens and the general public which may be both excited by and feel powerless in the face of scientific advance" (Matthewman 2011, p. 120). There is also a need to better mobilize the interests of organizations that have acted traditionally as bulwarks against other forms of ideological dominance – in particular trade unions, community groups and other areas of civil society such as non-governmental organizations, voluntary groups, charities and the professions. There is also room here for the more prominent inclusion of oppositional groups that make use of digital media, such as 'indy media', hacktivist and other alternative technology movements. The aim here, then, would be to encourage the closer involvement and interaction between mass publics of educational technology that have hitherto been too disaggregated and remote to establish sustained connections.

In all these cases, it is important that these publics are involved in a manner that moves beyond 'tokenistic' processes of being 'consulted', 'informed' as to what is 'best' for them or positioned in a reduced role of expressing 'learner voice' or 'consumer voice'. Instead, the aim here would be to openly discuss and facilitate the meaningful rearrangement of educational technology. As such, increased democratization of debate is a ready means of moving the culture of educational technology away from individualistic and towards collective concerns. Key to the success of these discussions and debates would be an emphasis on listening as well as telling, and an open-ended sense of a "power-charged social relation" of conversation rather than the predestined logic of 'discovering' some predetermined and preferred truth (Haraway 1991, p. 198). The aim of these conversations would be to challenge the legitimacy of current dominant understandings, to develop long-terms views on how digital technologies should and should not be embedded in education practices and to collectively consider and promote a 'good sense' rather than a 'common sense' about education and technology.

One of the first steps to enacting these conversations is debunking the notion of technological expertise. As Brian Wynne (1996) reasons, one does not need to know how a nuclear power plant operates in order to have an opinion on how they should be used in one's community. From this perspective, a powerful starting point for critical public engagement with an issue such as educational technology is to consider people who are currently positioned outside of expert debates as 'nonexperts' only in the sense of not having 'answers' or 'solutions'. Alternatively, these 'nonexperts' should be seen as still having valid views and concerns about education and technology. As Smyth (2011, p. 137) argues, "If we think about the role of the 'outsider' in these terms, then it becomes clear that the function is not about being an 'expert'. Rather, it is more about . . .

- starting dialogue among people and setting up amenable conditions;
- eliciting, collecting, researching and bringing together views from as many diverse viewpoints as possible;
- reflecting, refining and making sense of what is being spoken about;
- interrupting, suggesting, confronting and helping people to re-frame challenges;
- helping to bring into existence local solutions and actions and ensuring that successes are recognized and celebrated".

Once these conditions can be established, then there are a range of existing public and participatory techniques that can be applied to public engagement with educational technology. These include citizens' juries, expert panels, public hearings, consensus conferences and deliberation polling – all of which have been used with some success in areas such as environmental and health policy. While many of these techniques could be hosted through digital technology, it is important to note that the most effective forms of dialogue might well occur offline. As Richard Sennett (2012, p. 24) reasons, the "most potent political effect occurs when they stimulate and arouse people to act off-line, rather than containing them to experience on-screen". An important role remains, therefore, for the dominant twentieth-century institutions of information – such as the broadcast media and newspapers – to play a more confident role in leading informed and critical public debates about education and technology. All in all, raising the public profile of these issues would require a sustained and widespread publicity. While perhaps inconsequential in comparison to the commercial actions that underpin the digital education marketplace, these public activities might well offer a realistic means of supporting the emergence of collective forms of counterhegemonic resistance and action. As Nick Couldry (2010) reasons, there is little point in encouraging the development of citizen 'voice' unless it can be considered '*effective* voice'. Thus these should be seen not simply as mass-awareness raising activities but as efforts to position educational technology as a site of controversy, indignation and even moral outrage.

This politicization of educational technology could well lead to the identification of tangible, material forms of resistance, as well as encouraging more subtle cultural shifts. In this latter sense, one of the key areas for contestation and challenge should be the language of educational technology. As has been illustrated throughout this book, language is key to the maintenance of ideology, providing both an immediate vocabulary and underlying cognitive frame through which elite values and interests are protected (Thrift 1997). As past chapters have illustrated, much of the current language of educational technology fulfils this ideological function to great effect in often subtle and imperceptible ways. There is a need to challenge much of the language that currently shapes understandings of education and technology. For example, the dominant metaphor of the 'network' when discussing digital technology plays a subtle role in "impoverish[ing] our understanding of power" (Prey 2012, p. 253). The binary logic of being either 'connected' or 'disconnected' "provokes a one-dimensional understanding of power, one that fixates on an inclusion/exclusion binary and is largely blind to relations of exploitation" (ibid.). Similar gaps and silences are evident in individualist notions of 'one-to-one computing', 'personalized learning networks' and so on. Attempts therefore need to be made to 'uncool' these dominant concepts (Lovink 2011), and promote the use of alternate vocabulary that better describes the sense of conflict and contestation underlying the use of digital technology in education. Even at this subtle level of linguistic adjustment, powerful changes in understanding and action can be enabled. As Richard Pring (2010, pp. 86–87) concludes,

> How different the provision of education and training might be if we employed different metaphors, for the words we use embody the way in which we conceive the world, other people, the relationships between them and the way in which they should be treated.

II. Supporting State Governance and Regulation of Educational Technology

While an important area for change, care needs to be taken not to place an unrealistic burden on these popular participatory processes. Public engagement and the development of counterrationalities are crucial elements of acting against the currently dominant forms of educational technology, yet will be fully effective only alongside other more substantial changes to the governance and regulation of educational technology. In this sense, we should also consider the enhanced role of the state in being more directly involved in educational technology. As much of this book has discussed, state involvement in educational technology to date has tended to be limited. As David Harvey (2005, p. 79) describes, this is a basic condition of contemporary capitalism, where "the neoliberal state is expected to take a back seat and simply set the stage for market functions". Certainly, states have historically been involved in creating 'good climates' for the development of technology to take place, and acted as cheerleaders for the broad adoption of educational technology. Yet generally state actors have played minimal roles in actively shaping or directing the values and nature of technology use in education.

Arguing for increased state involvement in digital technology is certainly not a popular recommendation to make from either a liberal *or* conservative perspective. The roles of the state and state institutions are largely discredited in most discussions of the digital technology and the digital age. As Tauel Harper (2009, p. 125) observes,

> Amongst theories of techno-politics there is some trepidation when it comes to reconciling the state and technology. Many of the state's services seem to require an authoritative 'General' which carries the legitimacy and control necessary for the provision of community services such as education, security and common law over a geographical territory. Technology, on the other hand, seems to challenge the sources.

Yet as we approach the end of this book, the state appears to perhaps be one of the only institutions capable of directing, regulating and controlling educational technology along moral lines of ensuring socially 'fairer' outcomes. There has been little evidence to date that the groups that constitute 'civil society' are particularly capable of repelling or even mounting a visible challenge to the market dominance and capitalist shaping of digital technology. While undeniably 'noisy', the many voluntary civic and social organizations and institutions that promise an alternative to the commercialized, corporate forms of digital technology have been less successful in practice than they might have hoped. Indeed, it could be argued that these groups have failed largely to construct sustained alternatives to the dominant neo-liberal ideologies of educational technology, ultimately doing little more than "reproducing consent to capitalist domination" (Burawoy

2005, p. 324). A surprisingly strong case can be made, therefore, for increased state involvement and engagement with educational technology. Of course, this presumes a strong and engaged ideal form of state that is responsive to multiple interests and capable of "facilitating, promoting and protecting the conditions of participatory democracy" (ibid., pp. 324–325). We are not arguing, therefore, for a dirigiste arrangement of state-controlled technology. Instead, we are suggesting that digital education is subject to a greater amount of what Archon Fung and Erik Wright (2003) term 'empowered participatory governance' – that is, where government and state agencies are charged with being more responsive and more responsible to the conditions of digital education.

In this sense there are a number of areas in which the responsible state might be involved more centrally in the governance and regulation of educational technology. For instance, there may well be scope for increased state involvement in the commercial production and provision of educational technologies. As has been acknowledged throughout this book, digital technology is an area of society that is entwined inextricably with commercial and corporate interests. It is not realistic to imagine the mass development and production of digital technologies by the state. Yet there are a number of possible ways that states might play a more active role in determining the forms of digital education that are enacted within their domains. For example, it could be that state organizations play a leading role in the 'translation' work that surrounds the implementation of any technology within a social context – ensuring that the socio-technical 'conversion' of educational technologies is a collective rather than individual concern (see Kullman & Lee 2012). In this sense, the notion of the 'cultural screening' of information technologies raises the interesting suggestion of how states might be able to adapt digital technologies to the national and local contexts in which they will be used, and the groups of users who might benefit most from this use (see Babe 2012). For example, states may want to 'screen' out ideological elements of consumer capitalist culture that surround emerging technologies but may benefit only privileged groups who have the required economic, cultural and social capitals to benefit fully.

Alternatively, there may also be scope for states to develop publicly directed – if not publicly controlled – forms of commercial activity in digital education as part of companies' commitments to 'corporate social responsibility'. Instead of allowing multinational IT corporations to effectively usurp state governance of national educational technology provision, states can seek to restrict and regulate the educational activities of these companies – perhaps as recompense for being able to operate freely within other areas of society. Similarly, more could be made of the state's position as a major bulk purchaser of educational technology. Thus rather than accepting (and attempting to adapt) digital technologies designed for the business or home markets, more genuinely 'educational' technologies could be commissioned by the state that better fit the collective, common, public good. This could see the development of alternative architectures and formats of educational technology. Geert Lovink (2011), for example, proposes the 'dangerous design' of new technologies – such as social networks that are engineered to link people by difference rather than similarity, or games that actively reward non-competitive actions. There is clearly scope for the design and development of educational technologies that are intended to introduce an element of positive discrimination and redress existing inequalities and imbalances of power.

Aside from these instances of assuming a more central role in directing technological development, state actors might also play a heightened role in terms of the regulation of technology use within educational institutions. Partially, this would involve increased state commitment to maintaining and improving physical 'bricks and mortar' institutions of the school, college and university, rather than allowing digital technology to be seen as offering a viable alternative. Of course, this is not to overromanticize the capabilities of educational institutions that are currently hidebound by regimes of testing, monitoring and control. As Sennett (2012, p. 29) argues, "Human beings are capable of doing more than schools, workplaces, civil organizations and political regimes allow for". Yet this is not to say that the model of mass, compulsory, physical educational institutions cannot be reimagined and redesigned by state interests along more collective, publicly orientated lines that can perhaps offer a refuge from the worst excesses of contemporary digital culture. An often suggested issue (that continues to be worthy of serious consideration) is state-supported use of schools and universities for fostering what has come to be referred to in the US and UK as 'critical digital literacy' (akin to the Scandinavian term 'digital competence' and the Dutch term 'media wisdom'). This involves setting time aside within official curricula to allow teachers and students to make digital technology itself problematic, pay much greater political attention to the 'stuff' of digital culture and, indeed, consider many of the issues that have emerged over the course of this book. As Kellner and Share (2007, p. 4) describe, this form of education therefore seeks to "deepen the potential of literacy education to critically analyse relationships between media and audiences, information, and power".

III. Towards a Better Academic Analysis of Education and Technology

Finally, we need to also consider the role of academic researchers and writers within this newly controversial and publicly positioned field of educational technology. Certainly academic research in this area can be characterized as generally well-meaning but largely ineffective in its eventual political influence and outcomes. For example, academic researchers and writers have done little to challenge the ideological nature of educational technology over the past 30 years. Indeed, it could be argued that academic research has played a supporting role in sustaining the hegemony of educational technology by failing to embed its analyses within a wider recognition of the prevailing structures of domination and associated struggles. In this sense, the academic study of educational technology could be described as what Henri Lefebvre (1970/2003) calls a 'blind field' – that is, a site of misunderstanding, misrepresentation and misinterpretation of what are profoundly political issues.

This is not to claim that academics working in the area of educational technology are ignorant of the critical issues that pervade their field of study. Many academic writers and researchers working in this area are politically astute, liberally minded liberals who are trying to make the world a better place. Some would consider themselves to be radical thinkers and political activists in other areas of their lives. Yet most have developed an unconscious but pronounced critical blind spot when it comes to education and technology. Perhaps distracted by the allure of digital technology and its promises of radical transformation and liberation, most academics are happy to overlook the problematic, dysfunctional realities of most technology use in education. The best that the academic literature on education and technology has offered to date is the championing of the "all-too-easy liberal-democratic alternative" (Žižek 2008, p. 6) that is offered by the digital forms of 'soft capitalist' ideals such as participation, self-organization and cooperation. More concerning still is the continued tendency within the educational technology literature to take pleasure in subverting and undermining mass forms of formal education – an antischool agenda that can be traced from the writings of Seymour Papert in the 1980s to more recent celebrations of 'connectivism'. Some of the most popular and influential academic accounts of education and technology struggle to hide their disdain for formal education, and their default assumption that education is best organized along informal lines of discovery, play and 'hard fun'. These may have been radically countercultural approaches in the 1960s and 1970s, but now should be seen as profoundly in step with contemporary dominant ideologies.

So how then could academic research into education and technology be strengthened and better organized to provide an effective critique of dominant forms of digital education? Certainly, there is a need for academics to ask better questions of education and technology, to have more nuanced discussions and be more confident in acknowledging the uncertainty of the topic. In this latter sense, an increased 'technological modesty' within academic discussions of education and technology would surely be welcome – that is, "having a sense of the whole and not claiming or obtruding more than a particular function warrants" (Postman 1992, p. 119). This suggests the need to 'de-scientise' educational technology research – that is, to encourage the greater acknowledgement that some things can only ever be discussed and problematized rather than demonstrated and proved. Thus, academics need to be more confident in posing awkward questions, and to conduct research that addresses the 'messy' realities of educational technology use *in situ*. These activities differ from current preoccupations with producing evaluations of best practice and speculative reports of potential applications in an attempt to keep up with the 'marketing machinery' of digital technology (Lovink 2011). Academics working in the area of education and technology also need to be confident of being critical rather than consensual, and prepared to disagree openly with one another and draw attention to substandard work and argumentation. At present, such self-scrutiny is largely absent from what has become a cosy, self-congratulatory field of practice – reminiscent of the 'accomplice paranoia' that characterizes the world of contemporary art. As Campanelli (2010, p. 43) describes,

> In other words, this is a scene that constantly eludes the possibility of critical judgement, and leaves space only for friendly, necessary, convivial, sharing of nothingness. In such a context, open dissent is seen as utterly inappropriate. Nothing is allowed to disturb the quiet harmony of a community that in fact comes together for comfort rather than to confront.

Aside from encouraging greater dissent and confrontation, there are a number of conceptual ways in which academics working in the area of education and technology might better approach the topic. Certainly there is a need for academics to be properly political (with a big 'P' and a little 'p') in their analyses of education and media. This is not to say that writers and researchers have wholly neglected the issue of politics in their previous work, but more emphasis clearly needs to be placed on the politics of class and collectivism. There is also a need for academic discussions of education and technology to frame 'new' technologies in a historical manner – therefore attempting to make sense of what has already happened with technology rather than anticipating what is about to happen. Framing the development of education and technology within a historical perspective can have many benefits – revealing how preceding technologies often have ramifications for later technologies, as well as offering clearer understandings of the meanings and significances attached to technologies before they become seen as inevitable, invisible and somehow 'natural.' Looking back over the history of education and technology might also counter the common tendency to "over-estimate the short-term impact of new technologies – and to under-estimate their long-term implications" (Naughton 2012, p. 9).

The academic study of educational technology would be also strengthened by a broad and rigorous engagement with theory. There are many theoretical approaches and traditions that currently are underutilized in the educational technology literature, yet might support the building of better questions, highlight otherwise neglected issues and act both as a point of reference and a point of correction. As well as engaging with unfamiliar theory, there is also a need for better use of the theoretical traditions that have hitherto been favoured in academic accounts of education and technology. In short, there are a number of ways that researchers might improve how they 'do' theory with regard to education and technology. Following on from these theoretical concerns, there is also a clear need for academic researchers to take a broad approach to research methods and methodology, while also maintaining an awareness of the quality and rigour of their research. Researchers should be making use of the methods of data collection and analysis that best fit their research questions of the moment, rather than methods that simply reflect personal convenience or habit.

Finally, in terms of engaging in academic work that seeks to make a practical difference to the conditions that it describes, inspiration could be taken from the area of critical participatory design – where usually excluded 'end users' are involved in the development and production of technological artefacts and practices in ways that better reflect their interests, needs and values (Iversen, Halskov & Leong 2012; Eubanks 2011). Following on from our earlier discussions, it is also likely that the academic study of education and technology needs to become more deliberately public in spirit – that is, engaging in the production of work that moves away "from interpretation to engagement, from theory to practice, from the academy to its publics" (Burawoy 2005, p. 324). In this spirit, more thought can perhaps be given to how writing and research in education and technology can span the boundaries between academic work and public engagement, and therefore become more publicly facing and 'deliberative' in character (see Goodson & Schostak 2014). What scope is there for academics working in the area of education and technology to engage in critical forms of public scholarship that provide "a disruptive but necessary voice in democratic debate" (Lauder, Brown & Halsey 2009, p. 580)? What role is there for methods of public research such as citizen panels, consensus conferences and science shops that seek to put academic research out in wider nonacademic communities? How can a critical 'public understanding of education and technology' be stimulated and supported through academic writing and research?

Above all, then, the academic community needs to be willing and able to champion all the critical issues raised throughout this book. Up until now the advocates for critical digital issues within public discourse have tended to be technologists, activists and hackers – not groups traditionally imbued with power or influence with the political or economic classes. While academics are hardly the most influential of groups within the cultural establishment, their heightened critical presence in educational technology debate and discourse should be pursued to a far greater degree than it is at present – not least in terms of the relative freedom granted to academics to think about digital issues in a more creative and less constrained manner.

Conclusions

These are all complex and contentious issues that clearly require further thought beyond the pages of this book. The underlying aim of all the tentative suggestions outlined in this chapter is to strengthen people's resistance to the sense of inevitability and certainty that often surrounds educational technology. All these suggestions are therefore concerned with shifting the prevailing mindset that surrounds education and technology, and beginning to address the problems of educational technology in a different manner that relates to actual concerns and real-life circumstances. Whether any of the suggestions might lead to tangible change is uncertain. In many ways this is not the primary purpose of raising these particular ideas. Instead, what is most important is that these ideas act as powerful starting points for beginning to think otherwise about education and technology. If these types of discussions take place more frequently, then plausible alternatives will present themselves more frequently. As has already been stressed, these are not issues that have any straightforward, immediately identifiable solutions.

So what has been achieved by *distrusting* educational technology? This book has attempted to open up the 'black box' of educational technology. By thinking consistently against educational technology, this book has highlighted some of the bigger (but less obvious) connotations and implications of the apparently 'commonsensical' act of integrating digital technology into education – not least the ideologies of neo-liberalism, libertarianism and the 'new' economic arrangements of contemporary capitalism. Worryingly for those already working in this area, the book has shown the efforts of well-meaning and well-intentioned technology-using educationalists to be often "dis-articulated from progressive movements and re-articulated to the neoliberal and neoconservative agendas" (Apple 2010a, p. 196). At best, then, current forms of educational technology appear to be doing little to challenge or disrupt the prevailing reproduction of social inequalities that characterize contemporary education.

There are, of course, a number of caveats and limitations to this analysis. First and foremost, it should be noted that this book has provided a predominantly Western analysis, rooted in European, North American and Australian contexts. While many of the arguments made in this chapter may well hold true for the more routinely digitally mediated societies of Japan and the Southeast Asian 'gang of four' (i.e., Singapore, South Korea, Taiwan and Hong Kong) as well as the high-tech urban regions of South America and South Africa, it is important to note that this book does not present a totalizing analysis. What differences would be seen, for example, if considering educational technology with Chinese or Arabic characteristics? How do these concerns translate in the context of more authoritarian regimes where state intervention into digital technology is more commonly associated with less benign practices such as overt censorship, surveillance and oppression? The need remains for the arguments raised in this book to be carried over into more nuanced and localized analyses. Moreover, it must be acknowledged that this book has focused its critical concerns primarily in terms of class, and has had relatively little to say on matters of gender, identity, sexuality, race and ethnicity. These omissions are largely due to the availability of such analyses elsewhere, rather than any deliberate oversight or ignorance.

Yet perhaps one of most important caveats to our analysis is that of longevity. An inevitable shadow that blights any claim of techno-social understanding is the impending development of new domains of technology in areas that nontechnologists find it difficult to respond quickly to. One of the main reasons that the social sciences were relatively slow to respond to the 'digital revolution' of the 1970s,

1980s and 1990s was an unwillingness within disciplines such as sociology to give up on confronting the major 'political technologies' of class struggle that had dominated the first half of the twentieth century – that is, what Rainie and Wellman (2012) call the 'big machines' of the industrial era such as factories, mills and military technology. While the social sciences are now beginning to 'catch up' with digital technologies and the issues associated with them, there is a corresponding need to begin to consider what the *next* wave of technological change might mean for education. If we can be sure of one thing, then the education of the twenty-first century will not be influenced and shaped solely by digital technologies. While the past 30 years have been characterized increasingly by the development of digital technology, the next 30 years look set to be characterized increasingly by the development of *post*digital technologies of many varieties. An upcoming challenge for the critical study of education and technology is to make critical sense of what is to come. This will undoubtedly include what Steve Fuller (2011) calls the 'converging technologies' of the nano-, info- and cogno-technosciences, as well as biomedical and genetic engineering, and the 'green' technologies. These post-digital technologies are likely to be associated with another 'long wave' of capitalist development (Harvey 2010), perhaps with altered ideological implications other than have been described in this book. There is clearly a need for an ongoing and sustained critical analysis of education and all forms of 'new' technology for a long time to come (see, for example, Lee & Motzkau 2014).

These future challenges notwithstanding, it is hoped that this book has gone some way towards redressing the narrow debates and understandings of digital technology that characterize the area of educational technology – offering a problematic and pessimistic perspective on an area of education that is rarely afforded such scrutiny. As an exercise in critique, it is perhaps unsurprising that this has resulted in a book without an uplifting ending, or even an especially neat set of conclusions. At best, everything that has been written in this book should be treated as a question – as Holloway (2002, p. 215) puts it, "an invitation to discuss". Approached along these lines, one of the key threads of discussion running throughout the past eight chapters is the need for everyone involved in education to develop a heightened sense of realism about what digital technology is, and what digital technology is not; about what technology can do in education, and what it cannot. These are important contentions and controversies that need to be nurtured throughout the next few years as education becomes ever more digitally defined and digitally delineated.

REFERENCES

Aarseth, E. (2005). Game studies: What is it good for? *International Digital Media and Arts Association Journal*, *2*(1), 3–7.

Adorno, T. (1981). *Minima moralia: Reflections from a damaged life*. London: Verso.

Agger, B. (2004). *Speeding up capitalism: Cultures, jobs, family, schools, bodies*. Boulder, CO: Paradigm.

Allen, A. (2011). Michael Young's the rise of the meritocracy: A philosophical critique. *British Journal of Educational Studies*, *59*(4), 367–382.

Amin, A., & Thrift, N. (2005). What's left? Just the future. *Antipode*, *3*(2), 220–238.

Anderson, C. (2009). *Free: The future of a radical price*. New York: Hyperion.

Andersen, C., & Pold, S. (2011). The scripted spaces of urban ubiquitous computing: The experience, poetics, and politics of public scripted space. *Fibreculture*, *19*, 110–124.

Appadurai, A. (2005). Commodities and the politics of value. In M. Ertman & J. Williams (Eds.), *Rethinking commodification* (pp. 34–45). New York: New York University Press.

Apperley, T. (2009). *Gaming rhythms: Play and counterplay*. Amsterdam: Institute of Network Cultures.

Apple, M. (1979). *Ideology and curriculum*. London: Routledge & Kegan Paul.

Apple, M. (1986). National reports and the construction of inequality. *British Journal of Sociology of Education*, *7*(2), 171–190.

Apple, M. (2007). *Markets, standards, God, and inequality*. Seminar given at Institute of Education, London, 5 June.

Apple, M. (2010a). *Global crises, social justice, and education*. London: Routledge.

Apple, M. (2010b). The measure of success. In T. Monahan & R. Torres (Eds.), *Schools under surveillance* (pp. 175–192). New Brunswick, NJ: Rutgers University Press.

Apple, M., Ball, S., & Gandin, A. (2010). Introduction. In M. Apple, S. Ball, & A. Gandin (Eds.), *International handbook of the sociology of education* (pp. 1–11). London: Routledge.

Apple, M., & Jungck, S. (1990). You don't have to be a teacher to teach this unit. *American Educational Research Journal*, *27*(2), 227–251.

Aronowitz, S. (2008). *Against schooling: For an education that matters*. London: Pluto.

Arora, P. (2012). Typology of web 2.0 spheres: Understanding the cultural dimensions of social media spaces. *Current Sociology*, *60*(5), 599–618.

Arvidsson, A., & Colleoni, E. (2012). Value in informational capitalism and on the internet. *Information Society, 28*(3), 135–150.

Ashton, D. (2011). Awarding the self in Wikipedia. *First Monday, 16*(1–3). http://firstmon day.org

Atkins, D., Brown, J., & Hammond, A. (2007). *A review of the open educational resources movement: Achievements, challenges, and new opportunities*. Menlo Park, CA: William and Flora Hewlett Foundation.

Atkinson, P. (2010). *Computer*. London: Reaktion.

Augé, M. (1995). *Non-places: Introduction to an anthropology of supermodernity*. Translated by J. Howe. London: Verso.

Austin, R. (2005). Kwanzaa and the commodification of Black culture. In M. Ertman & J. Williams (Eds.), *Rethinking commodification* (pp. 178–190). New York: New York University Press.

Babe, R. (2012). Theodor Adorno and Dallas Smythe: Culture industry/consciousness industry and the political economy of media and communication. In D. Berry (ed.), *Revisiting the Frankfurt School* (pp. 91–115) Aldershot: Ashgate.

Bacon, S., & Dillon, T. (2006). *The potential of open source approaches for education*. Bristol: Futurelab.

Baier, K. (1986). *The moral point of view*. Ithaca, NY: Cornell University Press.

Ball, S. (2007). Reading Michael Apple: The sociological imagination at work. *Theory and Research in Education, 5*(2), 153–159.

Ball, S. (2012). *Global Education Inc.: New policy networks and neoliberal imaginary*. London: Routledge.

Banaji, S. (2011). Disempowering by assumption. In M. Thomas (Ed.), *Deconstructing digital natives* (pp. 49–66). London: Routledge.

Barab, S., Gresalfi, M., Dodge, T., & Ingram-Goble, A. (2010). Narratizing disciplines and disciplinizing narratives: Games as 21st century curriculum. *International Journal of Gaming and Computer-Mediated Simulations, 2*(1), 17–30.

Bartle, R. (1997). Hearts, clubs, diamonds, spades: Players who suit MUDs. *Journal of Virtual Environments, 1*(1). www.brandeis.edu/pubs/jove/HTML/v1/bartle.html

Bauman, Z. (2001). *The individualized society*. Cambridge: Polity.

Bauman, Z. (2010). *Forty-four letters from the liquid modern world*. Cambridge: Polity.

Bauman, Z. (2011). *Collateral damage*. Cambridge: Polity.

Bauman, Z. (2012a). *On education*. Cambridge: Polity.

Bauman, Z. (2012b). *This is not a diary*. Cambridge: Polity.

Beck, U., & Beck-Gernsheim, E. (2002). *Individualization: Institutionalized individualism and its social and political consequences*. Thousand Oaks, CA: SAGE.

Beck-Gernsheim, E. (1998). On the way to a post-familial family: From a community of need to elective affinities. *Theory Culture and Society, 15*(3–4), 53–70.

Becker, K. (2011). The magic bullet: A tool for assessing the evaluating learning potential in games. *International Journal of Game-Based Learning, 1*, 19–31.

Beer, D. (2009). Power through the algorithm? Participatory web cultures and the technological unconscious. *New Media & Society, 11*(6), 985–1002.

Bell, M., Smith-Robbins, S., & Withnail, G. (2010). This is not a game – Social virtual worlds, fun, and learning. In A. Peachey, J. Gillen, D. Livingstone, & S. Smith-Robbins (Eds.), *Researching learning in virtual worlds* (pp. 177–191). London: Springer.

Beller, J. (2011). Cognitive capitalist pedagogy and its discontents. In M. Peters & E. Bulut (Eds.), *Cognitive capitalism, education and digital labor* (pp. 123–150). Berlin: Peter Lang.

Benjamin, W. (2007). The storyteller: Reflections on the works of Nikolai Leskov. In *Illuminations*, translated by H. Zohn (pp. 83–110). New York: Scholcken (Original work published 1936).

Benkler, Y. (2006). *The wealth of networks: How social production transforms markets and freedom.* New Haven, CT: Yale University Press.

Bennett, W., & Segerberg, A. (2012). The logic of connective action. *Information, Communication & Society, 15*(5), 739–768.

Benson, L., & Harkavy, I. (2002). Saving the soul of the university: What is to be done? In K. Robins & F. Webster (Eds.), *The virtual university: Knowledge, markets and management* (pp. 169–209). Oxford: Oxford University Press.

Berdou, E. (2008). *Managing the bazaar: Commercialization and peripheral participation in mature, community-led free/open source software projects* (Unpublished doctoral thesis, London School of Economics).

Bergquist, M., & Ljungberg, J. (2001). The power of gifts: Organizing social relationships in open source communities. *Information Systems Journal, 11*, 305–320.

Bernstein, B. (2001). From pedagogies to knowledges. In A. Morais, I. Neves, B. Davies, & H. Daniels (Eds.), *Towards a sociology of pedagogy: The contribution of Basil Bernstein to research* (pp. 363–368). New York: Peter Lang.

Bezroukov, N. (1999). Open source software development as a special type of academic research. *First Monday, 4*(10). http://firstmonday.org/issues/issue4_10/bezroukov/

Bigum, C., & Kenway, J. (1998). New information technologies and the ambiguous future of schooling: Some possible scenarios. In A. Hargreaves, A. Lieberman, & M. Fullan (Eds.), *International handbook of educational change* (pp. 95–115). Berlin: Springer.

Bijker, W. (2010). How is technology made? That is the question! *Cambridge Journal of Economics, 34*, 63–76.

Bishop, B. (2009). *The big sort.* New York: Mariner.

Blank, G., & Reisdorf, B. (2012). The participatory web. *Information, Communication & Society, 15*(4), 537–554.

Boellstorff, T. (2008). *Coming of age in Second Life.* Princeton, NJ: Princeton University Press.

Bogost, I. (2008). The rhetoric of video games. In K. Salen (Ed.), *The ecology of games: Connecting youth, games and learning* (pp. 117–140). Cambridge, MA: MIT.

Bogost, I. (2011). Persuasive games: Exploitationware. *Gamasutra*, 3 May. www.gamasutra.com/view/feature/6366/persuasive_games_exploitationware.php

Boltanski, L., & Chiapello, E. (2005). *The new spirit of capitalism.* Translated by G. Elliott. London: Verso (Original work published 1999).

Bolter, J., & Grusin, R. (1999). *Remediation: Understanding new media.* Cambridge, MA: MIT.

Bonal, X., & Rambla, X. (2003). Captured by the totally pedagogized society: Teachers and teaching in the knowledge economy. *Globalization, Societies and Education, 1*(2), 169–184.

Brabham, D. (2010). Moving the crowd at Threadless. *Information, Communication & Society, 13*(8), 1122–1145.

Branco, M. (2006). Free software and social and economic development. In M. Castells & G. Cardoso (Eds.), *The network society: From knowledge to policy* (pp. 289–304). Washington, DC: Johns Hopkins University, Centre for Transatlantic Relations.

Braverman, H. (1974). *Labour and monopoly capital.* New York: Monthly Review Press.

Brehony, K. (2002). Researching the 'grammar of schooling': An historical view. *European Educational Research Journal, 1*(1), 178–189.

Brennan, T. (2011). Intellectual labour. In M. Peters & E. Bulut (Eds.), *Cognitive capitalism, education and digital labor* (pp. 1–22). Berlin: Peter Lang.

Brighouse, T. (2003). Comprehensive schools then, now and in the future: Is it time to draw a line in the sand and create a new ideal? *FORUM*, *45*(1), 3–11.

Bromley, H. (1997). The social chicken and the technological egg: Educational computing and the technology/society divide. *Educational Theory*, *47*(1), 51–65.

Brown, P., Lauder, H., & Ashton, D. (2011). *The global auction: The broken promises of education, jobs and incomes*. Oxford: Oxford University Press.

Bruns, A. (2008). *Blogs, Wikipedia, Second Life and beyond*. New York: Peter Lang.

Buckingham, D. (2006). Studying computer games. In D. Carr, D. Buckingham, A. Burn, & G. Schott (Eds.), *Computer games: Text, narrative and play* (pp. 1–13). Cambridge: Polity.

Buckingham, D. (2011). Foreword. In M. Thomas (Ed.), *Deconstructing digital natives* (pp. ix–xi). London: Routledge.

Buckley, C., Pitt, E., Norton, B., & Owens, T. (2010). Students' approaches to study. *Active Learning in Higher Education*, *11*(1), 55–65.

Bugeja, M. (2006). Facing the Facebook. *Chronicle of Higher Education*, *52*(21), 27 January, p. C1.

Bulut, E. (2011). Creative economy: Seeds of social collaboration or capitalist hunt for general intellect and imagination? In M. Peters & E. Bulut (Eds.), *Cognitive capitalism, education and digital labour* (pp. 151–168). Berlin: Peter Lang.

Burawoy, M. (2005). The critical turn to public sociology. *Critical Sociology*, *31*(3), 313–326.

Burawoy, M. (2011). On uncompromising pessimism: Response to my critics. *Global Labour Journal*, *2*(1), 73–77.

Burnett, J., Senker, P., & Walker, K. (2009). Introduction. In J. Burnett, P. Senker, & K. Walker (Eds.), *The myths of technology* (pp. 1–22). Berlin: Peter Lang.

Caillois, R. (2001). *Man, play and games*. Chicago: University of Illinois Press.

Calhoun, C. (1998). The infrastructure of modernity: Indirect social relationships, information technology, and social integration. In H. Haferkamp & N. Smelser (Eds.), *Social change and modernity* (pp. 205–236). Berkeley: University of California Press.

Cammaerts, B. (2008). Critiques on the participatory potentials of web 2.0. *Communication, Culture & Critique*, *1*, 358–377.

Campanelli, V. (2010). *Web aesthetics: How digital media affect culture and society*. Amsterdam: NAi.

Cape Town Open Education Declaration. (2007). *The Cape Town Open Education Declaration*. www.capetowndeclaration.org

Carmichael, P., & Honour, L. (2002). Open source as appropriate technology for global education. *International Journal of Educational Development*, *22*(1), 47–53.

Carr, D. (2006). Games and narrative. In D. Carr, D. Buckingham, A. Burn, & G. Schott (Eds.), *Computer games: Text, narrative and play* (pp. 30–44). Cambridge: Polity.

Carr, D., Oliver, M., & Burn, A. (2010). Learning, teaching and ambiguity in virtual worlds. In A. Peachey, J. Gillen, D. Livingstone, & S. Smith-Robbins (Eds.), *Researching learning in virtual worlds* (pp. 17–30). London: Springer.

Carr, N. (2010). The web shatters focus, rewires brains. *Wired*, June. www.wired.com/magazine/2010/05/ff_nicholas_carr/

Cassidy, J. (2006). Me media. *New Yorker*, 15 May. www.newyorker.com/archive/2006/05/15/060515fa_fact_cassidy

Castells, M. (1996). *The rise of the network society*. Oxford: Blackwell.

Castells, M. (2001). *The internet galaxy: Reflections on the internet, business, and society*. Oxford: Oxford University Press.

Castells, M. (2006). The network society: From knowledge to policy. In M. Castells & G. Cardoso (Eds.), *The network society: From knowledge to policy* (pp. 3–22). Washington, DC: John Hopkins Centre for Transatlantic Relations.